KENTUCKY DERBY DREAMS

Also by Susan Nusser

In Service to the Horse:
Chronicles of a Labor of Love

KENTUCKY DERBY DREAMS

THE MAKING OF THOROUGHBRED CHAMPIONS

Susan Nusser

Thomas Dunne Books ⚎ St. Martin's Press
New York

THOMAS DUNNE BOOKS.
An imprint of St. Martin's Press.

KENTUCKY DERBY DREAMS. Copyright © 2012 by Susan Nusser. All rights reserved. Printed in the United States of America. For information, address St. Martin's Press, 175 Fifth Avenue, New York, N.Y. 10010.

www.thomasdunnebooks.com
www.stmartins.com

Design by Meryl Sussman Levavi

ISBN 978-0-312-56990-7 (hardcover)
eISBN 978-1-250-01149-7 (e-book)

First Edition: April 2012

10 9 8 7 6 5 4 3 2 1

For Michael, Geneva, and Antonia

In memory of Amelia Barjuca Nusser

Contents

Acknowledgments

Without the Taylors—Duncan, Ben, Frank, and Mark—this book would not have been possible. With all gratitude, I thank them for sharing with me their horses and their horsemanship, their farm, their business, their families, and their lives.

I am equally as grateful to the Taylor Made employees who allowed me to observe, put up with my being underfoot, answered questions, and shared their expertise, their pleasure, their frustration, their failures, and their successes. I continue to be awed by their horsemanship, their knowledge, and their deep respect for and understanding of the horse.

For showing me the farm's nightlife—from delivering foals to finding good hideouts to spot owls—I thank the night-watch staff: Dan Kingsland, Charlie Barron, Terry Pellin, Barb Burton, who was especially useful in identifying those foals that would be interesting to follow, Dave Mayo, and Burt Hamm.

The divisional managers, whose horsemanship and knowledge could fill any number of books, helped me understand the rhythm of the farm's days and seasons, to see the horses as individuals, and established an atmosphere of candor and respect that enabled me to uncover the farm's stories. Taking care of the broodmares were Scott Kintz, broodmare manager, and divisional managers Steve Avery, Bob White, and Lindsey Terrazas. Ever patient on the yearling side were John Hall, yearling manager, and divisional managers Cesar Terrazas, Tom Hamm, and Tanner Tracey. Stallion manager Gilberto Terrazas was equally informative about the management of the stallions.

A thousand-acre Thoroughbred breeding farm is crawling with equine professionals who have made it their life's work to care for these animals. To those women and men who found themselves in the middle of a book project and still, willingly, taught me what they could of their profession, I am also grateful: Dr. Bart Barber, Dr. Lori Henderson, Dr. Dale Brown, Farriers Bobby Langley, Andre MacDonnell, and Bobby's son, Logan, and nephew Ben, Dr. Fatima Wazir, and massage therapist Susan Rodgers. At Rood and Riddle, I need to thank Dr. Rolf Embertson and his knowledgeable and informative assistant, Starlee Smith.

Blessed are the grooms who care for these horses, and to whom the horses turn for comfort and friendship: José Mario Ramirez, Chilo Escobar, Freddy Lucas, Elfuego Lucas, Lisandro Perez, Miguel Ramirez, the Taylor children—Marshall, Danny, young Joe—Dominic Corbin, and Noelle Duff.

Thank you to the interns who shared their learning curves and their inside information: Arielle Cheshire, Taylor Shealy, Juan Rodriguez Salto.

And a special thank-you to Barrett Midkiff, who was present at all places and at all times, and therefore falls into a category all his own.

I'd like to thank the staff in Taylor Made's office who found the time in their already-overbooked days to track down information that I needed: Sue Egan, Bonnie Flanery, Cathy Welch, Annie Padron, Patrick Mahan, Cara Adkins, Audra Tackett, and Hunter Houlihan. Special gratitude to Mark Brooking, marketing director, who steered this project from its initial proposal to wrapping up final permissions. Thank you to Sheri Pitzer, who helped with the photos, and Jeff Hayslett, who agreed, against his better judgment, to introduce me to his clients the Lewises, the Pollocks, and John Fort of Peachtree Racing. And a special thank-you to Finn Green, who shared not only his knowledge but also his great love of these horses and this business.

The narratives of these horses' lives could never have taken shape without the permission of the women and men who owned them. I am grateful for their stories, for their candor, for their willingness to sustain their passion for their horses and their sport in the face of financial turmoil: Sam and Jo Pollock, Beverly and Jeff Lewis, Rod and Lorraine Rodriguez, and John Fort and his Peachtree Racing.

With everything else they had to do, Taylor Made's traveling encampment still made time to answer questions and show me how the sales work. For their willingness and expertise, I need to thank Jamie McKechnie, Tammy Frasier, Iris Ziegler, Cordell Anderson, Ignacio ("Nacho") Martinez, Sheri Murphy, Leandro Cortez, Dean Proefrock, Louis Germany, Jose ("Hollywood") Merced, Julie Davis, and Ellen Kim, and an additional thank-you to Frank and Kim Taylor and their children, Gracie and Chris.

Industry professionals, from agents, breeders, and trainers to rescuers helped me fill out the larger portrait of the industry, and I'd like to thank them for their time and for their expertise: Diana Pikulski, Susan Dyer, and Susanna Thomas, the Thoroughbred Retirement Foundation, Tom Ludt, the Thorougbred Retirement Foundation and Vinery, Ltd., Michael Blowen of Old Friends and Niall Brennan of Niall Brennan Stables, Ryan Mahan and Beau Black of Keeneland, and Missy Robertson and Susanne Johnson of Copper Cap Farm.

Without Keeneland's Library and Archive, I would not have been able to find the early material about Thoroughbred racing in America. In addition to being extremely knowledgeable and helpful, Keeneland's librarians Cathy Shenck and Becky Ryder maintain a serene and joyful working environment at the library. I am deeply grateful for the time I was able to work there.

This project was completed with support from Carroll University, whose faculty generously provided me with grant funding for travel, and where my colleagues, especially Lilly Goren and Allison Reeves Grabowski, never failed to express their encouragement.

My agent, Lisa Bankoff, made all things possible by keeping faith, and my editor, Marcia Markland, offered excitement, faith, and important early encouragement.

And finally, I am grateful that the writers for the industry publications the *Daily Racing Form*, *The Blood-Horse*, the *Thoroughbred Times*, and the *Thoroughbred Daily News*, the Paulick Report, and the Rail blog are such well-informed and good writers. And a special thank-you to Glenye Cain Oakford, who gave me a place to stay in Lexington and spent hours listening to and telling stories. Her knowledge, her humor and wit, and her insightful writing in the *Daily Racing Form* not only taught me about the business but revealed another dimension of the relationship between horses and humans. Much of this book has been informed by her work.

KENTUCKY
DERBY
DREAMS

Foaling Season

1

February 2009

BROODMARE MANAGER SCOTT KINTZ IS ON THE phone. In khaki jeans and a burgundy baseball cap and ski jacket embroidered with the name of his employer, Taylor Made, he stands with his feet wide apart and planted firmly in the middle of the lane between the two barns of Whitehouse upper. It's 7:00 A.M. on a frosty February morning and as he's talking, he's watching a broodmare named Maddie's Charm, who has just been turned out with her new colt. Only days old, the colt is already leaping and bucking at her side, puffs of steam coming out of his nose as he races around his paddock. Scott, whose family has been raising and training racehorses for three generations, lives on the farm with his wife and four children. He likes Maddie's Charm very much; her colt, he's not so crazy about.

It's February 12, early in the foaling season, and the seventy-mile-an-hour winds that whipped through the bluegrass last night have left the farm looking scoured: dust blown out of the driveways, the dull midwinter grass blasted at its roots and standing upright. The sky is sparkly, cold, and clear, and, surprisingly, the storm didn't leave any damage behind. As Scott listens to his early-morning messages, he keeps an eye on the grooms who are leading the mares out to their paddocks.

The Taylor Made Farm rolls out over a thousand acres in Nicholasville, Kentucky. The farm is divided into three divisions: stallions, yearlings, and broodmares. The broodmare division under Scott's management has fifteen barns, all but three of which have twenty-six stalls. The fifteen barns are themselves split into sections: Whitehouse (four barns), Springhouse (three barns), Ivywood (two barns), Bona Terra (four barns), and a catchall category called Casey, which includes the barns where the maiden and barren mares are housed. In all, Scott has his eye on about three hundred mares during the foaling season. On a hillside dotted with identical brownish-reddish broodmares, he can pick out each one by name, knows their pedigree, and, for most of them, can tell you what their siblings are up to.

This morning, he's waiting for Dr. Bart Barber from Rood and Riddle Equine Hospital, one of the two largest vet clinics in Lexington. During the breeding and foaling seasons, which roughly coincide, every mare on the farm will get an ultrasound when she's coming into heat so they can schedule her trip to the breeding shed; she'll get another two days after breeding to make sure she ovulated, a third at fifteen days to make sure the egg was fertilized, and another at twenty-eight days to be sure it's still there. Rounds begin around 7:00 A.M. and include the managers of the different broodmare divisions and, when they're not taking care of horses elsewhere on the farm, two young vets from Rood and Riddle.

The barns of Whitehouse are converted tobacco sheds, and slivers of pale winter light slice though the spaces between the wide boards. The asphalt aisle, covered with interlocking rubber mats, is messy, straw from the mares' stalls spills out as they are led to their paddocks, and their hooves make a soft *whop, whop, whop* on the rubber mats. Spotting Barber's white truck coming up the lane, Scott pulls the phone away from his mouth and shouts to the groom in barn B: "Juan! We need Universal Peace in a twitch!"

Barber gets into the barn before Scott, who's still on the phone. Juan, an Argentinean student who is part of Taylor Made's intern program, rolls the grain bin out to him. There's a worn plywood board over the top that converts the bin into a rolling table for Barber. On it are a portable ultrasound machine, two plastic totes of supplies, a box of latex gloves, and another box with rectal sleeves. Seeing which horse Barber was aiming for, Juan and the other groom have caught and twitched the mare—slipping a loop of rope over her lips and torquing it down with an attached pole—and she's standing quietly, her ears flopped to the sides. In 1984, Dutch researchers concluded that the twitch was effective not because it was a painful form of restraint, but because it released endorphins—a kind of equine acupressure. It's believed that horsemen adopted this method of controlling horses after watching wild dogs bring down zebras by first latching onto their muzzles, after which the zebras would become still and calm, allowing the pack to close in on their flanks.

Scott walks into the barn and describes how he and his nine-year-old son, Nick, stopped the family's trampoline from blowing into the mares' paddock in last night's winds. Leaning back, his arms straight in front of him, knuckles white, Scott demonstrates for Steve how hard it was to hold on to the trampoline. Nick, he says, was almost off the ground.

Steve has his back to Barber while he listens to Scott's story, grinning. The two men have known each other for twenty-five years. In the past, Scott and his family stayed with Steve when he worked for Gainesway, and Scott says the first thing he did when he became broodmare manager at Taylor Made was to bring Steve on board.

Barber pulls on a fresh rectal sleeve, squirts some lubricant on his hand, and works it inside the mare's rectum, scooping out manure and tossing it into her stall, and then pushes in the ultrasound probe. Universal Peace looks fine, but she isn't coming into heat, despite having given birth two months ago. Scott would like to see the mare get pregnant soon.

Universal Peace, the men decide, will need hormone injections to cycle her back into heat. Ninety percent of the mares, Scott says, are short-cycled in this way.

Whitehouse upper A and B, Whitehouse lower, Springhouse middle, Springhouse lower, Springhouse upper, Ivywood A and B. Across East Hickman Road to Gullette, Casey, Bona Terra D, C, A, then B, and finally Mackey Pike, with a stop at the quarantine barn if need be. The order is the same every morning, but rarely do they have to hit all of the barns. The mares are sorted by their due dates, so by the time Ivywood's mares are ready to foal, for instance, the Whitehouse mares are done. Once Bona Terra C is ready, Bona Terra A is done. And they don't deliver foals in every barn; some of the barns are the ones they move the mares to after they've given birth. During rounds, everyone travels from barn to barn in their own trucks—a four- or five-truck caravan on most mornings. Scott's includes his old dog Silks, who props her feet up on the toolbox mounted behind the cab and barks joyously into the wind.

By the time they get to Casey, they've dropped Steve, who stays in his division, and have been joined by Dr. Lori Henderson, the Rood and Riddle Equine Hospital intern, and first-year associate, Dr. Dale Brown. Lindsey Terrazas, who recently had her own baby, meets them at the big double doors, clipboard in hand.

The team gets through the mares in Casey quickly and moves up to Bona Terra D—a small barn, just fourteen stalls—housing barren mares, those who skipped a pregnancy last year and may be having trouble getting into foal this year. The mares in this barn are agitated. They pace and weave, sink their teeth into the stall ledges or their buckets, and suck in great gulps of air, called "cribbing." They pin their ears when approached.

Lori scrubs up the hind end of a mare named Hishi Diva while Scott checks in with Lindsey about a newly hired groom.

It doesn't have to work out, Scott says, they'd like to give it a try.

Once the mares are palpated, Barber, Lori, or Dale—whoever performs the procedure—predicts, within half a day, when the mare is going to ovulate. The divisional managers, Lindsey, Steve, or Bob White, write that down on their records, and Scott uses his radio to call Sue Egan in Taylor Made's office so she can book the time with the stallion. The Jockey Club, the registry for all horses who want to race in North America, requires that all registered Thoroughbreds be bred via live cover. In theory, this protects the breed from having too few stallions dominate the bloodlines. It also protects the value of those stallions by ensuring that their genes remain a somewhat rare commodity. Historically, this may have contributed to genetic diversity in the breed, because up until the 1970s, stallions could only breed to about forty or fifty mares a year. Most stud fees come with a live foal guarantee, and it used to take multiple trips to get a mare pregnant. But advances in reproductive technology—the use of hormones to regulate the mares' cycles and the use of ultrasound, common since the 1990s, to predict ovulation—mean that where it once took multiple covers to get a mare pregnant, it now usually takes just one. As air travel has become more accessible, top stallions are also flown to the southern hemisphere during the off-season. Top stallions now breed to between 150 and 200 mares a year, says Duncan Taylor, CEO of Taylor Made Farm. If they're going to the southern hemisphere, that's another hundred. "So you take that over ten years," he explains. "You know there's a lot of that blood available in the population." To be this productive, farms can't miss an ovulation cycle, or they'll have to wait eighteen to twenty days for the mare to come into heat again. The universal birthday for all Thoroughbreds is January 1, and mares have an eleven-month gestation cycle, so to produce a viable racehorse, mares need to be bred between early February (breeding sheds typically open around Valentine's Day) and late May. Researchers at the University of Kentucky's Gluck Equine Research Center who've analyzed the relationship between reproductive efficiency and the financial value of broodmares reported in a 2009 study in the *Equine Veterinary Journal* that over a seven-year investment period, "live foals must be produced in all but one year to yield a positive financial return." Drift—mares getting pregnant later in every subsequent foaling season—means that for the 60 percent of mares who *don't* get pregnant every year, they'll come up barren every 3.4 years. Profitability, then, for the owners of the broodmares lies in getting them pregnant early and often. Though he's never heard it discussed by the Jockey Club, Duncan says that there are some in the industry who think that horses might be better off if people in the breeding business were restricted to, say, eighty mares a year.

The stallion owners, says Ben Taylor, who directs Taylor Made's stallion division, fill a horse's book and then keep a list of people who might also want to breed a mare to that stallion. If they have an empty slot in the horse's schedule—a Tuesday afternoon, for instance—they get on the phone and try to fill it. Sue Egan is competing against any number of people who are aiming for the same half-day window, so the farm can't wait until the end of rounds to start booking its mares.

Scott turns down his radio and tries to get Miranda, who, like Juan, is another one of the farm's interns, to tell a funny story about yet another intern's early-morning mishap while leading in the foals over the weekend. It's an elaborate story and Miranda misses the punch line, which is something about the intern lying on the ground, waving her arms and legs like a bug. Barber, who has heard the story already, tells her to go back and tell it again. Lindsey is smiling because she's already heard the story, too. In fact, everyone on the farm has heard it, because it's been passed around for two days. But no one has yet heard it from Miranda, who started it, and if there's one thing this team likes to do, it's have a big laugh.

Lori is only half-listening as she manipulates the probe inside the mare, searching for her follicles. Lori already has her veterinary degree, and many young veterinarians would have already begun their careers. But Lori, and Dale before her, have extended their training with the Rood and Riddle Equine Hospital internship. The Thoroughbred industry, with its deep pockets, not only drives the technology and the treatment models for equine veterinary science, it also provides a high quality, high volume practice opportunity for interns like Lori.

The downside for Lori is that Bart Barber, who is supervising her work, is very, very good, and very, very fast, and the staff at Taylor Made Farm is very, very knowledgeable. Not only is deference to her education not automatic, it's also part of her job to take whatever teasing Scott and Barber want to dump on her while she's learning her job. One of her talents is her ability to handle that teasing with good humor. Lindsey is waiting on Lori.

Miranda still hasn't gotten to the punch line because just remembering the story is making her laugh, and in the midst of this, Hishi Diva rocks back on her heels and rears up.

They give up on the punch line. Lori finds the follicles. Lindsey writes the instructions on the chart and they snap off the ultrasound and load the gear into the truck.

"You're getting through these mares quickly," Scott says to Lori.

"You're welcome," Lori reminds him, trying to prod a little gratitude out of him.

"Thank you for doing your *job*," Scott replies, teasing, that gratitude not yet forthcoming.

Lindsey is done and goes back to Casey as the team heads over to
Bona Terra. In his book, *Joe Taylor's Complete Guide to Breeding and
Raising Racehorses,* Taylor, who was the farm manager at one of Kentucky's first huge commercial breeding farms, Gainesway Stud, before
his son Duncan started Taylor Made, offers a compendium of wise
farm-management practices. Not only should paddocks not have any
corners in which galloping horses can get trapped but the fencing
should follow the natural contours of the land. Taylor Made's blackboard fencing gallops up and down hills, through gullies, and around
trees. The barns are situated to make turnout convenient and safe, and
so it is the farm's roads that go in last, accommodating first the horses'
need for natural terrain and then the humans' need to get from point
A to point B in a straight line. The caravan motors slowly over the
curving blacktopped roads that connect the four barns of Bona Terra
B, then heads to the most distant corner of the farm, an older barn that
fronts on Mackey Pike and is contiguous to the rest of the farm only
by its back pasture. To get there, they drive down a narrow and wind-
ing public road along Hickman Creek, passing houses, where Scott's
truck is chased by a black Lab and a golden retriever who have been
lying in wait. Silks barks frantically at them until Scott gets away.

Lindsey is in charge of all the odd barns: Casey, which is full of
just the horses owned by Aaron and Marie Jones; Gullette and Bona
Terra D, which house the barren mares; and Mackey Pike, which
houses the maidens. Just off the track, these mares are sleek and fit,
their manes and tails silky. Their whiskers have been shaved off and
the long fur on their legs trimmed. Soon enough, they'll look like the
rest of the mares: shaggy, their bellies dropped, covered in nicks and
bumps from living outside with their girlfriends, their slender legs
stocked up with fluid, and, for the most part, calm and friendly. But
right now, they're racing-fit and hyperalert. The grooms, who don't
know how well they were handled on the track, can't always catch
them in their stalls. In this barn, everyone slows down. Older, smaller,
at the edge of the woods, Mackey Pike seems less like it belongs to

Kentucky's leading consignor of Thoroughbred yearlings for sixteen years in a row, a farm that's grossed over a billion dollars in sales, and sold three hundred graded stakes winners, including thirteen Breeders' Cup champions, and more like a neighborhood barn, in which a handful of friends have gathered on a cold and sunny Thursday morning in February to sit and talk about their horses.

Barber is leaning against the wall; the sunbeam coming in through the double doors stops just at his feet.

"What would you rather do, Dale?" Dale is finishing up an ultrasound. "Win the Masters or pitch the winning game seven of the World Series?"

"World Series or winning quarterback in the Super Bowl?" Barber asks, amending his own question.

Scott wants to know if you also get MVP.

"Definitely MVP," Barber says.

"Winning the Super Bowl or president of the United States?" Scott asks.

"I'd rather be Bill Buckner than president." Barber shakes his head.

Someone points out that they've left out the Derby.

"Winning trainer/owner at the Derby or the winning quarterback?" says Scott, offering a new dilemma.

They look at their feet, silent. The other choices were between equivalent fantasies, but they know what it's like to be a trainer. Scott has trained horses in the past, and his brother and stepbrother train them now. For these two men who've placed their families at the center of their lives, they understand the costs and risks of being a trainer.

"I would say trainer," Scott begins, "except for . . . your life is . . . to be that kind of trainer . . ." The thought goes unexpressed, but everyone knows what he's talking about.

Meanwhile, the grooms have been unable to get Dale's mare back into the stall. She planted her feet on the way in and they backed out and circled her, hoping to trick her into walking right back in, but she planted her feet even farther away and is now refusing to budge. Scott and the vets stare at the grooms, who are tugging, clucking, and shoving ineffectually, mildly curious about how they're going to resolve this dilemma.

The problem with being a quarterback, Barber explains, is that you know at some point that your career is going to be over. You know that someday you'll throw your last pass. But being a trainer, there's always a shot. "There's always another horse out there that might be the one," he says.

"My grandfather used to say," Scott adds, "a man with a two-year-old in the barn will never commit suicide because that could be the one."

It's an old horseman's story. They all tell it and they all kind of believe it. Any horse on the farm right now could be that one. You never know.

🐎

Eight P.M.: Dan Kingsland, Taylor Made's night-watch manager and chief midwife, is patrolling the farm. It's cold tonight, but much calmer than last night, when Dan watched a transformer in the distance pop orange and then go dark, taking with it a string of lights on the horizon, and wondered if he was going to have to deliver foals by flashlight for the second time this season. The first was about two weeks ago, when an ice storm knocked out the power *and* the farm's generator. The branches and trees taken down by that storm have already been cut and stacked along the lanes, and they loom up in the headlights of his truck as he prowls the farm tonight.

An intern named Arielle opens the big double doors of Bona Terra B when Dan arrives. Dressed in flannel-lined overalls, a Taylor Made parka, and smarty-pants librarian glasses, Arielle worked at a Denver bookstore before she came to Taylor Made. She has parked two large bags in the Bona Terra office, one with her snacks for the evening and the other with books she wants to read.

The foaling kit—a red plastic toolbox with sterile gauze, pulling straps, Banamine, an enema, a thermometer, and an antiseptic naval dip—sits on the straw bales outside Marwood's stall. There's a stainless-steel bucket in the sink, ready for hot water and disinfectant, and plasma in the freezer, to be thawed once the foal is born. All the Taylor Made foals gets plasma when they're first born to help boost their antibodies and protect against common infections.

Every barn that has mares approaching labor has someone sitting up with them. A barn is considered "hot" when they've got mares close to their due dates who are also showing the early signs of labor—heavy udders and waxed teats, dropped bellies, elongated vaginal openings. There are additional watchmen who patrol specific sections—Bona Terra on one side of East Hickman Road, and Whitehouse and the yearling division on the other. Dan keeps his eye on the entire farm and is present at almost all the foalings. On his nights off, or when he's got too many mares foaling at once, Charlie Barron, who's worked nights for Taylor Made since 1987 and who used to be the night-watch manager until stepping down a few years ago, picks up those responsibilities. Everyone used to keep in touch via radio, and Arielle has hers on and in its base in the office. But when the power went out two weeks ago, it took out the radio transmitter, and everyone switched to cell phones for the night and hasn't switched back. Arielle says she misses the chatter, the friendly voices coming to her in the dark, reporting on all the activity from the other lonely quarters of the farm.

Dan is in Marwood's stall, running his hand over her back, feeling where the muscles have gone slack over her hind end. He murmurs to her as he runs a hand over her distended belly, peers under it at her udder, whose teats are waxing heavily. Marwood's vaginal opening is elongated, and she's shifting her weight from hoof to hoof, but other than that, she's calm. Her body is cool to the touch and her skin smooth and without the popped-up veins that indicate the start of contractions. Marwood leans her butt against her water bucket and sighs. The whiteboard outside her stall lists her due date and then her name, Marwood, followed by that of the sire, More Than Ready. Written that way, it reads more like a description than a lineage. For three nights now, Arielle has been convinced that this mare is going to go into labor, but Marwood is holding out. Leaning on her bucket, her head low, her lips dangling, she just looks like she wants to sleep. Dan pats her sympathetically and heads off for his rounds.

Horses generally give birth at night, and Dan would even close that down to a four-hour window between eight and midnight. He thinks it's an evolutionary remnant—being born during that time frame gives the foal the most amount of time to gather its strength before it'll have to get up and run away from predators during daylight hours.

The night crew works a twelve-hour shift: six to six for the crew and seven to seven for Dan so that there's managerial overlap. The Chevy

S-10 that he drives from barn to barn stays running because it's too ter-rifying to imagine what would happen if the night-watch manager's truck wouldn't start. The interns rotate through a night shift as part of their training, and the day grooms who want the higher hourly wage switch to the overnight hours. They check the horses every fifteen minutes—Taylor Made's goal is never to have a mare deliver alone. To trick the mares' bodies into coming into heat early by making them think the days are getting longer, they leave the lights on until eleven o'clock. As Dan drives over the farm's dark roads, the foaling barns loom up out of the darkness. The lights beaming out through the high ventilation windows, and the long panels outside every stall, make them look like giant spacecraft that have settled into the bluegrass hollows.

The first deliveries of the year were in Bona Terra A, whose lights Arielle can see just across the paddocks from her barn. Her roommate and fellow intern, Tailor, sits up in Bona Terra A, and she's had a rough season so far. One of her mares had laminitis—the disease that felled Barbaro—and was so sickly that by the time she gave birth, her foal weighed only sixty pounds. Both mother and foal died. In one stall, a dark colt by Roman Ruler nurses on a draft horse.

In another stall, a Thoroughbred filly nurses on a chunky but kindly Percheron mare. Right after she was born, this filly's mother was shipped back to England to be bred to a stallion there. The first nurse mare didn't produce enough milk and the filly developed ulcers. Now, Tailor thinks, she's a little needy. When she enters the stall, the filly crowds up against her, demanding attention.

In the corner stall, a big flea-bitten gray mare named Holy Niner has given birth to a Successful Appeal filly, whose right hind leg is turned forty-five degrees in its hip socket. The mare stands in her stall, relaxed, eating hay, while her dark brown filly sleeps in the corner. She won't, Tailor explains, be with the farm much longer. The joint can't be operated on because it's way up in the hip, and though the filly can walk on it now, eventually the bone grating on bone will be too painful. They're giving it time to see if something happens with the joint, she says, that will make it possible to operate, but it doesn't look likely. The filly had a difficult delivery. They had to put the pulling straps on the foal—the turned leg caught inside. Holy Niner was so exhausted, says Tailor, "she lay back an hour before she ever got up." It was three hours before she had the strength to stand long enough to let the baby nurse. For now, she looks pleased with her sleeping baby. "No." Tailor shakes her head. "She doesn't see any problem with her baby."

Friday the thirteenth, 8:00 A.M.: Bart Barber is leaning on a straw bale in Whitehouse B, waiting for Lori Henderson to finish performing a Caslick's on a mare named Sayitwithfeelin. Scott, standing nearby, is on the phone. It's cold and bright, and the sunlight from the big double doors rolls halfway down the aisle, which is scattered with bits of straw that fell off the bodies of the mares and babies as they headed out to the paddock. Barber is warning Lori to always double-check information from the grooms and especially the interns, who are famously misinformed. A few years ago, he tells her, an intern told a visiting journalist that the foals who died on the farm were buried in back of one of the paddocks, even though everyone knows their bodies are sent to the lab for a necropsy. "Don't listen to the interns" is his advice.

The Caslick's is a routine procedure in which the edges of the mare's labia are sewn together, closing down the opening to the vagina to keep debris from getting sucked inside by the negative pressure created by the weight of the developing fetus. Caslick's procedures, like routine postbreeding lavages, are one of the ways that modern farms prevent infection and keep their pregnancy rate up above 90 percent. In the wild, it's closer to 60. Lori has done these procedures before. She comes to Rood and Riddle from Texas, where she went to vet school and worked with Quarter Horses. The problem with the Thoroughbreds is that they have Caslick's procedures so regularly that the flappy, soft tissue gets trimmed away often, leaving less room for the stitches. In a year, Lori will be able to perform these procedures quickly and routinely, but in the meantime, Scott has nicknamed the Caslick's that Lori does "The Henderson Procedure."

Sayitwithfeelin is bored and she fidgets and hassles Juan. Lori has given her a mild sedative and needs to inject an anesthetic into the area she wants to stitch. While the grooms get the mare settled, Lori stands a little to the side, holding the syringe. Barber taps the toe of his boot with the long foil-covered cardboard tube that they use to look all the way inside to a mare's cervix. He suggests that Lori tuck her elbow up to her body instead of letting it flap out like a wing. That way, if the mare kicks, she won't end up with a needle in her face like he did once, a long time ago, making his face totally numb for the rest of the day.

Scott looks up from his phone. He and Lori stare at Barber.

"Seriously?" Lori asks.

"Yeah." Barber's tone suggests it wasn't funny.

Lori and Scott shoot each other a look that clearly indicates that they think it *is* funny.

The mare, now numb and sedated, has had the soft flaps of her vulva trimmed more than once today. There's a pool of blood at the mare's feet, streaks of it down her legs, and smears of it on Lori's overalls.

"Lori!" Barber calls out. "That mare is actually leaning against the door." Sighing with boredom, Say It with Feelin has propped her hip against the door frame while she patiently waits for Lori to find a chunk of skin into which she can anchor her stitches.

Barber wants to know what everyone is doing for Valentine's Day. Lori, perhaps unwisely, volunteers that last year, while she was still in Texas, she and her boyfriend went to Hooters. Scott, Barber, and Juan all burst out laughing.

"I was starving," she explains. "It was the only restaurant in town that didn't have a two-hour line."

Scott wants Barber to look at a mare named Kimchi, who colicked around 4:00 A.M. She doesn't seem to be in serious pain, but she is lying around. Barber gestures to the grooms to get her ready while he sleeves up.

"The mare's worth a fortune," Scott comments.

With one hand in his pocket and the other feeling around in her rectum, Barber stares at the floor in concentration. "Lot of stuff going on all over in here." He frowns.

He gestures to Lori to examine the mare. She feels the distended colon but pulls out, afraid that she'll rupture if it she pushes too hard. By himself, Scott is keeping Kimchi and her four-day-old foal under control.

Barber checks Kimchi's gums for dehydration and rubs her face sympathetically. She closes her eyes and pushes into his hands. Barber gives her a shot of acepromazine to relax her, and Scott tells Juan to get her out into the paddock, where she can move around. If she doesn't get a lot better in a couple of hours, Barber warns, she'll have to go to the clinic.

It takes four trucks to transport four people and one dog the eighth of a mile downhill to Whitehouse lower. Scott thoughtfully backs his up to the horses' loading ramp so Silks, whose muzzle has gone gray and whose eyes have frosted over with cataracts, doesn't have far to jump to get down to the ground.

While they're palpating mares, Barber quizzes Lori about types of bacteria and the conditions they cause. Steve Avery, grinning, his blue eyes twinkling, keeps beating her to the answers. Barber prompts her again, and she smiles. "I'm not going to answer," she tells him. "Because if I'm wrong, I'll have to live with Steve being right."

The grooms are chatting in Spanish, their conversation intelligible only to Steve, because no one else speaks more than a little Spanish. Scott is giving a play-by-play of his son's "awesome" basketball game last night, while Barber is trying to find out from Lori, and now Dale, who's just arrived, how other people are doing in Rood and Riddle's diet contest. He is not winning.

Dale has one hand inside a mare and is listening as Barber and Scott retell Lori's Hooters story for his benefit. Half-distracted by the monitor and nodding sagely, he says, "Hooters are huge in Texas."

Before they leave Whitehouse, Scott calls ahead to Lindsey, but they still arrive at Casey before she does.

"Where have you been?" he asks, teasing her as she rushes down the aisle with her clipboard.

"Sorry! Sorry!"

Tall, thin, patient, and the only one of Taylor Made's broodmare managers who doesn't gossip, Lindsey is a graduate of Taylor Made's intern program. Because she's patient, she's often assigned the grooms who drive everyone else nuts. She met her husband, Alberto, a stud groom, while she was working as an intern, and has married into the farm's second dynasty—that of the Terrazas family. Eduardo Terrazas first started in the business twenty-five years ago, and before he had his own farm, Terrazas Thoroughbreds, he worked for Taylor Made as the stallion manager. He was succeeded in the position by his cousin Gilberto Terrazas. Alberto's nephew, Cesar, manages the Eagle Creek section of the yearling division. And now Lindsey and her husband have started another generation of Terrazas born on the farm, and into the business.

At Bona Terra D, the team runs into the apprentices of the farm's farrier, Bobby Langley. If they were working with any other horses besides these Thoroughbreds, they would be journeymen, not apprentices, but Bobby Langley keeps them trimming and assisting for the first four or five years of their apprenticeship—even when his apprentices are his son, Logan, and his nephew Ben. Logan and Ben scramble to get out of the way while Dale sets up the ultrasound. After scrubbing the mare's bottom with gauze and disinfectant, Dale, not seeing a garbage can anywhere, tosses the dirty gauze to the floor, where it lands with a splat.

They're in and out quickly, teasing the farriers the entire time, and then whisk away like rock stars, leaving the apprentices standing in the aisle. On the floor is the clipboard that Logan and Ben failed to get out of the way before Dale tossed the gauze, and now their notes are splattered with disinfectant and poop.

"Hey," they protest to the backs of the departing vets.

Since no one is in a rush, when they get to Bona Terra A, Barber turns palpating over to Lori. Watching her set up her equipment, he threatens to nickname her "the Great Delay."

She looks frazzled.

"You're probably my favorite intern," he tells her.

"Really?" Lori smiles, pleased. "Thanks."

Scott and Barber check on Holy Niner and her crooked-legged filly. They agree that the leg has gotten better. The filly will be fine, Scott says.

"She'll be an athlete," Barber adds.

Turned-around legs are not uncommon. If the foals get hung up on the way out of the mare, like this one did, their ligaments get stretched. As the soft tissue hardens up, her leg will go right back into place. All she needs is stall rest and some time.

They turn around to watch Lori. She's still probing, trying to get something to appear on the screen.

"It's a little like fishing," Barber says helpfully.

"At least fishing, you catch something once in a while," she replies.

Friday, February 13, 8:05 P.M.: A big chestnut mare named Cherry Bomb has just gone into labor in Whitehouse upper. The mare is a favorite of her owner, John Fort, who runs Peachtree Racing. He says she was the most beautiful filly he had ever seen in training but that she never quite reached her potential as a racehorse. Cherry Bomb retired two years ago, and her first pregnancy ended in a late-term abortion. This foal, sired by the sprinter Henny Hughes, is her first.

Despite the cold, she is sweating. The veins in her shoulder have popped to the surface and she's circling her stall, agitated. Dan and Elfego, the groom sitting up in Whitehouse tonight, have removed her water and her grain. Terry Pellin, one of the night-watch patrollers, has brought out the foaling kit. Cherry Bomb's tail has already been braided. Braiding it keeps it out of the way, and during the day, when the grooms use binoculars to check on the mares in their paddocks, they can easily see if a mare who's close to her due date has sneaked away to give birth in some hidden corner.

Cherry Bomb props out her front feet and pushes her back down toward the ground in a pelvic stretch that eases her contractions. She acts like she wants to lie down, but she doesn't. She's urinating frequently, but her water hasn't broken yet.

Elfego takes Cherry Bomb's head, circling her around the stall. Her friend, Resplendency, who lives across the aisle and has the same due date, looks on with interest, her face pressed up against the stall's bars, her ears pricked.

Dan slips on a sleeve and gets a hand inside the mare, checking to see if the foal is in the right position—nose first, head lying on the front legs, little hooves poking out. He's not worried that it's upside down, because they turn on the way out. And he wants to be sure the hooves aren't poking up where a mare's contractions might push one though her rectum. He's also on the lookout for red bag—a bloody placenta pushing out in advance of the foal, indicating that it's already separated from the uterine wall and the foal inside is without oxygen.

The thin white tissue of the mare's amniotic sac bulges out of her vagina. Sheer and glistening, the veins run over its surface and the foal's thin legs and small hooves are visible inside. Cherry Bomb is still circling. She moves to the wall and starts to lie down. Dan and Elfego chase her away, clucking, yelling, and tugging on the lead shank. Mares like to get right up against the wall for labor, but then their butts are too close to the corner of the stall, where their foals are mushed up against the wall when they come out.

Dan slips a hand inside her again, and this time her water breaks, pouring out of her in a great gushing stream. She lowers herself to the ground with a grunt. She rocks from side to side, her back legs held out stiffly beside her as she presses down and tries to push out the foal. Stretching and pushing, stretching and pushing, and then at 8:32 P.M., a nose pokes out of her vagina and Dan grabs hold of the front legs, timing his tugs on them with her contractions.

Cherry Bomb plants her feet in front of her and pushes up with her head and neck, pulling at the contracting muscles of her pelvis, pressing her great orb of a belly into the floor. Elfego and Terry have joined Dan and all three of them are tugging now, inching the foal farther into the world with every contraction. With a groan and a deep sigh, Cherry Bomb gives a last push and a chestnut filly sluices into the world on a slimy mat of fluid, placenta, tissue, and blood.

Because foals are usually named by their new owners sometime before their second birthday, the foals on the farm are known by their mother's name and the year of their birth. As long as she's on the farm, Cherry Bomb's bright red filly will be known as Cherry Bomb '09.

Already, she's struggling to get up. Cold, wet, blinking in the harsh light, she's in the uncomprehending shock of all newborn mammals who slip out of the watery caves of their mothers' wombs and into the hard, cold light of the world.

Cherry Bomb's legs are curled underneath her and she is staring at the baby lurching and collapsing around her stall as if she wishes she would just lie down. Terry has the foaling log and is keeping track of the labor, the delivery, and will note the time when the foal gets to her feet and stays there.

At 8:57, the mare heaves herself up. Elfego carefully folds up the placenta hanging down her back legs, tying it up to itself so the mare won't step on it and rip it out as she moves around. With a bucket of warm, sudsy water, Dan washes the mare down gently, congratulating her. He cleans off her teats and then Cherry Bomb has one more contraction and the placenta drops to the ground.

Dan spreads it out on the aisle floor, looking for tears, discoloration, hard spots, or anything that might indicate a problem. Days, weeks, even months from now, if something goes wrong with this foal, everyone will recall this placenta, wondering if there was a sign.

Satisfied with his inspection, he folds the sloppy, wet mass into a black garbage bag. After it's weighed, he dumps it at the end of the aisle, where the lab will pick it up in the morning.

Together, Dan, Terry, and Elfego put the stall back together. While Cherry Bomb licks her baby clean, they fork out the manure and the wet, bloody straw into a pile three feet high in the middle of the aisle. The outer window is closed to keep the wind from blowing on the baby. Once her mother's tongue has licked off the afterbirth, Cherry Bomb '09 fluffs out like a duckling. Her baby coat and the clean straw are all she needs to keep warm.

Forty-three minutes after arriving in the world, Cherry Bomb '09 is up and wants to nurse. Her mother pins her ears and moves out of range, waiting for the baby to get a little steadier on her feet before she lets her latch onto her tender udder. By 9:40, the filly is still trying to nurse. Her head is bumping around under her mother's belly, her tongue flicking in and out; she's in the neighborhood but hasn't yet found what she's looking for. Cherry Bomb swings her big head back toward her foal and nickers softly. When the filly makes rough contact, Cherry Bomb squeals and moves out of the way.

"Your mommy's a meanie," Terry says, sympathizing with the foal.

Cherry Bomb has sucked up her belly, as if she's trying to hide her sore udder from the foal. Terry is in the stall, holding the mare, and the filly starts nibbling Terry's leg.

"I'm not your mama," Terry tells her.

Cherry Bomb pins her ears as the foal gets closer, and Terry gives the lead shank a sharp little snap. "Quit," she growls. Pressing one hand against the mare's shoulder, Terry soothes her. "Whoa," she says, and then, enthusiastically, "Good girls!" as the filly finally latches on and sucks.

Outside the stall, Terry makes the final notes on the foaling report, then replaces the water and grain in the stall. Everyone else is already gone, and Terry turns off the stall light, leaving mare and foal to sleep in the clean, dark stall.

On Saturday morning, Barber and Scott want to get their rounds done quickly. It's Valentine's Day and both their kids have games today.

They have about thirty-five mares to palpate this morning. At the height of the season, around March, they'll have as many as eighty. No matter how many they have, Scott jokes, rounds take the same amount of time. When they have more, "we just move faster."

Barber is tossing the dirty gauze right and left as he cleans the mares. When he's finished, he snaps off his gloves and shoots them into the garbage can in one move. He's using his teeth to get the sterile wrappings off his equipment faster. With the grooms already holding the mare, Barber spots the garbage can behind Juan and banks the dirty, wet gauze off the wall and into it. The splat hits Juan in the face.

"Hey!" Juan protests in a long drawl, and Barber actually looks a little remorseful.

"Well, the can is over there. What am I supposed to do?" he says, defending himself.

"I don't know," Juan says, wiping his face with his upper arm, never letting go of the mare's tail, which he's holding on to. "Put it in your pocket."

Barber smiles and takes the pace down a notch. He has his older daughter, McKenzie, with him this morning. When he reaches for something, she has it ready.

"She's the best tech he's got," Scott says, adding, "She doesn't run her mouth."

As they're about to finish with one division, Scott calls ahead to the next, letting the manager on the other end of the line know that they're on their way and that they're in a rush. When they get to Gullette, Lindsey is ready, the mare already twitched and with her bottom turned toward the door. As they're palpating, Scott is on the phone with Dale. A foal was born to a jaundice-positive mare last night—her colostrum will contain antibodies to him. They'll be gone after sixteen hours, and the foal can then nurse normally, but in the meantime, he needs colostrum from the supply that the farm banks, as well as milk replacer. The mares are checked two weeks before delivery to see if they're jaundice-positive, and this mare's test had been sent to the lab, but the foal was premature and they didn't receive the results until this morning. Scott and Barber are worried about how much milk the foal got, and Scott wants to see if the mare was jaundice-positive last year, in which case that information should have been communicated to the night staff.

By the time they get to Mackey Pike, they're ahead of schedule. Barber is setting up outside the stall of a maiden named Light My Fire Baby. In the corner of the stall, the groom is struggling to get hold of the mare's head. She's lifted it out of reach.

"She's kind of piggy," the groom says. "She doesn't like the twitch."

"I don't blame her," Lindsey says. "I got my finger stuck in there before. It hurts."

Lightmyfirebaby, Scott notes, is a celebrity. She won a race on the Animal Planet show *Jockeys*.

Down the aisle is another potential celebrity. Time Reveals All has returned from an early trip to the breeding shed and her date with Curlin. Horse of the Year in 2008, winner of the Preakness, the Breeders' Cup, and the Dubai Cup, world record holder for most earnings won—$10.5 million—Curlin is this year's most fashionable stallion, and because of the early breeding date, Time Reveals All may have been his first official mare.

Glancing at the notes that were forwarded from the breeding shed, Lindsey jokes that they got a good cover on the *fourth* jump.

"Well," Barber says sympathetically. "That Curlin. He's just learning."

Time Reveals All gets a special congratulatory pat as everyone passes her stall.

Barber sets up across the aisle. The groom enters a stall and comes racing right back out.

"She ran you right out of there," Barber says, annoyed, and without looking up.

The groom goes back in the stall and swats at the mare with the end of the lead shank.

"That's more like it," Barber tells her.

The mare pins her ears and evades the groom. "Somebody stronger than me want to take a crack at this?" she calls out.

"McKenzie?" Barber calls jokingly to his fifteen-year-old daughter.

Scott walks into the stall and in seconds has slipped the twitch over the mare's lip and backed her up to the stall door.

Standing at the mare's hindquarters, Barber is focused on the ultrasound screen, trusting that Scott will keep her under control.

"She's terrified, isn't she?" he asks Scott without looking up.

The mare has calmed down a bit, as if she's comforted by Scott's authority and the proximity of his big body. Her ears tip toward him. She's not quite relaxed, but she's not fighting him, either. Calm, efficient, quiet, the body language of both Barber and Scott says that everyone needs to focus on their jobs.

The rest of the maidens are out in their paddock already. It's sunny and cold, the grass under their feet tramped down and brown, though in one week of spring rain and warm weather, it will bloom into a lush, thick green. As Barber packs up his gear, the mares in the paddock suddenly break into a gallop. Digging in, they tear across the grass and turn to head up the hill. Tails floating out behind them, their necks stretched, they're racing toward an imaginary finish line; the pounding of their hooves thrums the walls of the barn.

"I love that sound." Barber's gear slides out of his hands and he stares out the door. The others turn to watch; Scott is in the doorway. When the girls reach the crest of the hill, they turn and tear back down it.

"It's like the brumbies." Scott's talking about the horses in *The Man from Snowy River*.

"Or *Lord of the Rings*," someone adds.

"I've never seen it," Scott says.

The others are aghast. "You've never seen it? You gotta see it."

The mares are racing directly for the fence. In a close pack, the lead mare is running for her life, ears back, nose stretched out, and they're heading straight for the fence at the bottom of the hill.

"Whoa, whoa, whoa!" Scott, Barber, and Lindsey all move forward, waving their arms above their head, trying to get the mares to turn before they crash though the fence.

The mares pop their legs out in front of them, putting on the brakes before the curve. They arch their necks, slowing to a trot and shaking their manes prettily as they scatter over the hill.

Colic and labor look a lot alike. At 8:30 P.M. on Valentine's Day, Dan Kingsland is in the stall of Arianna's Passion, trying to figure out which of the two she's experiencing. Arielle called Dan around 8:00 P.M., when she first noticed the mare in distress. She was gassy and uncomfortable and Dan gave her a shot of Banamine—an anti-inflammatory that has a mild sedative effect. Arielle walks the mare up and down the aisle for about ten minutes and then puts her back into her stall. The mare is breathing hard, sweating, and her veins have popped up. This might be labor, but her udder is still small, and she's not due for another week. She has a history of colic and has already had two surgeries.

Agitated, head down, she's pawing the floor of her stall, scraping her toe on the cement that's at the edge of the rubber mat. She'll scrape her toe down doing that, and Dan and Arielle add more straw, but she just paws it up. In the stall with her, Dan is texting this information into a report. He holds the phone in front of him, his glasses propped on his forehead while his thumbs operate the keys. When he's done, he waits and watches.

Summoning Scott to the barn at night is not something that's done lightly. There will be a few hundred foals born this year; if Scott is summoned to every labor, he'll get no sleep at all from January to April.

While Dan is watching the mare, Arielle chides her to stop pawing. Without looking at her, Dan tells Arielle that the mare won't stop until she feels comfortable. The mare tries to lie down, then changes her mind and straightens up. Arielle turns her around and Dan peers into the birth canal with a flashlight, hoping to see what's going on. Switching tactics, Arielle rubs the mare's face.

"It's terrible; it's terrible, I know," she coos.

"Something's definitely wrong," Dan concludes. He's talking to himself as much as to anyone else. "She's not pushing. She's acting like a red bag. When I reach in there, there's something very tight. I don't want to reach up in there."

He calls Scott.

The mare tries to lie down again, and Dan and Arielle clap and cluck to her, getting her up and moving. Her gums are pale when Dan checks them, suggesting dehydration and blood loss. They wait in silence for the sound of Scott's truck. The night is cold, calm; the sound of yelping coyotes drifts in from across the paddocks. Silently, another watchman, Dave Mayo, slips into the barn and joins the vigil.

The headlights of Scott's truck slice through the gap in the double doors. He's wearing jeans and a parka and has a stethoscope around his neck and a vet kit in his hand. His progress down the aisle seems slow, as if he's pushing back a wall of tension. The relief that he's arrived is palpable. He says hello softly and nods. In the stall, he repeats Dan's examination: checking the mare's gums, listening to her heartbeat, listening to gut rumbles that tell him she's digesting her food. He feels her belly, checks her bag. Arianna's Passion submits to the exam, periodically tossing her head in discomfort. Scott checks her hooves for heat. When he opens it, his vet kit is filled with preloaded paste syringes of xylazine—a sedative that's stronger than the one she's had but that acts faster. He gives her some, and when Arielle unclips the lead shank, the mare is calm, but her sides are heaving. Everyone watches her in silence.

Scott calls Dale. Her heart rate is fifty-three, he tells him. Gums are pale. She's got gut sounds. She's had xylazine. He can't get the foal to move. "I just can't feel him move," he tells Dale. "If she hadn't had two colic surgeries already, I'd be less worried."

"The good broodmare manager," Joe Taylor wrote in his book, "genuinely likes the mares. He understands them and knows how to read their body language. He has the necessary devotion to endure the long hours and sleepless nights of the breeding season."

Scott phones Barrett Midkiff, the farm's van driver, to let him know they might need him tonight. On call twenty-four hours a day, Barrett arrives within minutes when he is summoned from where he lives on the farm, his slacks pressed, his hair combed, bright-eyed under his Taylor Made cap, his thin frame moving energetically. He's fifty-nine and has been with Taylor Made since 1991.

"Her brother is about to run at Mountaineer," Scott says to no one in particular as he waits for Barrett to answer. Arianna's Passion turns toward Scott and instinctively, he props out his knee so she can rub her head against it. Barrett has picked up on his end and Scott warns him that he might need to take a horse to the clinic tonight.

When he hangs up, Arianna's Passion raises her head toward him and he lifts her chin, looking under her lip at her gums.

"Ohhhhhhhhhh. Shit." He calls Barrett back and tells him to get dressed.

Arianna's Passion has moved closer to Scott and is rubbing her head on him while he texts information over his phone.

At 10:00 P.M., Dale walks in the door in track pants, layers of shirts, and a down vest. He's wearing glasses and looks tired. Repeating Scott's exam, he listens for gut sounds, checks her heart rate, and looks at her gums. He wants to know how long it's been since the last sedative.

Arielle turns Arianna's Passion around so that her hind end is outside the stall. Dale is careful getting his hand inside of her and stares at the ground in concentration.

"I called Barrett and told him to get dressed," Scott says.

The mare groans. "He's down there," Dale says, pulling out his arm. He doesn't like the color of her gums, either.

"Could be an adhesion causing problems," Scott suggests.

"It's definitely not an impaction."

The men walk away. Arianna's Passion nickers at them.

When they return, Dale has wide-gauge surgical tubing and Scott is on the phone, summoning Barrett.

Holding one end of the surgical tubing in his teeth. Dale starts feeding the other end down the mare's nose. Using a hand pump, he pumps in water from a bucket that Arielle has filled for him. Next to it is an empty bucket into which the fluid from her stomach is going to drain.

"She could be colicky," Scott says. "She's pretty stoic."

Once Dale has gotten the water into her, he suctions it back out and fills the other bucket. It pulls up reflux, and the yellowish fluid starts to run through the tube.

"There. That feels better," Scott says.

Arielle volunteers that the mare didn't eat much dinner. The reflux, Dale says, is probably from the morning. He sniffs the end of the tube and says, "Phew."

The fluid, which is getting thick and brackish, with streaks of black, is a normal color, says Dale. You just don't normally see it coming back out of the horse. The fluid is getting too thick for the tubing, and to draw it up, Dale puts the end of the tube in his mouth and siphons up. He pops it out of his mouth, gagging and spitting.

"That's terrible," Arielle comments.

Dale nods. "Good for her, though."

Fluid starts gushing through the tube and the mare lifts her head and swats her tail. "Hang in there. Hang in there," Dale croons.

The fluid fills the contractor's bucket.

"There you go, sweetie," Scott says. "How's that feel?"

The mares are so stoic, Dale says, that they often wait too long before they let anyone know they're in danger.

The bucket is almost full, and Arielle loosens the twitch and the mare lowers her head. Her eyes are half-closed and her ears are flopped to the sides. She looks drained, but she's clearly more comfortable. Barrett arrives, backing the trailer up into the aisle. He's upbeat and businesslike as his long, skinny body hustles around the back of the trailer, letting down the ramp and opening the gate.

Dale pulls out the tube and Arielle leads Arianna's Passion out of the stall and up the ramp onto the trailer.

Everyone thanks one another and Dale calls the clinic with his diagnosis. Scott lingers in the office, leaning back against the counter, his arms crossed over his chest, while Dale runs scalding water and antiseptic through the tubing.

"She's a hell of a broodmare," Scott says. It's his highest compliment.

Dan has left to check on the other horses, and Arielle's spirits have lifted. Although everyone knows better, it always feels like a horse that gets to the clinic is going to be okay. But Dale and Scott are still grave. The mare is twenty-one, carrying what is probably her last foal, and she's already had two colic surgeries. Neither of them will be surprised when the clinic tells them that the mare is hemorrhaging. By morning, both Arianna's Passion and her foal will be dead.

On the other side of the farm, business goes on. At 12:22 A.M., Angela's Love '09 splashes to the ground just twenty minutes after her mother's water broke. Dan and Terry drag the dark bay filly off the wet and bloody straw while Angela's Love, still lying down, snaps her head from side to side, alternately licking her baby and pinning her ears at Dan.

"I don't want your baby," he tells her. "Not yet anyway."

With a shudder and a tumble of debris, Angela's Love heaves herself to her feet, pacing around the foal, still licking. The filly already has her legs propped out in front of her, and with a push from her hind end, she lurches toward the open stall door.

"Don't come out here, baby," Terry tells her. "You'll piss off Mama."

The baby splats to the ground, legs splayed. Her mother nickers to her and the filly lurches to her feet, only to splat down in the straw again. The mare is weaving from side to side; her foal looks stunned.

Dan is forking the wet straw out of the stall while Terry gets the filly out of the way. The night has turned bitterly cold. They've already shut the stall's outside door to keep the wind off the baby, and they want to get the clean and dry straw down as quickly as possible. The baby, given an enema just after birth, poops. Her tongue moves frantically, feeling the air and everything it comes in contact with. Terry writes on the foaling report, "Good foaling. Poor blood supply. Mare jumped up right away."

Jumping up right away, for anyone who reads the report, will indicate that the mare was anxious and unsettled.

"Mare, mare," Dan coos.

Terry is trying to sponge her off, but she's mad, tossing her head and pinning her ears.

"Terry is being nice," Dan tells the mare.

Once mare and stall are clean, Terry and Dan slip out the door.

"All yours, Mama," Terry says. "Bad girl."

In the aisle, Terry smoothes out the gray, veiny placenta. Its horns are intact, there are no tears, and its good color will be noted in the report. They flip it inside out, showing the bloody interior. Dave says that where he grew up, farmers called the inside-out placenta a "bloody pair of long johns."

Terry sits, keeping vigil. Alone in the barn now, she'll note the time that the foal gets up and nurses. Splay-legged, unsteady, a little stunned and uncomprehending, the filly is on her feet again. One leg slides slowly, inexorably, out from underneath her.

"You get that leg under you," Terry promises, "and we'll call you standing."

The foal is mad. She's kicking her front feet out in front of her, and when she does finally get up again, she starts inching her way around the stall.

"Look at her," Terry says. Tongue flicking, trying to nurse on everything she gets close to, she's taking careful steps around the perimeter of her stall—finding her balance in a new place before she moves on to the next.

"This baby is so careful," Terry says. "Usually, they just throw themselves around the stall, but she's just inching around."

She's marooned herself in the corner, face against the wall, unable to back up. She suckles the wall hopefully, then, dissatisfied with that, figures out how to get to another corner, and then seems to sense that her mother is in the middle of the stall. She takes a cross-step in her direction.

"Side pass!" Terry says. "Are you going to do dressage when you get older?"

When Terry enters the stall, the mare rocks back onto her haunches, weaving, her ears pinned.

"Don't," Terry growls.

Terry clips on the shank and holds her still while the foal approaches. The baby presses up against the mare's body, and Terry keeps her from wandering away again. After forty-five minutes of trying to nurse on everything in the stall, Angela's Love '09 finally finds her mother's udder and her first meal.

At 5:50 A.M., the last foal of the shift arrives in Bona Terra A. Sliding into the world on a carpet of spongy tissue and warm fluid, the dark bay colt out of Clay's Rocket lands in the straw, lifts his head, and blinks in the bright light and cold air.

"Welcome!" says Dan Kingsland. "Good morning! Rough trip?"

2

Early Spring 2009

IT'S EARLY MARCH AND THE PEAK OF THE FOALING season. The mares in Bona Terra A are done, and at night, the barn is dark and empty. Bona Terra B still has mares that need to deliver, and some newborns who are too little to be outside overnight. Arianna's Passion's stall is being used to store hay and straw.

On the Whitehouse side, Steve Avery has moved his early-foaling mares from Whitehouse upper to Whitehouse lower. The Springhouse mares have been moved from the upper barn to the middle and lower barns. Ivywood, the most distant of the broodmare barns, is open, its stalls full of mares who have recently given birth to their foals, or are about to. At night, as Terry Pellin drives her rounds on the White-house side, the truck's lights strafe the aisles of the empty barns, startling the raccoons, possums, and skunks that prowl, trying to get into the feed rooms. Taking a smoke break outside of Ivywood, Terry hears a pack of excited coyotes down by the stream. Their yelping rises in pitch and volume but doesn't quite drown out the desperate screaming of whatever animal they've gotten hold of. Inside the barn, the horses are alert, heads raised, their ears pricked, listening.

"That's the thing I hate about sitting up in this barn," Terry says. "I hate coyotes. I hate wildlife. I'm terrified of the dark. I don't know why I work nights."

So far this year, she's delivered three foals on her own. "I'm very proud of myself," she says. Once the coyotes calm down, Ivywood goes quiet. The radio beeps from time to time, but the only other noise is the sound of the mares groaning and passing gas, or swishing through straw and splashing their muzzles in their water buckets.

It's Saturday morning, March 7, and Steve Avery stands in the doorway of Whitehouse lower, watching Juan struggle to get a mare and foal through the paddock gate. The foals are bigger and stronger now and don't always want to be led. Steve watches passively, as if there's nothing he can do to help, like holding open the gate.

Juan is excited because Old Fashioned, the gray Unbridled's Song colt out of a mare named Collect Call, whom Juan takes care of, is an early favorite for the 2009 Derby. He quickly rattles off what he knows about the mare: Her first foal, a 2004 filly by Fusaichi Pegasus, sold to Sheikh Mohammed bin Rashid al Maktoum for $2 million. Old Fashioned, her 2006 foal by Taylor Made stallion Unbridled's Song, sold for $800,000 at Keeneland. Last year's Ghostzapper colt didn't meet his reserve. Collect Call's got some maintenance issues, like navicular, a degenerative hoof disease that's pretty common in Quarter Horses, but less so in Thoroughbreds, and requires some special care. She's one of the few mares on the farm who wears shoes. But, says Juan, mares like Collect Call "pass on their class," and the Empire Maker colt at her side right now looks just like her.

Lorraine Rodriguez, who owns Collect Call with her husband, Rod, says that they set a high reserve on last year's Ghostzapper colt—$635,000—because her husband "wanted to keep something of Collect Call" to race on his own. He's started his training in California, though, Rodriguez says, laughing, they haven't gotten around to naming him yet. Strategically, she has a hard time explaining how they pick stallions for their stakes-winning mare. They talk to the Taylors, look at pedigrees, visit the stallions in Kentucky, and pick the one that they like the best. Juan suspects that the decision to breed Collect Call to Curlin this year is because of his commercial value. Empire Maker, he says, is the kind of stallion you pick when you want to race. Rodriguez doesn't even think it was that strategic. With a sigh, she says jokingly, "Oh, I don't know. It was the way the sun shone on him that day."

Collect Call is the couple's first Thoroughbred of this caliber, and the only one they keep in Kentucky. They breed cattle and cutting horses on their California ranch and got into Thoroughbreds at the urging of their vet. The business is new to Rod, a native New Yorker, who, Lorraine says, would be "happy in the city with a dog and a cat," but she's been around Thoroughbreds her whole life. Her father bred, trained, and raced them on the northern California fair circuit. Growing up, she says, "we always had a Thoroughbred in the backyard."

They bought Collect Call at a dispersal sale and she went on to win or place in graded stakes races, including the Kentucky Oaks, where she came in third. "We always thought she could give a little more," Lorraine says, but they never figured out how to get her to do it. Not really a pet, or even very affectionate, Collect Call, says Lorraine, "is a princess." When she was racing, she began every training session with a good long look around the track, as if she were surveying her domain. Since retirement at age four, "she's been a fabulous broodmare for us."

Collect Call was bred to Curlin seventeen days ago, and Barber is doing an ultrasound on her this morning to make sure that she's not carrying twins. Before ultrasound, he says, twins were the number-one cause of spontaneous abortion in mares. Now there's a really low rate because the vets pinch off the extra fertilized egg. While he probes, her colt ducks his head down under his mother's belly, taking the measure of the space, as if it's just occurred to him that he could escape by going *underneath* her. He has white socks behind and a broad white blaze down the center of his face. "That mare," Lorraine says, "has a tendency to put pretty into all her offspring. They all have a little bit of chrome."

By 8:50 A.M., the talk has already turned to basketball. Scott segues from basketball to his daughter's dance competition. The team is skeptical about the idea of dance as a sport, but Scott is adamant that it is. In fact, it's the competition of it that makes it fun to watch.

Dale is palpating Apple Juice Tea, and behind his back, her colt makes a break for the door. Dale kicks out a foot behind him, blocking the colt. "Get in there, rat!" he says. Dale also saved the groom from having to buy a box of doughnuts for everyone—the penalty for bonehead mistakes, like letting a foal slip out the door, accidentally thawing out a freezer full of plasma, or lavaging the wrong mare.

Barber has brought his daughter Ashton with him today, and she doesn't share her sister's enthusiasm for the work. "Did you come to sit on the straw or did you come to do something?" her father asks her.

By the time they get through Whitehouse and into Casey, Lindsey is ready for them. Aidan, now four months old, is bundled up and tucked into a BabyBjörn. Clipboard in hand, Lindsey is ready for work, but everyone has to play with the baby first. Scott, who's thirty-nine, and whose kids range in age from nineteen to three, scrunches down, googly-eyed, and tickles Aidan under his chin.

The vets made such little progress on their last diet contest that they've started another one. Because everyone wants to get done early, Barber is palpating the mares. Ashton looks bored, and he throws a wet gauze at her. She picks it up while she's playing with her phone and throws it back at him. He smiles and gets back to work. Inside a stall, Lori chats as she draws blood on a mare. Behind Lori's back, the foal steps quietly into the empty door frame and pokes his nose out, as if he's preparing to escape.

"That's not good." Scott grins, but Lori spots the foal in time, prodding him back into place.

When they pull up at Bona Terra D, a mare is whinnying frantically.

"Hey, Lori," Barber jokes. "You get to palp that one down there," he says.

"Which one?" she asks.

"The one blowing fire."

With nothing to do, Dale goes hunting for the new kittens. One of the barn's two cats is pregnant and has gone missing. No one has found the litter yet.

They caravan to the last barn, and Scott hands the clipboard to

Dale so he can get to his son's basketball game. Dale makes the scheduling calls while Ashton, bored, blows the surgical gloves up into balloons. Barber's phone, whose ringtone is the theme from *The Good, The Bad and the Ugly*, rings from the front seat of the truck and Ashton answers it for him. She hands it to Barber, who wants to know who it is.

"It's your best friend," she says.

"Your mom?" Barber reaches for the phone.

"No," Ashton replies, and walks away.

Dale and Lori snicker.

They move on to Mackey Pike, where, after getting an update from Lindsey, Barber observes that three of the mares who've been to Indian Charlie this season have come up empty. The stalls are already clean, and once they're done, everyone, including Lindsey and her baby, can go home for the afternoon. As they're packing up, Lindsey's phone rings.

"The kittens were born!" she tells everyone as they head out for their weekend.

Monday morning, Lori and Dale start their rounds at 6:00 A.M. They try to get their routine work done in time to meet up with Scott and Barber, who begin their rounds around 7:00. Originally from Texas, Lori came to Rood and Riddle because someone she worked with had Thoroughbreds. "One thing I really, really like," she says, "is that the horses here are easy to work with because they're handled all the time." In Texas, she mostly worked with Quarter Horses, who are not as intensely managed as the racehorses.

She's in Springhouse upper, checking on a mare named FaMulan who's not eating and has a low white blood cell count. There's something not quite right, and Lori is wondering if she'll break out with colitis.

She moves on to Whitehouse upper, where she needs to lavage a mare. While holding the mare for her, Juan tells her about last night's weekly poker game at the yearling manager John Hall's house.

"I don't think he won a game with a legitimate hand last night," Juan says about Steve Avery.

"He likes to bully the pot." It's a nickel-and-dime game and Steve admits that he gets bored and stirs up the action to keep it interesting. "I beat him with a pair of twos," Juan says, and Lori laughs.

She catches up to everyone else at Whitehouse lower. Sometimes, for fun, she times how long it takes before the conversation switches to sports. After greeting everyone, Scott returns to basketball. "That was, like, three minutes," Lori jokes.

Barber wants to know how she's doing on the diet contest.

"I lost six pounds," she says brightly.

"I want to be in a diet contest with honest people," he replies.

Almost a month old, and Cherry Bomb's filly looks good. Big and athletic, she has the bright red coat of both her dam and her sire, Henny Hughes. They've moved to Springhouse upper and Barber is palpating Cherry Bomb before her scheduled date with Midnight Lute tomorrow. In the next stall, Kimchi's colt whinnies for his mother, who's away at the breeding shed.

"Where's your mama, buddy?" Steve Avery puts his fingers through the stall grating for the colt to nuzzle. "She's been gone a long time. You'll be okay."

At Casey, they meet up with Lindsey, and lose Lori, who's been called to the yearling side. The team has gotten wind of something going on with the interns, but Scott can't get any gossip out of Miranda. A pretty blond Wisconsin girl, Miranda is usually an excellent source of information, but this morning she's silent and blushing. Scott is suspicious.

"If we get to Elizabeth," he warns her, "and she's full of stuff, we'll know you're holding out."

Before they leave Casey, Barber wants to look at Glenarcy's foal. The January foal by Master Command has a sore hoof and has been on stall rest. She's almost sound when she walks out, and they decide that she can go out with a hoof pack. Miranda, who led her down the aisle, turns slowly to lead her back to where five people, Barber, Lori, Dale, Lindsey, and Scott, stand shoulder-to-shoulder, heads tilted, appraising the filly's walk.

Before they head to the next barn, Scott runs through the messages on his phone and reminds the team that it's the time of year when they need to be on the lookout for caterpillars.

In 2001, the Kentucky breeding industry experienced a massive die-off of their foal crop. Tom Riddle, senior partner at Rood and Riddle, and a reproductive specialist, was at Taylor Made, palpating mares, when he noticed two in utero foal deaths on the same day. By Derby Day of that year, the entire industry was affected. What response the industry was able to muster, Rood and Riddle credited to Taylor Made, which was willing to go public with the disaster on their farm. In a deeply paranoid industry, there were smaller farms all over the region that couldn't afford to reveal that something was killing their foals and risk the immediate departure of every one of their clients. By the end of foaling season, about two thousand of the foals conceived that year had been lost and about six hundred near-term foals had been aborted late and were unable to survive. Total loss to the industry was estimated at around $330 million.

They've never figured out conclusively what caused the die-off, but the culprit appears to have been some combination of a distinctive frost/warming cycle, eastern tent caterpillars, fungus, and cherry trees. The weather coincided with an infestation of tent caterpillars so dense that the roads looked like moving carpets. The caterpillars were attracted to the cherry trees, and the farms where they grew had an especially vigorous infestation. Taylor Made ended up cutting down 580 trees on the farm, and every year, around this time, everyone is on the lookout for caterpillars. Often when Frank Taylor expresses his anxieties, the team responds like he's a mother hen, but not even Scott jokes about mare reproductive loss syndrome, or MRLS.

"*Eastern* tent caterpillars," Barber says, reminding everyone of yet another scourge from that troublesome part of the country. For the record, he also hassles Lori for being from Texas.

At Bonna Terra D, Hishi Once More has backed out of Miranda's reach and raised her head. When Miranda reaches for her, she pins her ears and snakes her head toward her. She's dancing from hoof to hoof as if revving up to charge.

Miranda is tentative, unsure, and Scott and Lindsey counsel her to be firm.

"Stop it!" Miranda shakes her finger at the mare. "Stop it right now!"

When everyone stops laughing, Scott takes the twitch from Miranda, and in one motion, he enters the stall, grabs the mare's lip, and slips the twitch over it.

At Bona Terra A, Holy Niner's crooked-legged foal isn't crooked anymore. While Lori palpates the big flea-bitten gray mare, Scott tells division manager Bob White that he can give the filly a little tranquilizer and then turn her out with her mother. It will be the first time the filly has been outside since she was born, almost six weeks ago.

"What do you think, sweetie?" Scott asks the foal. "You're going to see a whole new world." He rubs her face. "You're a pretty girl," he murmurs. "You're a good girl."

"I feel bad that Steve can't golf," Barber says suddenly. "That's the only halfway normal thing he does. He never leaves the farm." Steve has a shoulder injury, which will keep him from playing golf this summer.

On her tiptoes, pressed hard up against the rear end of the mare, Lori is up to her armpit in the mare's rectum and has found her ovaries.

"That was very good, Dr. Henderson." Barber is peering over Lori's shoulder at the monitor's screen. "And I kind of giggled when I gave you this great big mare."

"Book her in four days," Lori says confidently. "Check her in two."

They move on to a mare named Heiress Apparent, whom they've nicknamed "Bobtail" because before she came to Taylor Made, someone wrapped her tail too tightly, left the bandage on, and her circulation was cut off. Instead of a tail, she now has a stump.

Her behavior is consistent with that of a horse who's not been handled well. They need to culture her because she's not getting pregnant, and she's going to need to be tranquilized before they can get close to her. Two grooms are at her head, one with the twitch. As they turn her hind end around, both Lori and Dale are about six feet away, as if they plan to get the tranquilizer in her by throwing the hypodermic like a dart.

"Be careful." Barber grins.

She's not as difficult as she first seemed, and when they're done, they head to Bona Terra A, where Elizabeth doesn't have any gossip, either. Scott is unconvinced, and the bright red spots in Elizabeth's cheeks belie her claim that she doesn't know anything. After she graduates from the intern program in June, Elizabeth will return to Ireland for law school. When she graduates, she'll join her family's bloodstock business. Her family, like the Taylors, puts a high value on horsemanship that's learned in the barn. If the Taylor children want to work for the family business, they have to go to college, or at least spend two years working for someone else before they can expect to be part of the business. It mirrors the deal Duncan made with his brothers. After an initial period of being paid a pittance, if they stayed with it, they'd become an owner. Every one of his three brothers took him up on the offer.

As Elizabeth is blushing and claiming ignorance about what Scott is convinced is a new intern romance, Madonna Lilly's foal, who's behind Elizabeth, steps up to the door frame and, with mincing, careful steps, slips out the door and into the aisle. Spindly-legged and slightly confused, she looks around as if she's not quite sure what to do with herself now that she's free. Everyone goes silent.

Registering their silence, Elizabeth follows their gaze past her own shoulder and spots the filly behind her, who's easily corralled and led back into the stall with her mother.

"Ahhhhhhhhhh," they chide Elizabeth. "Doughnuts for everyone tomorrow."

"Really?" she asks.

"Really."

"All right. Straight to the hips, but doughnuts it is."

🐎

The mares in Bona Terra B are way ready, and at eight o'clock that night, Sazerac Song's water breaks. Charlie Barron, Taylor Made's senior midwife, who's been working night watch on the farm since 1987 and held Dan's job until he stepped down a few years ago, arrives on the scene by accident, having been sent by Dan to fetch some Banamine. The mare lies down with her side to the wall and pushes until the foal's feet appear and then stands back up again. Her placenta is already pushing out of her vagina. Full of yellowish fluid, red-blue veins coursing over the outside, it swings behind her as she moves around her stall. Charlie and Arielle are trying to keep her from lying down against the wall. After ten minutes with no progress, Charlie gets his hand inside of her to check for the foal's nose.

"We have very few mares who just lie down and foal like they're supposed to in this barn," he complains.

The mare settles down in the straw again, and Charlie has the foal's feet and cannon bones clear. Sazerac Song nickers and looks back toward her butt.

"You ain't had it yet," Charlie tells her. "It's going to take a little more work than that."

The mare keeps pushing up onto her belly like she wants to get up. She grunts a couple of times and then peers around at her butt again.

"You ain't never going to get that head out like that," Charlie says, then looks up at Arielle. "Until she gets ready to do something, there ain't nothing I can do to help her."

Her foal is okay where it is. It doesn't need to breathe on its own until its rib cage is out. Then, if it takes too long, there'll be trouble.

"Get over there and push," Charlie says to the mare. "I'm gonna help you."

The foal slides out and Charlie lifts up his head and squeezes the mucus out of his nose.

"I didn't come over here to foal a mare," he complains to Arielle. "I came over here to get that Banamine."

Before he heads out, he drags the foal up to the mare's nose. "There you go. You just lay right there and lick it."

While the mare is lying down, he ties up her bag and then heads out to his truck. The temperature has dropped down to near freezing, but the two days of warmth have brought early color into the grass. It's still March, winter still in the air, but the days are getting longer; thin slivers of pink light stretch across the horizon.

Over on the Whitehouse side of the barn, Dale is trying to get some milk replacer into another jaundice-positive foal. He's tugging the baby's halter. "Sit up, buddy," he says. "We'll fill your belly; then you can lie down."

Into a feeding tube whose end is taped to the filly's halter, Dale has stuck a 60cc syringe. Once he starts squirting, the filly suddenly stands still. Her tongue pokes out of her mouth; she's suckling and looks mystified.

"Does that feel weird?" Dale asks her. "Your belly getting full and you're not doing anything?"

The filly has to wear a muzzle, which keeps her from nursing. Dale notices that it's on upside down, with the big holes on the bottom instead of the top. He leans over and whispers to the filly, "I'll switch that around for you."

Two hours later, Dan is back in the barn for the filly's next feeding. This time, Lasandro holds the filly's head while Dan gets the first syringe into the feeding tube. "We are so hungry," he murmurs to her. "We are so hungry. I know. I know."

Lasandro fills up another syringe, but the filly's eyes are already drooping. "All of a sudden, I need a nap," Dan says, speaking in the filly's voice. Behind him, Barb Burton, another member of the nightwatch staff, is stripping the mare, squeezing what milk she has out of her teats. Seeing Barb, the filly pins her ears and stamps a foot. Dan laughs and talks in her voice. "I want to do that! Look at those ears. I'm so mad!"

The next night, March 12, at 8:50, 9:15, and 10:00 P.M., three mares in Bona Terra B deliver their foals. Dan and Arielle run from stall to stall, tugging out first one foal and then another and then another. They wash bottoms, administer enemas, clear nostrils, and dip umbilical cords in antiseptic. They drag the hundred-plus-pound animals up to their mothers and then slip away, leaving the mares in peace to nuzzle and lick their babies. Burt Hamm arrives at some point to help with cleanup, releasing Dan to text in a lengthy report while Burt and Arielle get the barn back in order. City Fire is jaundice-positive and so Dale is summoned again. Willow Run is rearing up in the stall, ears pinned, and Dan wonders briefly is she's going to attack her own foal. He turns the light off in her stall, everyone moves away, and she settles down.

The City Fire colt's brief biography is already noted on the foaling report: "9:15. Bay colt. Jaundice-positive. Hard foaling. Hung up at ribs, stuck at hips/cord broke in delivery."

Dale arrives by 11:15 in a T-shirt, baseball cap, and purple track pants. All business, he looks worn-out. He feels the foal's ribs, making sure they weren't broken, and listens to his heart.

"All right, kiddo," he says, preparing the colt for the unpleasant-ness of the catheter and feeding tube.

Dan wraps his arms around the foal lengthwise, squeezing him into his chest. He leans over the foal's back, using his upper chest and shoulders to keep the foal from leaping upward. Behind Dan, City Fire is rocking from hoof to hoof and snapping her head from side to side like a whip's lash.

"C'mon, sweetie," Dale implores her.

She's swinging her nose over Dan's head, aggressively pushing up against his back. He ignores her. Dale calls her a little bit of a freak. "Stop!" he says

"Mom, stop!" Dan adds. "We're not hurting him. I promise. I promise."

The mare gets too close and stomps on Dale's foot. He's too tired to even react and just pulls it out from under her hoof. Slowly, he slides the feeding tube down the colt's nostril. City Fire has settled into a more subdued fretting—one that everyone can live with. Dan is clearly in range of her whiplashing head, but she hasn't hit him yet. He holds the colt's head close to his own and pulls him into his chest, pressing down on the colt's spine with his chin. Arielle is holding the colt's head with the lead shank and Dale is crouched close, trying to insert the catheter. The foal jigs forward, jigs back, but they've got him boxed in. He tries to go up, but Dan increases the pressure of his chin, push-ing the foal back down. Left with nowhere to go but down, the foal crumples his legs and slides to the ground. Dan, Arielle, and Dale go down with him.

City Fire is still hovering, but her curiosity about this heap of bod-ies in her stall has momentarily calmed her. Ears pricked, her head low, she snorts gently over their backs. Dan grabs hold of the foal's ear and Arielle is the first to untangle herself and stand up, followed by

Dale. Dan is still on top of the colt. Feeling that Arielle is off his neck, and thinking he can get free, the colt throws his head out and gives a mighty kick with his back leg, a hoof landing on Dale's shin.

"Ow," Dale says.

The colt lurches to his feet.

"You're a firecracker, kiddo," Dale says, coming back at him this time with the milk replacer.

The foal gets his head down and bucks, loses his balance, and crumples to the floor again, taking Dan with him. Dan lies atop him for a moment, catching his breath while the colt calms down and then sighs.

"I'm tired," Dan declares when he's back up on his feet. "I already had to pull this colt out of that mare tonight," he reminds everyone.

Having managed to get the plasma into the foal, Dale is now feeling for the colt's esophagus, making sure that he's threaded the feeding tube into his esophagus and not into his trachea, where the milk replacer, once it goes down the tube, would drown him. Once the tube is in, Dale sucks on it to make sure there's negative pressure. With a 60cc syringe, Dale slowly injects the colostrum through the feeding tube and the colt suckles, the tip of his tongue pressed between his lips, his mouth suckling even though the fluid is bypassing it and going straight down his throat. After the first feeling of a bellyful of warm food, the foal snaps alert and tries to throw himself to the ground again. "Don't do it," Dale warns, hanging on to the syringe. "You're a pistol," he tells him.

A warm front moves in the next day, raising the temperature into the seventies and releasing the scent of spring that's been lying under the winter cold. It won't last long, but for now the ground expands with the warmth, the air smells like sweet dirt, and everyone straightens up, the night warm enough to stop hunching over against the cold.

After almost a year of being pregnant, Don't Read My Lips finally goes into labor. She's looked ready for days—her foal shifting and pushing her belly out to one side. Her tail is braided and wrapped and she's pawing the ground. Eighteen years old, with some successful foals behind her, the mare has not bloomed with this pregnancy. Outside, the killdeer screech to one another as they swoop from one paddock to the next. Dave Mayo is on watch tonight, covering the shift for Arielle, who has the night off. Lasandro calls from Springhouse, where a mare is colicking, and Dan has to leave, radioing to Charlie (who doesn't have a cell phone) that Dave is going to need help at Bona Terra B.

Dave, who moved to Kentucky because there were no jobs left in Ohio, has always been around horses, but this is the first time he's worked with them at this level. When he's on watch, he sits in the aisle because he wants to be able to hear the mares. He's the nighttime naturalist, the person to go to when you hear a weird noise and want to know what it is. In the long silent stretches, he wonders about UFOs and the Fourth Reich, and sometimes spooks the interns by talking about them. Unlike his colleague, Burt Hamm, who retired here from North Carolina, where he was a juvenile probation officer, and who passes his shift tinkering with his little hobby farm in his imagination (his current obsession is in getting some Tennessee Fainting goats because he thinks they're cute), Dave's settling into the bluegrass has been fraught with anxiety. He bought a foreclosed property, not realizing that everyone in his neighborhood was part of the same family, and sees his property as a shared resource. Just a few days ago, one of his neighbors cut down a tree in his yard.

He's sitting on a straw bale across from Don't Read My Lips, and next to him, Key to the Cat's chestnut filly has pressed her head up against the stall grating, ears pricked in his direction. He sticks his fingers through the grating for her to play with, flicking up her lips as she nibbles them.

"Is Dan upset for nothing, or do you got something that's ready to go?" Bandy-legged, in a Taylor Made cap, his belly round and tight as a basketball, Charlie Barron bursts through the double doors and swaggers down the aisle. When a delivery goes bad, Dan says, Charlie is the one you want handling it.

He stands outside the stall, watching the laboring mare. Dave is next to him. Having heard the call on the radio, Burt walks in the door and leans on the stall wall. Apropos of nothing, Burt blurts out, "I ran over Bob's dog today."

This is not the first time someone has run over Fiona, Bob White's little rat terrier, who chases cars. Scuffing their feet, both Dave and Charlie confess that they've almost run over her themselves. They're fond of her. She runs up to Bona Terra B from the little house down the hill where she lives with Bob and his wife, Mary, and then gets stuck because she's too afraid to go back in the dark. Eventually, Bob or Mary will wander up the hill to retrieve her.

While the men look at their feet and then turn back to the mare, Burt slips out the door.

"Aw jeez," Charlie shouts, throwing the stall latch. "She's a red bag." Dave jumps in after him and takes the mare by the halter.

"She had a big old bloody bag," Charlie explains. He's got surgical sleeves on both arms and is reaching into the mare. Her placenta has already separated from the wall of her uterus. The foal doesn't have any oxygen and he needs to get hold of the bag and break it so they can get the foal out. Bloody up to both biceps, he's also trying to turn the foal around, because it's upside down.

Charlie pushes against the bag, trying to break the mare's water, and when it bursts, it drenches the front of him.

"Oh shit! Dan, now I know why you wanted to leave. Damn it," he says to the mare. "You got me wetter than hell!"

He's still trying to turn the foal. Big gassy farts are coming out of the mare as he relieves the pressure from all the fluid.

Don't Read My Lips is down, but she's not pushing hard enough. The foal's legs are poking out, but her labor isn't progressing. They can't wait for her. Charlie and Dave wrap the foaling straps around the foal's front legs, looping them around the pasterns. On the other end of the straps are metal handles, and they hold on to these, leaning back, pulling hard as the mare contracts. Together, coaxing her all the way, they pull out a chestnut colt with three white stockings and a star.

Charlie grabs the colt's nose, squeezing hard and stripping out the mucus with both hands. They watch to see if he takes a breath. Don't Read My Lips stays down. Her head is up, ears pricked toward her colt, but she trusts the men who are handling him. When they're sure the colt is breathing, Dave drags him forward, where Don't Read My Lips can reach him with her warm tongue.

Burt reappears in time to clean the stall. He went to check on Fiona and happily reports that the dog is going to be fine.

*

Don't Read My Lips is jaundice-positive. The colt can't drink his mother's milk for another twelve hours or so, until after the antibodies are gone. He needs colostrum and milk replacer and he also needs plasma. This year, Dale says, Rood and Riddle discovered that the plasma and the milk replacer were reacting badly to each other, though the reaction is easily avoided by giving the plasma first. Since the foals have to eat right away, that means that Dale has to come out to the barn immediately for every jaundice-positive foal.

Dan tells Dale he doesn't think the foal looks right. He's breathing heavily and he doesn't have any energy. Dale isn't as worried as Dan. In the stall, Dan shows Dave how to hold a foal still for the catheter and Dale gives the chestnut colt a quick physical: temperature, reflexes, making sure the ribs weren't broken when the colt came through the birth canal. While Dave keeps his arms wrapped around the foal, Dale slides a catheter into his neck, attaches the bag of plasma, and squeezes it in.

Dan lingers in the office after Dale has left, filing his report. The foal is still lurching around his stall, breathing heavily, and suddenly he collapses. Dave yells for Dan and they both rush in, yelling. Dan grabs the foal's mouth, checking his airway, and Dave starts slapping the foal's butt and side, trying to get him up. They cluck to him and tug on him and shove on his butt, but the colt has stopped breathing, and a moment after a final convulsive kick of his hind legs, he also stops moving. Silent, the men stare down at him. Dan leans over and checks for a pulse while Don't Read My Lips looks over his shoulder. She noses forward as they leave the stall, closing the door behind them, leaving her alone with him. She runs her nose all over her colt's body, sniffing, snorting, prodding. On the phone with Scott, Dan watches her. "I don't know," he says into the phone. "I don't know." He's silent, listening, and then says, "All right, Scott," and hangs up.

Don't Read My Lips is standing over her foal protectively, and Dan and Dave give her a few more minutes with him before they enter the stall and drag the foal out by its legs. They leave him in front of the stall door, where she can still see him and sniff him through the grating. Her ears are pinned in confusion as she sniffs his body. She nickers to him, and the Tale of the Cat filly across the aisle, who's been playing with Dave all night, nickers back. The mare paws at the bottom of the grating, and then she's still, as if she realizes he's not going to get up.

Dan and Dave drag the body around the corner, near the barn's main entrance. In the morning, the lab will come and pick it up for a necropsy, but not before the morning shift's grooms and interns arrive and find a dead foal in the doorway.

Once the colt is out of sight, Don't Read My Lips starts to whinny for him. Her body tense, head high and pressed up against the stall bars, looking in the direction that her colt was dragged, she emits a strange high-pitched keening, her whole body quivering. She's not frantic or even that loud, but her wail is steady, coming in waves, one right after the other, for half an hour, and then she stops. Ears pricked, she listens, her body waiting for a response, and when it doesn't come, she drops her head and circles her stall, sniffing, paying special attention to the spot where she delivered her colt, and the spot where he lay down and died.

Across the aisle, shaken, Dave watches her. He's wondering if there's something he could have done, or should have seen, that might have changed this outcome. He's the only one on the farm who wonders this. Across the aisle, Don't Read My Lips is moving around, but more slowly, as if she's tired and has come to some conclusion in her mind.

Trouble with the horses, Dave says, stresses him out.

3

Summer 2009

 IT'S MAY AND THE SEASONAL PENDULUM SWING IS
about to move the farm activity from the broodmare side
to the yearling side. Except for a few stragglers in Springhouse upper and Ivywood, the mares are done foaling. At the yearling
barn, John Hall and his section managers, Cesar Terrazas and Tom
Hamm, are getting the yearlings who were born in 2008 ready for the
sales season that begins in July with Fasig-Tipton's sale in Lexington, followed by their select sale at Saratoga in August, and concludes with the
granddaddy of yearling sales, Keeneland September, which takes place
over two weeks and catalogs over four thousand horses. That's followed a
little over a month later by Keeneland's equally huge November bloodstock sale. Leftovers get cataloged in the Keeneland's January Horses of
All Ages Sale. The two-year-old sales, in which the farm does not partici-
pate, start in February, giving the farm a break from sales season while
foaling season gets going again.

The paddocks are profoundly green, scooped into amoeba shapes
by the blackboard fencing that runs over ridges, shoots down gullies,

and races up the hills. Plopped here and there in the middle of all this green are the upright gray rectangles of the barns, topped by their burgundy cupolas. The mares have shed their winter coats and are fat and shiny, most of them in shades of brown and red. They doze in their paddocks and switch their tails as their foals play: Compact peanut shell–shaped bodies on spindly legs, racing one another across their paddocks, heads dropping to buck gleefully, or rearing up to paw the air with hooves the size of big teacups.

"I hate this." Steve Avery leans over Lori's shoulder as she does an ultrasound on the last mare in Whitehouse who doesn't have a confirmed pregnancy. The breeding sheds are only open for a few more days, so any mare who isn't pregnant has probably missed her chance for the year—all expenses, no income. Even if you were to try to breed her back, she'd have a very late foal, one that might not mature enough to race as a two-year-old, which is when the careers for the most successful racehorses begin.

They're all staring at the monitor, which comes up blank.

"Shoot!" Steve turns away from the empty screen.

Taking advantage of an opportunity to tease Lori again, Barber reminds everyone that he has a 70 percent higher success rate than Lori when he follows her exams. "Find the cervix"—he's taken over the probe and Lori stands at his side, watching the screen—"and go straight forward to the bifurcation."

A small gray orb appears on the screen. "It's right there," Barber says.

"You must have moved it," Lori jokes.

Barber wants to see a lame filly, who is brought out of her stall.

"This is going to be your disaster of the year," Barber tells Scott.

The groom jogs off to find a hoof pick.

Barber leans over, propping the filly's hoof on his knee and pinching it with circular metal tongs called "hoof testers."

There's a new Rood and Riddle intern named Casey with them this morning. In June, the entire industry shifts as the new batch of interns arrive. Though this year, Taylor Made will not be taking on any new interns for their program on the farm for the first time in over a decade. The difficulty of securing visas since 2001, the lack of interest from American students, the cost of running the program during a recession, and the size that it's grown to have finally led the brothers to end the Taylor Made intern program. They do so with some regret. Joe Taylor was especially proud of the program. Frank Taylor, the brother in charge of the day-to-day operation of the farm, remembers an accounting done some years ago that found that something like 70 percent of Kentucky's farm managers had been trained by either his father or by someone who had been trained by his father.

But Rood and Riddle *will* be taking on new interns. Dale will be moving on from the farm, and Lori, all teasing aside, has developed the skills and the confidence to replace him as the farm's regular veterinarian.

Casey is so new that she doesn't even have overalls yet. She's in low-riding jeans and a spotless pink polo shirt.

"Casey," Barber calls to her. "Lame foal. What are your differentials?"

"He could be septic?"

"Yeah, you always want to check that."

"Abscess?"

Barber doesn't answer.

"Out of screw?"

"No screws," he says.

"Sesamoid fractures?"

"Okay, now you've hit two."

Juan has reached the end of the aisle and is turning the filly around. As she walks toward everyone, her head bobs every time her left front foot hits the ground.

"He could have raging physitis?" Casey's guessing.

"What's wrong with this foal?" Barber demands. He's trying to get her to see the whole animal, to notice that her legs are crooked when she walks. Talking out loud, he thinks the source of the problem is in the filly's fetlock.

"Get some bute," he tells Steve. "Put some mud on it. Leave her up until tomorrow."

Casey is invited to palpate one of the nurse mares. The nurse mares come from a farmer down the road who goes by the name of Archie. His entire business is providing nurse mares and teaser stallions—the support staff of the Thoroughbred breeding industry. Foals born on his farm are fed milk replacer by the bucket, while their mothers are leased out to places like Taylor Made for their foals who either lose their dams or have dams who don't produce enough milk. Teaser stallions are used to test a mare's readiness for breeding, but they are not allowed to actually breed unless the farm needs to get a nurse mare pregnant. It's Taylor Made's responsibility to return Archie's mares to him pregnant.

She's not pregnant, and sitting on a hay bale, Steve glumly reports that he's one for three on nurse mares this year.

Casey manages to palpate the mare without getting manure on her shirt.

By the time they get to Bona Terra D, Scott and Dale have caught up. Dale was over with the yearlings, and Scott was out at a satellite facility called Just A Beginning. A new kitten meets them at the door. "What kind of lazy cat has only one kitten?" Barber asks.

Lori, feeling the cat's belly, sheepishly mumbles something about finding the time to spay her.

"Lori," Barber chides. "We put you in charge of the nurse mares and the barn cats."

They're not terribly busy this morning, but they do need to be done by 11:30, when they have their monthly meeting with Frank Taylor. They grumble about it and nag one another like a bunch of kids who have to go see the principal.

The last barn before the meeting is Bona Terra C. There are a couple of mares to palpate and a foal to sex for an owner who wants to know if he's getting a colt or a filly. It's a colt, and Barber leaves the mares to Lori. Lavaging one of them, they notice that her fluid is discolored. Barber points out that the other mares who've gone to the same stallion also come back from the breeding shed with discolored fluid, but so far, none of them has shown up with an infection.

Lori wonders if it's because the stallion's farm uses an extender—a supplementary fluid that helps increase his fertility rate.

Scott is pleased with Lori's judgment and her confidence in expressing it. "You might be right."

Still trying to get the mares finished, Lori needs one of the long cardboard tubes they use to peer down at the mare's cervix. Realizing she doesn't have one, she jogs down the aisle to her truck.

Scott and Barber, standing shoulder-to-shoulder, their arms crossed over their chests, tilt their heads in the universal stance of people who evaluate horses as they jog. Barber points out that Lori is crooked.

"Straightens out as she goes, though," Scott observes.

"She's a toeing-in thing when she starts, though, isn't she?"

Focused on the task at hand, Lori doesn't notice that they're watching her and is smiling when she comes back from the truck. She finishes the mare's examination, and Casey and Bob White, the manager for this division, start hauling gear back into the truck. Leaning against the weight of the ultrasound machine in her hand, Lori follows them. Catching up, Scott asks her what they're doing at the next barn.

Lori draws a blank. She has to look at her notes, she tells him. They're in the truck.

"You're about to take over this big ship," Scott reminds her with a smile. "You better know what you're doing."

Frank isn't going to make it to the meeting. Since Casey is sitting in his chair, Scott assigns her the responsibility of being Frank.

The first item on the agenda is the relative cost of the various brands of supplements. After the September 2008 yearling sale, Geoffrey Russell, Keeneland's director of sales, went on record with the statement that the market was in a correction. Prices were dropping in response to a decade's worth of overproduction and overpricing. The recession, which either prompted the correction or is simply coinciding with it, means that so far, no one really knows how much the market is going to drop before it stabilizes. Already some of the more marginal farms are starting to fold. Even the very deep pockets of Sheikh Mohammed, ruler of Dubai, and those of Coolmore and its owner, John Magnier of Ireland, which have been chiefly responsible for the massive payouts for top yearlings for a decade or more, seem to be feeling the impact of the recession.

The profits from the mare-boarding part of the operation are marginal at best. Where the farm makes its money is on the 5 percent commission it takes when it consigns the horse. When those commissions drop, as they have, there's less of a cushion for the boarding operation.

This year, everything is on the table. Every expense is being reevaluated: cosmetic surgeries, supplements, treatments, staffing, maintenance.

They're questioning whether or not the supplement they use to prevent ossification around the foal's joints is worth the expense.

Tucking her chin into her chest and lowering her voice, Casey says, "I don't know . . . two times the amount. I don't like that."

It's so close an imitation of Frank that everyone bursts out laughing.

"She's right-on," Scott says.

If the owner requests the more expensive treatment, the team agrees, then they can have it, but it will no longer be fed routinely.

"Still no sign of MRLS," Barber says, moving on to the next item.

"One thing you did for us that I like," he says to Sue Egan, the boarding assistant who keeps track of the mares' records, "was track the pregnancies that we lost."

Sue thinks that Frank's assistant, Bonnie Flanery, tracks that now, but Bart points out that she tracks the abortions; he wants the early fetal losses, as well. Scott would like to map and color-code the losses so if there is a pattern, they'll be able to see it right away.

They'll track the mares after twenty-eight days, and after Derby Day, when, they agree, they'll be able to see the patterns.

"I think we just ought to be keeping track of them," Scott says. "Like Glenarcy was empty at twenty-eight, she would go on the numbers, but fifteen days later, when she got back in foal, she would come off that one and drop up, and that would change. At the end of the year, we could say, 'Look, on May fifteenth, we had ten in this category; now we're down to eight, so we got two of those back.' Does that make sense?"

Sue thinks they could add the number to Bonnie's weekly breeding report.

"Not only that," says Scott, who is getting more enthusiastic about this idea. "Because she sends it to Pat and Mark and Ben and Duncan, maybe they would see that and not be so alarmed that we're losing pregnancies."

Outside the windows, a breeze is fluttering the trees and drifting into the office. It's peaceful and lazy outside. While Scott, Barber, and Sue figure out how to track data, the rest of the team looks lost in thought.

The next item is on a new sheet of paper. "What are we looking at? The mortality log?" Scott asks. "So how do we read this thing?" He nudges Casey. "That's your line. How do we read this thing?"

The mortality report is a running tally of the horses who've died on the farm. The most recent is a colt who was killed in a pasture accident on the yearling side.

"You guys did a good job getting the horse up there," Barber says to yearling manager John Hall, who takes part in these meetings. "Did, umm, did he get tranqued when he was turned out? Was there anything in hindsight?"

"Yeah. That's what Tom and I talked about," John says. "The regular protocol. You tranquilize two colts and put them out together and it turns out the colt they put him out with was a poor choice. I don't think anybody realized he'd gotten that aggressive with other horses. They were both tranquilized: a cc of Ace, a cc of Rompum. They dropped their heads pretty good. It's the same protocol. We've been doing it a long time."

The owner of the colt was understanding.

The account manager for the horse, they all agree, did a good job of keeping the owner informed every step of the way. Scott departs from the agenda to talk about a crushed hock.

"So is that thing done?" Scott's referring to the horse. "Is it a giveaway? For sure? That's a darn good foal. What do you think, Dr. Henderson?"

Lori has already talked to Rood and Riddle's specialist, who doesn't think the horse will stand up to training.

Barber wants to know if it's a colt. Lori and Scott tell him it's a filly.

"He's talking about giving her away." Scott is referring to the owner. "I don't want to give her away." He pauses. "But if that hock isn't going to be any good . . . If that hock's going to end up . . . You hear so many stories about awwwhhhh, when he was a baby, they x-rayed it and said it'll never be a racehorse and then it won this race. . . . So I *hate* giving up on babies on X-ray issues that early."

"Let me work on that," Barber says.

"Okay."

There were a couple of dummy foals—foals that don't get enough oxygen during the birth process. One never had a chance from the start. Scott asks Dale about the other. "That was the big, thick placenta. That was the placenta that had the black horn, right, Dale?"

Barber and Dale are counting the mortalities on their spreadsheet. "How many mares did we foal this year?" Barber asks.

"Close to two fifty," Sue says.

"Nine," Dale says, counting the number of foals that died. "That were actually full term, or stood."

"I got ten," Barber says. "But then you take out the foals that were born dead. . . . Well . . ."

"I came out and gave plasma right away," Dale says, referring to one mare. "That was a few hours later. It stood."

"There's not much you can do about that," Barber says. "Take that one off." He ticks off the others who were born dead or severely compromised. "So foals that were born healthy that we later lost, there's only three of them. One's a colic—not much you can do about that." That leaves them with two, he thinks, who might have been saved.

Bigger and bolder, the foals are getting harder to catch in the morning. At Springhouse lower, there are twenty-four mare and foal pairs split between two paddocks. The gates to the paddocks are right near the barn, but where the foals like to hang out is a long walk uphill. The mares are at the gate, ready to come in and eat, but the foals are testing their independence and refuse to come down from the top of the hill. Their mothers look at the grooms as if to say, *You* go get them.

The grooms leave the horses they can't catch until last. The mares linger by the gate, and the grooms, stooped low, walk quietly into the paddock. They whistle softly, sing a little, anything to arouse the interest of the foals, who, overcome by the curiosity and desire for connection that led them to being domesticated in the first place, tiptoe forward, their noses outstretched. Ever patient, the grooms stay still, letting the foals sniff, and then slowly they raise their arms under the foals' chins and quietly snap the lead shanks into place. Thus tricked, the foals either accept their lot or stamp their little hooves in consternation.

In Whitehouse lower, Juan and a new groom named Jacob West have already fed and turned out the mares, leaving behind the few that Barber and the team need to check out. They pull out the foals to poultice their legs, a practice recommended by Joe Taylor in his book. The medicinal mud not only hardens up tendons and ligaments, it also keeps the flies off, so that foals aren't stamping their feet and risking injury. Jacob stoops over with a big tub of poultice and, while Juan holds on to the horse, smears the mud downward, coating the foal's legs. Once it dries, it will take a couple of days for it to flake off, and then they'll replace it.

They've got a problem colt in their barn, a dark bay by Tale of the Cat who's puny: At four months, he's the size of a two-month-old. The grooms have nicknamed him "the Great Dane." He is listless and has low-energy, though the farm can't find anything wrong with him. He's had all the problems a foal could have: He was crooked and needed screws in his ankles. He had sesamoid fractures, and a tendon that's slightly bowed. He won't go to the sale—too many problems—so his owners are going to race him. But Juan and Jacob think he has bigger problems.

"He's lazy," Juan says. "He's the laziest horse I've ever seen."

"I bet my life savings," adds Jacob, "if you walk down there now, he'll be lying down."

He is—sprawled on the straw, eyes closed.

When he turns him out in the morning, Juan says, he doesn't race off like the other foals. He just stares up the hill, as if he's thinking, I gotta walk up this hill. I gotta walk.

The grooms repeat an industry truism as if it's their own insight. "A bad foal generates a lot more bills than a good one."

After rounds are completed and Steve has seen Barber and Scott off, he evaluates the foals in his division. With over a hundred mares, he's got too many to do on a daily basis, so he does a couple of barns a day. In Springhouse middle, as the grooms take the foals out of their stalls, they pause so Steve can look at them, and as they walk away, he centers his gaze on them so he can evaluate their walk.

Like everyone else, Steve likes a good shoulder—the depth of it indicates the length of the horse's stride. He also looks at the gaskin— the muscle mass between the point of the horse's thigh and the back of his hip. The straightness of the horse's legs, which most horsemen believe has less to do with the horse's ability than other factors, also needs to be evaluated. At around three months, there's an important developmental window in the foal's life in which surgeons can intervene to straighten the horse out. Foals who either toe in or toe out too severely have screws put into their fetlocks to stabilize them. As they grow, the screws stabilize the bones on one side of the fetlock, allowing the other side to catch up.

The foals are also getting their first lesson in how to stand still and be the subject of an appraising stare. They will be evaluated like this for the rest of their lives. Their pose and their walk is their currency—as important to their futures as it is to those of runway models.

Steve likes the Cherry Bomb filly. "She's athletic," he says. "She's got a lot of what you want." Ultimately, people who evaluate conformation are led by their own instincts and an overall impression. Steve does his own evaluations, but Scott does them, as well. Dictaphone in hand, he prowls the barn for an hour here and an hour there. His monthly reports, coupled with photographs taken by the farm's photographer, Sheri Pitzer, are sent to the foal's owners.

Steve has moved to Springhouse lower, the grooms riding with him in the back of the pickup. They pull the mare and foal pairs out one by one.

"Most of them look like average horses," he says, and then grins. "But they could be champions. You never know." He watches a few more foals go out the door with their mothers. "Every now and then," he adds, "you get a bad one."

At the end of this aisle is one of the farm's rock stars, a mare named Folklore. By Tiznow and out of a mare named Contrive, who also belonged to one of the farm's clients, she was bought by Bob and Beverly Lewis, owners of 1995 three-year-old champion filly, Serena's Song, and Derby winners Silver Charm and Charismatic. Bob Lewis died in February of 2006, at age eighty-one, and his horses are now owned by the Robert and Beverly Lewis Trust and managed by his widow, Beverly, and his son, Jeff.

As a two-year-old, Folklore was the Juvenile Fillies winner in 2005 and was retired at three, after she sustained a stress fracture during the Santa Ynez stakes. Retired late in the season, she didn't get pregnant that year, but in 2007 they bred her to Unbridled's Song. The colt she produced, says Jeff Lewis, "was beautiful," but about a week or so later, he "died without explanation, despite Taylor Made's best efforts to figure out what happened." He was found dead in the paddock, and they've never figured out what happened.

The chestnut colt in Folklore's stall now, who is squared off at Steve, his chin lifted like a pugilist, is by Distorted Humor. He's small and fierce, but Steve says, "If you didn't know who this was, you might not be inclined to pay much money for him."

"*Hay lista*," Steve tells the grooms, and the Folklore colt heads out to the paddock with his mother.

Lindsey likes to use the afternoons to get stuff done. It's almost June, and the foals who haven't yet shed their baby coats need to be clipped. They're in their stalls, napping in the early-summer warmth. The foals are sleepy, sprawled out at their mothers' feet, and the grooms have to tug at them to get them up. They spank their bottoms and cluck to them until the foals lift their heads, blinking at the grooms with their big eyes. It takes an extra effort to get their legs out in front of them because they're so long. The grooms pause to make sure the foals are balanced, before they lurch upward, leveraging their big butts forward. Once they're on their feet, they stretch like dogs, bowing down onto their front legs, their hind ends in the air. One groom clips and the other holds the lead shanks. The foals are getting bigger fast, and are now eye level with their grooms. Angela's Love's filly stands quietly as her sun-bleached baby coat is shaved off, revealing a dark, smooth coat underneath. She and her groom gaze at each other. Leaning forward, he plants a kiss on the whorl of white hairs in the middle of her forehead.

In Whitehouse upper, Juan and Jacob have finished feeding the mares out in their paddocks. Even this is according to Joe Taylor's directions. "Place all the mineral blocks in a row," he wrote in his book, "about sixty feet apart. Starting at the first mineral block, put down a small flake of hay and pour the grain ration on top of the hay. Walk 25 to 30 feet toward the next mineral block and put down another hay/grain pile." Juan and Jacob's improvement on this procedure is the use of the tractor—Juan driving and Jacob balancing on the trailer as it bounces along, tossing the hay and grain out behind it. From a distance, it looks as if the mares have agreed to eat in a nice straight line.

It's almost the end of the shift, and Juan and Jacob are waiting to go home. The other grooms, separated from them by class and rank, are gathered near the doorway, the radio quietly playing salsa music. Jacob is on top of a hay bale, leaning back against the wall, his long legs stretched in front of him. He quit a career in banking to come work in the barns, and already the Taylors are exposing him to the financial aspects of the business—he's been to sales meetings and shares the brothers' insights with Juan. He'll be going to the sales in September, but he's a big guy and makes the yearlings look small by comparison, so he won't be allowed to show them to the customers.

Juan has opened the door of another of the farm's rock stars— Alidiva. Foaled in 1987, she won three of five starts and earned a respectable sixty thousand dollars by the time she was retired. In 1997, as a broodmare, three of her foals won Grade 1 races in the same year, earning her broodmare of the year honors in both Ireland and Italy. At twenty-two, with a Giant's Causeway filly at her side, she's pregnant with what Duncan believes will be her last foal. She's owned by Charles Wacker, who lives in South Africa and directs the management of Alidiva and his other horses through Duncan Taylor and Wacker's assistant, Georgette Simon.

Alidiva's filly is curious, and Juan can't keep himself from playing with her. He steps into the stall and waits. She pricks her ears and steps forward, one delicate hoof at a time, while Alidiva stands with her back to them, staring out the window toward her paddock. The filly creeps slowly around her mother's body, nosing out toward Juan's extended hand. He moves, and she jumps back toward her mother. Juan pursues her, getting a hand on her halter, petting and cooing until she's relaxed, and then he lets her go, sliding the stall gate closed and dropping in the peg that locks it in place.

Outside, the cars that pick up the grooms are circling the farm's lanes. Crowded and running rough, they're full of men in Taylor Made shirts and khakis. Tied by family and neighborhood, they ride in together from Lexington, the drivers disgorging passengers all over the farm before they park in front of their own barns. Juan and Jacob each have their own cars, beaters that rev up roughly before they drive away.

The radios off, the grooms gone, stillness creeps over the barns. It's quiet enough to hear cars whooshing by on East Hickman Road. The mares crop the grass, occasionally coming close enough to the fence so that you can hear the sound of it tearing. At their sides, the foals leap and gallop away, already racing one another, though their bodies are still too small to produce the heart-racing pounding that they will when they're older. Closer and more insistent is the twittering of birds in the rafters. Starlings and sparrows swoop in and land on the wooden beams and swoop out, bits of pilfered straw in their beaks. The night-watch crew hasn't arrived yet, but the divisional managers are around—finishing up paperwork in their offices, driving down the lanes from one barn to the next. At Taylor Made, the horses do not often go for more than an hour without being the subject of someone's gaze.

In Whitehouse upper, Alidiva has been left inside because she and her filly are going to the clinic first thing in the morning. The filly, who is sprawled in the straw, asleep at her mother's feet, is going to have screws put in her fetlocks. Alidiva stands with her back to the door of her stall, gazing out the long vertical window that faces the front of the barn. The mares in the paddock have moved over the rise and Alidiva can no longer see them. Tense, alert, ears pricked, she stares out the window in concentration, as if she's listening for the sound of their movements.

The day of Alidiva '09's surgery is cool and damp. Barrett arrives a little before six. The mares are still asleep in their paddocks, lying down, some of them with their backs pressed up against each other, and snoring softly. The sound of the trailer rattling by, hollow and empty, rouses them and they heave to their feet with deep groans, snorting dust out of their nostrils and nickering to one another, as if they're pleased to find that they've woken up in the company of friends.

According to Barrett, he's made 209 trips to the clinic this year. His worst are the nighttime runs on icy roads. This winter, with a mare colicking in the trailer, it took him half an hour to get down the ice-coated lane from Bona Terra to East Hickman Road, a drive that normally takes about two minutes. He stuck one set of wheels on the grass and progressed by inches, never letting the wheels completely give up the traction they had until he got to the road.

By 6:15, Barrett is on the road with two mares, Alidiva and Uaintseennothinyet, and their two foals and is weaving into Lexington's commuter traffic. Because it's Lexington, the commuters are used to horse trailers during rush hour. Even this late in the season, mares are being shipped to breeding sheds, and the roads are populated by the boxy, short-bodied horse vans, which are coated with transfer-print advertisements for local stallions.

The first to arrive at Rood and Riddle, Barrett curves past the main entrance and pulls up in front of the first angled and elongated parking space. A technician greets him and they walk Alidiva and her filly down the ramp and into the holding stalls—metal and wire enclosures under a roof, a prefab garden shed set up as a tack room in the middle of the row.

Starlee Smith, assistant to Dr. Rolf Embertson, one of Rood and Riddle Hospital's equine surgeons, arrives with her clipboard. She checks the foal in while two of the interns behind her are laughing. It's the annual prank day—the last day of the internship—and for this year's prank, the interns have appropriated the partners' parking spaces. In one, a bicycle sits propped on its kickstand.

Starlee examines Alidiva '09 and gives her antibiotics. Even though the foal and the mare are separated by just a few feet, the mother is stressed. Behind the wire fencing, Alidiva's lips are pressed together and she's snorting and whinnying softly to her foal. The Taylor Made foals, says Starlee, are some of the best-behaved ones that the clinic handles.

Like Barrett, the other drivers wear the insignia of their farms. They greet one another over coffee in the clinic's well-appointed waiting room. Like everyone else's in the industry, their hair is neatly trimmed, and though the drivers work with animals, they look scrubbed, their boots in good repair.

The procedure that will straighten out Alidiva's fetlocks costs twelve hundred dollars for the first leg and three hundred dollars for the second. Even in a down economy, says Starlee, most owners will pay for the screws and wire procedure. Bidding on even modestly priced horses goes up in five-thousand-dollar increments. If those straight legs get someone to bid one more time, the surgery will have more than paid for itself. And if your horse's crooked leg causes someone to go elsewhere, the cost to the seller will be far more than the twelve hundred dollars for the surgery.

Embertson arrives at 8:30 in slacks and a Hawaiian shirt. Since Barrett got there first, Alidiva '09 is the first in line. Embertson watches her walk up and down outside the stalls. Scott sent her in for one ankle, but Embertson thinks she needs both of them done. Starlee gets Scott on the phone and he agrees with the vets' recommendation. He moves on to evaluate the next foal, Uaintseennothinyet, while Alidiva and her foal are walked into the clinic.

As a twenty-two-year-old broodmare, Alidiva is not unfamiliar with this clinic, but she's still stressed. She passes through the double doors to the cavernous space inside. The technician leads her to the doorway of a padded room where a hoist hangs from the ceiling. Both she and her filly are given a sedative. Alidiva's head droops and her technician talks to her gently, scrubbing the mare's neck with her fingers and patting her. Her filly gets a second injection and sinks to her knees, the technicians supporting her as she slowly crumples to the floor. Once her filly is down, Alidiva is led away. She goes quietly.

A resident maneuvers the hoist over the filly and the technicians roll her body back and forth over the hoist's straps. The hoist lifts her onto a gurney with a black Tempur-Pedic pad. It's concave in the middle and its sides are high, shaped to support a horse that is lying on its back.

In the preoperating room, a breathing tube is inserted into the filly's mouth. She will breathe on her own throughout the surgery, but the tube ensures that she will take a full breath instead of panting shallowly. Her front legs are tied to poles on the corner of the gurney, while her back legs splay to the sides, like those of a cat who's fallen asleep on its back, belly exposed.

Watching through an observation window as the technicians shave her legs, Barrett comments on the filly's white stockings. "That's going to be a nice-looking yearling," he says. "Some woman is going to talk her husband into paying a lot of money at the sale."

The techs are using the filly's belly as a table for their antiseptic and gauze-filled canisters, balancing them between the flat part of her belly and the inside of her thighs. Alidiva '09's belly rises and collapses rhythmically. More technicians and another resident arrive, one finishing her coffee, the other spooning up the last of her yogurt from a paper cup. Masks on, they cover the filly's feet in blue booties. Having used up all the gauze in the stainless-steel canisters, they're now scrubbing her down with Betadine from a flat pan on her belly.

Dr. Embertson consults a whiteboard with the day's surgeries. He does fetlocks on the same day.

Alidiva's outside in her temporary stall. She's nervous but not frantic. Returning from checking on her, a tech reports that she's a very sensible mare.

There are horses everywhere. The clinic looks just like a regular medical clinic, but instead of people in various stages of medical treatment, there are horses. A yearling plants his feet outside a room that he's being led into. His tech gives him a minute to look around at the padded walls, the crane above his head, the bank of beeping, lighted equipment along one wall, and then tugs his lead shank, pulling him through.

On the other side of the operating room, a stallion is being delivered, via crane, to a padded recovery room. The clinic's outer door opens and an intern whistles lightly, leading a brilliant chestnut colt with a shank over his nose down the aisle. "Watch your back on this one," she calls out as everyone gets out of her way.

Outside, Dr. Larry Bramlage, the TV networks' favorite go-to veterinary commentator, is watching horses jog. An expert in lameness and orthopedic surgery, he's surrounded by young interns who are watching a huge black warmblood with the floating gaits and swinging motion of a dressage horse jog in a circle.

In the operating room, Dr. Embertson wraps the filly's ankles in blue surgical cloths. Her legs are now suspended from a bar that hangs from the ceiling. Compression wraps are layered over the blue surgical cloths. With a scalpel, Dr. Embertson makes a small incision in the skin covering the filly's fetlock. Using a compact drill and bearing down, he drills a three-inch screw into the bone, cranking it down with a special screwdriver. He repeats the procedure on the left front leg and then leaves the room while the residents take X-rays.

When he returns, he stitches up the incision and covers it with a small bandage. Once he's checked the X-rays, he strips the latex coating off her legs and wraps them in layers of gauze. The vets recommend that the horses wear these bandages for fourteen days after the surgery. Bob White doesn't think they're much good after about three days because the horses live outside and the bandages get wet and muddy.

As Alidiva '09 is wheeled out of the operating room, Uaintseen-nothingyet is wheeled into it.

In the padded recovery room the techs heave the Alidiva filly off the gurney and onto thick floor mats. Her breathing tube will stay in until she swallows. The first male technician to handle her lays blue towels over her neck, which is wet with sweat. He leans back against her, lying over her neck to keep her from thrashing around when she starts to wake up. He opens up the sports section of the *Lexington Herald-Leader* while he waits.

In a few minutes, she starts to wake up, first by calling out in a high-pitched whinny, which shakes her whole body and jiggles the technician's paper. He keeps reading but lays a hand on her, letting her know she's not alone. He continues to lie on her even as she stirs. Not quite fully awake, she lurches forward, about to crash onto her nose, but the tech, on his feet now, grabs hold of her tail and keeps her from going down. He's run a rolled-up green towel through her halter and he's using that to keep her head up. With his free hand, he's using a sweat scraper to flick the water off her body.

She's wobbly but whinnying. The tech hangs on to her while she slips first to one side, then the other, catching her under her butt to keep her from falling. She's as cumbersome and wet as a big fish and he's trying to make sure she doesn't fall down.

He and another tech lead her back out to her mother, still wobbly. She's propped up in between them like she's headed out the door between two bouncers. Once she's back in her stall, her dam stops whinnying and hovers over her protectively. Baring her teeth at the other mares, she whips around the perimeter of the stall and then comes back to her baby. Next to her, Uaintseennothinyet is whinnying for her foal, who's still inside the clinic.

Alidiva '09 went into surgery at 8:20 A.M., and by 9:35, she's back with her dam and nursing. Once Uaintseennothinyet comes back out, Starlee gives them both a shot of penicillin and Barrett is cleared to take them back to the farm.

By nine o'clock that night, the farm has returned to slumber. There's just enough light out to count individual mares in the fields. On their next rounds, members of the night watch crew will have to use their spotlights. Flat gray clouds creep up on the eastern horizon and one huge cream puff of a cloud has a big hole in the middle, where lightning flashes orange. The mares are sighing and snoring in their paddocks. Frogs croak down by the creek and a motorcycle patters down East Hickman Road. A crescent moon hangs overhead and layers of lightning flash inside the huge clouds.

On quiet nights, Terry parks down by Springhouse lower. It's a good place to see without being seen. In between rounds, she smokes a cigarette and reads a book; her cell phone is largely silent—she seems to prefer horses to people. Terry's finishing up her second foaling season with the farm, and she is forever grateful to Scott for giving her a chance. "I didn't know anything about broodmares," she said. But she told him how much she wanted to learn and how hard she was willing to work. Now that she's learned how to deliver foals on her own, she wants to learn how to get inside a mare and turn around a foal that's upside down. But since foaling season is over for now, she'll have to wait until next year.

Pedigree

4

September 2009

SEPTEMBER 14, 2009, THE FIRST DAY OF KEENELAND
September, the yearling sale, falls on the one-year anniversary of the collapse of Lehman Brothers. Of the
5,189 horses cataloged for the 2009 sale, Taylor Made Farm is selling
564 of them, and 86 of those are in Book 1, the "select" horses.

For over a decade, Taylor Made has been the leading consignor at
this sale. Its best year was in 2006, when it sent 554 horses through the
ring for a gross of $62 million. At the other big sale that year, the No-
vember bloodstock sale, 410 horses went through the ring for a little
over $52 million. Total sales for that fiscal year, including the smaller
sales and the horses who didn't initially meet their reserves and were
sold privately afterward, amounted to $169.5 million. That was the fis-
cal year that pushed Taylor Made over the benchmark of one billion
dollars in cumulative sales. And those totals don't include the income
from their stallions, their shares in other horses, or the boarding.

By 2007, it was clear to everyone that the market was starting to slide, and the sales total from that fiscal year had dropped by $30 million, to $136 million, and the following year, 2008, they netted $104 million. Taylor Made rode this bubble up—in 1993, its total sales were just $19.2 million—and so those at Taylor Made are not surprised that they're going to have to ride it down. "We saw this coming," says Ben Taylor, the vice president of Taylor Made Stallions.

Like other agricultural products, there's a lag time between when a racehorse is produced and when it comes to market—two years. The horses coming to sale in 2009 were bred at the height of the market, when stud fees were at their highest. Some of those fees dropped for the 2008 breeding season, but the stallion syndicates didn't adjust their fees to the current market reality until the *end* of 2008. For this year and the next, yearlings are coming to a down market carrying stud fees that are two to three times higher than they are now.

The Keeneland sales pavilion, built in 1969, blossoms out from the sales ring at its center. Six hundred and fifty seats are divided into four sections. A windowed wall separates the arena from the rest of the pavilion, where there are offices and conference rooms, a media room, two dining rooms, an indoor and outdoor bar, and, in 2005, a renovated repository where buyers can review X-rays of the horses for sale.

Behind the auction ring, separated by giant double doors and built in 1980, is an indoor walking ring connected to the sales ring by a lead-in chute.

On Keeneland's 1,038 acres, there are forty-nine barns available to consignors, but the grounds can only hold sixteen hundred horses at a time. Big consignors like Taylor Made take over several barns, shipping in truckloads of horses every couple of days. As the horses from one set of barns sell and ship out, a new set comes in. Taylor Made, which has the largest number of horses, followed by Eaton Sales and then Lane's End, has its Book 1 horses in barns three and four, which are downhill and northeast of the pavilion. Book 2 horses, in barns 22 and 23, are uphill and southwest, and just behind them are barns 33 and 34, which hold even more horses. There are Taylor Made staff members, in their blue button-down shirts and burgundy ties, scattered all over the grounds.

At 7:00 A.M., on the first morning of the sale, the skies are the honest blue of baby's eyes; it's warm, but with the lingering nip of cool overnight air. The buyers have started their trek through the barns. Armed with their catalogs, some of them tucked into leather portfolio covers, pens in their pockets, or dangling from a string around their necks (the pen on a string is a popular Taylor Made giveaway), and trailing their retinues, they march with great purpose down the little rise between Taylor Made and the Lane's End consignment next door. Marching even more purposefully are the vets, endoscopes looped around their necks, followed by their assistants, twitches in hand.

Ready to receive them, eyes bright, smiles on their faces, hair smoothed into place, are the Taylor Made staff members and horses. The farm hires over a hundred temporary employees for the sale, fits them out in khakis, blue button-down shirts, the farm's signature burgundy tie embroidered with the silks of their most successful clients. At the welcome desk, a staff member takes the buyers' names, politely sounding out those that he is struggling to spell, types them into the computer, then on a touch screen that charts the horses' hip numbers (assigned sale number attached to the horse's hip), taps out which horses any given customer wants to see. The computer prints out a ticket, which is then passed to a controller. The controller gets the information to the right quad leader, and he, in turn, signals the grooms, who bring out the horses and hand them to the showmen, those grooms who are especially skilled at showing a horse to its best advantage. While a horse is being brought out, a front man lingers near the buyer with a laminated spiral-bound notebook that includes information and updates on every horse in that barn.

The Taylors, who've been the leading consignor at this sale for the past decade, came to the business because this is what they knew. While Duncan Taylor's brothers really liked horses, riding their ponies around the farm as kids, he says, "If I'd grown up in Detroit, I'd have done something with cars."

In his book, *Joe Taylor's Complete Guide to Breeding and Raising Racehorses*, Joe Lannon Taylor, the family patriarch, described their Kentucky roots. His mother was a Lannon, he wrote, whose family came from Ireland to farm. Like many men in the Thoroughbred business, Joe Taylor started out with trotting horses. More popular than Thoroughbreds, who were thought to be for the elite, Standardbreds were the common man's racehorse up until the mid-twentieth century. Unlike a Thoroughbred, whose breeding and registration was controlled by a central body, the Jockey Club, a Standardbred was any horse who could trot a mile under two minutes and thirty seconds. It was a very democratic standard, suggesting that it was possible for anyone with a fast trotter in the back paddock to have a champion racehorse. Their derby was the Hambletonian, still run every year at the Meadowlands in East Rutherford, New Jersey.

Joe Taylor's upbringing was a hardscrabble one. He quit high school, sharecropped, worked with horses, enlisted in the army, married Mary Emily Marshall—whom he revered and who bore eight children, two daughters and six sons, one of whom, Danny, died in a car accident in 1969, when he was just nineteen years old; another son, Chris, was killed in 1981 by a relative of one of the family's employees.

Joe Taylor worked on the track, struggled, and then paired up with Clarence Gaines of Gainesway Farm. As its farm manager, Joe Taylor went on to help Gainesway develop one of the most influential Thoroughbred stallion programs in the world, passing his management techniques onto multiple generations of horsemen.

Despite their influence on management and sales practices, the Taylors don't see themselves as the main decision makers in the industry. The Phippses, the Whitneys, the Hancocks, the Farishes, these are the blue-blooded aristocracies of American Thoroughbred racing. The Taylors, Irish Catholic, hardboots, are the upstarts and outsiders whose profits derive from the service they provide to their clients. "For better or for worse," explains Mark, the youngest of the brothers, "and some people won't like this, we didn't come from a background where we had the luxury of saying our goal is to improve the Thoroughbred breed and make this noble creature the best it can be. We came from a background of 'We have to pay the bills and we have to eat, and hey, maybe we can get into this horse deal.'" The Taylors are not shapers of Thoroughbred destiny. They are, Mark explains, "entrepreneurs and capitalists" whose business is to provide a service to those people who want to buy and sell racehorses.

By 8:30 A.M., the stabling area at Keeneland is crazy. The sale starts at 10:00 A.M., and though most of the decisions about today's horses have already been made, people are sneaking a last look and are starting on tomorrow's horses. Those horses who were raised at Taylor Made have been prepped for this sale for their entire lives. They've been groomed and patted, kissed and handled. When they're asked to walk, they're asked to walk exactly the same way each time—three firm pats on the neck, *whap, whap, whap,* and march. When they are turned, the grooms are always on the outside, never blocking the buyer's view, and when they signal the horses that they're going to stop, the horses have three strides in which to do so: one to slow, one to brake, and one to square off. Buyers are looking at only the horse they've asked to see, and not at the five or ten others who are out of their stalls and being shown to someone else. Most are behaving, but others are leaping, skittering, kicking, and bucking at the ends of their lead shanks. When someone yells, "Watch it!" those with their backs to the commotion respond to the threat just like a horse would: darting to safety and then turning to look at what they have run away from.

"Señor!" A front man named Raul calls to a groom who is returning hip number 544 to his stall. "Come back out with the horse, five forty-four."

The showman turns on his heel and walks back into the stall, clipping the lead shank onto the Speightstown colt. "One more time," he says. "Time for a walk. Time for a walk."

Hip number one, the first horse to be auctioned on the first day of the 2009 sales, is a gray filly by Mr. Greeley and out of Queen. She's owned by Sam and Jo Pollock.

"We had a mare named Contrive," says Jo Pollock, telling the story of how she and her husband, Sam, ended up with Queen. "She had a filly named Folklore." Folklore, who was bought as a yearling by Bob and Beverly Lewis, went on to win $945,000 as a two-year-old, including winning the Breeders' Cup Juvenile Fillies and was an Eclipse champion two-year-old. After Folklore's success, Jo says, the farm told her the mare was "too valuable to keep." And to their surprise, she brought three million dollars at the sale. Income from the sale of horses is taxed as regular income, and when her husband told her they were going to have to pay taxes on all that profit, she said, "I don't want to do that!" The way to avoid doing that is to invest the money in more horses right away. The tax penalty can then be spread out over several years, as those horses are sold off over time, or even depreciated if some of those horses lose their value. They spent $2.5 million on five horses, one of whom was Queen, and only one of those five "has produced the kind of foal we're looking for. Now I wish I had kept Contrive," Jo says.

Jo likes Queen, who will be sold in November at the bloodstock sale, and her foals. "I didn't *want* to sell any of them." But she can't afford to keep all of her horses. "They eat every day," she says. And there's boarding, as well as shoes, shots, and the vet. "It's amazing how much goes into a mare," she says. "If you pay a fifty-thousand-dollar stud fee, the foal really needs to bring a hundred and fifty thousand."

Queen's 2009 foal, by Street Cry, is on the farm, being prepped for next year. And this year's foal, for whom they paid a $75,000 stud fee for Mr. Greeley, will be the first horse, in the first book, in the first sale measuring the depth and gravity of a major market correction.

"Bummer for Queen," says Mark Brooking, Taylor Made's marketing and research director.

Already bathed and groomed on a daily basis, Queen '08 is led to the "top-off" station, where she'll have a final polishing before being sent up to the ring. The top-off station is at the end of the barn, where it's cool, dark, and quiet. Outside, the yearlings are marching and sometimes leaping for buyers; it's noisy and hectic, but at the top-off station, a groom named Sherry creates a peaceful and purposeful bubble around the filly. Sherry's a big woman, with a ponytail trailing down her back, and, presumably because she has no contact with the public, is allowed to wear her regular clothes—a T-shirt printed with a four-item checklist: I'M IGNORING YOU. I DON'T CARE. I'M NOT LISTENING, and, the final checked-off item, ALL OF THE ABOVE.

Like her mother and half sister, the Queen filly is a gray. Sherry walks around her methodically, calmly, talking to her and patting her, inventorying what needs to be done.

She starts with a spritz of ShowSheen, a coat conditioner that makes the coat shiny. It also makes it slippery, but no one's going to be putting a saddle on the filly. From her table of supplies, Sherry takes a bright white towel that she's hoarded away from the grooms, sprays it, and wipes the filly's face gently. Queen '08 closes her eyes and presses into the cloth helpfully. Deftly, Sherry flicks a disposable razor over the whiskers under the filly's eyes and on her lip, tickling it.

A groom named Herman holds the filly. When she hears a noise outside the barn, she tilts her head but keeps her eyes on Sherry. In the cool darkness, Sherry murmurs to her while she rubs baby oil onto her hands and then presses them against the filly's mane and forelock, shining and darkening them. With scissors, she trims away the filly's "poofies," the tufts of hair sticking up out of her ears. She smooths more baby oil into her tail and pushes her mane over from the opposite side of her neck.

The filly wrinkles her nose and snorts. "What's that smelly stuff I'm putting on you?" Sherry coos.

When she bends over to paint her hooves, the filly stamps the dirt. Sherry spritzes her with fly spray. "Now no more excuses," she tells her.

Being careful not to let the brush touch the dirt, Sherry paints mineral oil onto the filly's hooves, turning them dark and shiny. Methodically, slowly, she moves back to the filly's face and, with more baby oil on her palms, rubs it into the filly's eyelids and muzzle, softening and darkening the skin. Queen '08 snorts.

"I know, pumpkin," Sherry says to her.

For the finishing touch, Sherry passes a sheepskin fleece over the filly's coat to remove any brush marks and then rubs a dab of blue V05 into the darkest part of the filly's legs and hocks to "make them pop."

"Or course we all know," she adds, "there's some you don't want to bring attention to their knees and hocks."

A little Brasso to shine the halter plate and some mineral oil on the skin under her tail to clean and darken and she's done. Calm, relaxed, primped, and sparkling, the filly pokes her nose out for Sherry to kiss.

"Time to go?" Herman asks.

"If you want to mosey on up there," Sherry tells him, and just be-fore the filly walks out of the barn, Sherry uses the brush one last time to flatten out the little hairs in the crease above the filly's thigh.

Alert and calm, Queen '08 follows Herman up the lane that leads to the pavilion. They climb a sandy path up a short hill, cut through the middle of another barn, and enter the covered walking rings—two adjacent rings connected in the middle like a figure eight. A paneled wall closes in their center ovals, and behind it, buyers watch the horses walk before they enter the pavilion. From one of the shed rows, an-other yearling whinnies and Queen '08 whinnies back. On her toes, nervous and bouncy, she's alert but obedient as she follows Herman around the rings, walking counterclockwise around the top one, and then, as the rings fill up, moving to the bottom one and walking up and down one side only. On the other side, a filly by Rock Hard Ten is doing the same thing.

The middle of the ring is full of lookers. Most of them men, they wear khakis and jeans, polos and madras shirts, their weight planted evenly between feet that are sensibly shod, or they lean on the wall, their feet already tired, peering down through their reading glasses at their catalogs. When they signal, Herman sets up the filly so they can look.

A Keeneland security guard stationed at the ramp between the walking rings and the pavilion calls for hip numbers one and two. As the fillies head up the ramp, he shouts, "Horse coming! Watch your back!"

Queen '08, spooked by the sudden darkness of the pavilion, plants her feet and rears. Behind her, a Taylor Made groom who's been as-signed to the holding area materializes and taps a rolled-up newspaper against the ramp wall, sending the filly into the indoor walking ring, the Rock Hard Ten filly right behind her. They both look around and poop nervously. A Keeneland employee in khaki overalls sweeps the piles into a shovel and dumps them into a garbage can.

The indoor walking ring is enclosed by the same kind of paneled wall as the outer rings. On the side facing the sales ring, the ring narrows to a walkway, which, in turn, splits around a high wall, creating two chutes for the horses on deck, who, when their number is called, will pass through a huge sliding door and into the auction ring, passing on their left the auctioneer's stand, where, above their heads, sit the three auctioneers.

Once the auction starts, the crowd begins to gather at the walking rings, pressing in toward the chutes, where you can see the horses close-up, then watch them enter the ring, where they appear on the monitor sitting on top of the wall that separates the lead-in chutes.

It's also where the bid spotters can see you, and some high-profile buyers, like Sheikh Mohammed, bid from back here. It's also where there's a break in the wall, so anyone crossing from one side of the pavilion to the other can cut through without having to double back or leave the building. By the time Queen '08 enters the ring, Frank Taylor is standing in the middle of that intersection. He keeps an eye on his horse as it goes in, then watches it sell on the screen. Account manager Jeff Hayslett has shown up. The Pollocks are nearby, and Scott Kintz has arrived. Kintz likes the barn better than the sale, but he usually stops by for at least some of it.

At 10:10 A.M., ten minutes late, the loudspeaker crackles awake, the announcer reads the rules of the sale, the big double doors open, and Queen '08 is handed off to one of the green-jacketed Keeneland handlers. The announcer reads her pedigree and the buyers are summoned to start their bidding. Bidding opens at $10,000 and closes three minutes later with a $92,000 bid by Blandford Bloodstock of Great Britain. Frank, Jeff Hayslett, and Scott exchange a look of concern.

Queen '08 is led back to her stall. Her reserve price was met and the sale will go through, and at some point today, Blandford will send a van to pick her up. She'll never see the farm again, unless she is retired to it as a broodmare.

At the end of the day, Mark Brooking speculates that "this might be the worst day ever. Great for buyers. Bad for sellers." Keeneland's spin on the sale, delivered though their sales director, Geoffrey Russell, is that it's a bad economy and a market correction and that all in all, the losses really aren't that bad.

But they're pretty bad. Overall, by the time the sale is over two weeks from now, the market will be down about 40 percent. Taylor Made Farm will be the leading consignor again, with a gross of $27.9 million, down $20 million from last year and less than half of the $62 million of 2006. It's a harbinger of what's to come at the November bloodstock sale, which will represent even greater losses, dropping from $32.9 million in November 2008—the beginning of the recession—to $14.5 million in November 2009.

After the sale, Scott sends the last of the 2009 foals over to the yearling side. John Hall divvies them up among the seven barns under his care, sorting them by owner so that when the owners visit their horses, the farm can minimize the disruption to the horses' schedules. What horses like, what makes them feel secure and happy, is structure.

Sixty-eight years old, John Hall is a native New Englander. He's got one daughter in the business, the other is an engineer, and his son works in finance. His father rode hunters and jumpers on the New England show circuit and John grew up in the business. He moved into Thoroughbreds, but in the eighties, he realized that the racing industry in New England was "evaporating." He called the Taylors, whom he'd gotten to know through the yearling sales, and asked if a guy like him could get a job in Kentucky.

The brothers responded by telling him a guy like him could get a job at Taylor Made. Because he'd already worked with the yearlings, Hall explains, Frank started him out on the broodmare side so he could learn that part of the business. When Mark, who was managing the yearlings, took over as VP of public sales, John took over the yearlings.

His hands are gnarled from years of physical work and he is thin and slightly bent. Hall moves quickly, but with the stiffness of someone who's a little sore. He keeps his Taylor Made cap tapped down over neatly barbered white hair and his eyes are a bright Yankee blue.

When he first came to Taylor Made, the farm was in the business of breaking its own yearlings, but that practice has since stopped. "It was a business decision," Hall says. It made it easier to hire staff because they no longer needed to hire grooms who could also ride.

In the warm haze of an October morning, John Hall has his phone to his ear as he watches the 2009 yearlings come up from the paddocks outside Yearling Complex C. One of the newer barns on the farm, it's very prettily situated halfway down a rise. From the front, the paddocks swoop down to a little gulley and then up through a row of trees to a hill with nothing but trees and grass and the horizon. From the side door, where the yearlings are walking up from their paddocks in single file, each attached to its own groom, the view heads down and up a hill, nothing but paddocks and blackboard fencing and, in the early light before breakfast, the dark-bodied horses and their grooms walking single file up the lane between the paddocks. John Hall's house, where he lives with his wife, Debbie, and hosts his weekly poker games, sits on a rise behind the barn.

As the grooms lead the yearlings in one by one, they pause, giving John a chance to evaluate the foals. Sometimes they announce a horse's name, which is engraved on a brass plate attached to a leather neck strap, but sometimes they don't. In another month, John will know the hundred or so yearlings on the farm by sight. With him is Cesar Terrazas, the manager of the Eagle Creek section of the yearling division. As they watch, the Chartreuse yearling limps up the path from the paddock.

"*No bueno*," says his groom when he stops at the door.

"*No bueno*," John agrees. Placing the phone in its holder, he drops to one knee to feel the filly's leg as Cesar keeps an eye on the rest of the horses coming through the door. John sends the groom and filly inside. Twice as tall as the rest of the grooms, Jacob West, who is continuing his rotation through the stations of the farm as he completes his training, leads in a gray filly. John wants to know if it's Queen's 2009 filly by the Irish stallion Street Cry.

"It's fat and it's gray," Jacob quips. "It's Queen."

She also has crooked front legs. The left front one bows out, and the pressure is going to create uneven wear on her knee. The fuss about toeing in and toeing out is important mostly to people looking for perfectly conformed horses. But even buyers who are forgiving of conformation flaws don't like uneven knees.

But a 2006 study published in the *Equine Veterinary Journal*, conducted by researchers at the University of Glasgow, the University of

Bristol, and the British Jockey Club, stated, "There is remarkable inconsistency among putative associations between lameness and conformation attributes." Among the conformational flaws the team tracked from a yearling crop through their racing careers were being toed in and being back at the knee. Even the long-held belief that offset knees are associated with racing injuries did not seem to be borne out by the research. They found that "the statistical significance of these associations was weak." That said, the researchers *did* find that being back at the knee and being "tied below," or what Americans refer to as "over at the knee," were clearly heritable traits, even if their impact on soundness was unclear. Furthermore, the study stated, it's almost impossible to separate conformational traits from "other inherited traits that might affect performance, such as cardiovascular and respiratory functions and muscle fiber type."

What far outweighed any of these factors, the researchers found, was the horse's sire. "Overall," they wrote, "there was very little evidence to support an effect of conformational defects on racing performance. . . . Not surprisingly, the results of this study indicate that in this population of horses, racing performance was very strongly predicated by pedigree."

In November 2010, the *Thoroughbred Daily News,* published a report entitled "Do We Need a Sturdier Racehorse?" in which they polled professionals from all quarters of the racing industry about the measurable decrease in the average number of starts per racehorse, from 10.22 in 1970 to 6.2 in 2009. That number is more helpful in determining overall Thoroughbred health than an examination of the more dramatic events, like the televised breakdowns of Barbaro and Eight Belles. Wastage, fatal or career-ending injuries, in racehorses has always been high, but it's also been consistent for the past few decades.

While many critics both within and without the industry believe that surgically modifying the horses means that the breeders are hiding flaws that will be passed down to the next generation of racehorses, others, like James MacLeod of the University of Kentucky's Gluck Equine Research Center, claim, in the *Thoroughbred Daily News* report, that genetic changes just don't happen that quickly. "It is hard to arrive at a genetic explanation for a shift in the population as large and diverse as Thoroughbreds in such a short period of time." Other factors that might be worth more scrutiny, the report suggests, are the lack of uniformity in drug policy, and a dramatic change in training practices that has arisen as a result of sophisticated and comprehensive data collection that forces trainers to keep up a very high percentage of winning races so they don't lose their clients—thereby training their horses less often and less strenuously, and avoiding those challenging races that build a horse's fitness and ability but might also lead to a loss.

"Since I've been a kid," Mark Taylor says, "I've seen every guru in the world come around and come up with a way that they were going to fix that [crooked ankles]. From big huge extension shoes out to here and plaster and Equilox put on them and stuff." In his judgment, the surgeries are actually an improvement because they're not damaging ligaments and undermining the integrity of the foot and leg by applying "abnormal pressure loading" to try to straighten them out. "What I love about these screws . . ." he begins, then explains that the reason horses are crooked in their limbs is because one side of the growth plate is growing faster than the other. "What that screw does is, it closes the growth plate and shuts down the growth on the outside, so the inside continues to grow and pushes the leg back out. So you're not doing all this contortion activity with the foot. The foot is the foundation of the horse. You're just timing it out to where when that horse stops growing in that particular plate of the body, that the leg is as straight as can be. Once it stops growing, it is what it is on that day. . . . When you see a certain bloodline of a horse and say, 'Oh they're all pigeon-toed,' really what that means is that the outside of their ankles grows faster than the insides. I think it's a great procedure."

Stripping, done on the knees, frees up the slow-growing side by scraping the ligament away from the bone. Screws and stripping are the yin and yang of equine corrective surgeries.

Deciding if screws and wires in the ankles, or stripping the knees, are damaging the breed, Mark says, "That's not our job. If somebody wants to say, 'Hey, those things are illegal,' we won't do them. Whatever the boundaries are, we're going to operate within them."

Done with the yearlings in Yearling Complex C, John Hall heads over to Dayjur, an older, smaller barn just a few feet in off East Hickman Road.

The very thing that makes the bluegrass the bluegrass—a deep limestone base under the soil—is also what makes it so hard on the horses' hooves this time of year, especially when the region has had quick swings in the wet/dry cycle. During the wet weather, the horses' hooves get soft, and then when they dry out and harden up, grit and debris get trapped between the walls of their hooves, leading to abscesses.

The wing fractures, small breaks in the vestigial fingers of the horses' hooves, occur when a horse whose hoof and leg have been concussed only by soft footing switches suddenly to footing that's rock-hard. Right now, in every one of John's barns, he's got a horse with an abscess or a wing fracture in some state of treatment. Though common, the injuries can be serious if not treated properly. The bones might not heal correctly, abscesses can get infected, bandages abrade skin and can open painful and easily infected secondary injuries. But Taylor Made keeps the horses out, explains Mark Taylor, because "one of our core beliefs is that a horse needs to be outside as much as possible." When they go to the sales, he explains, "you can't take over some little papier-mâché horse that's got soft muscle, no bone, soft feet and no constitution to them. They need to be raised outside rough."

While he's on the phone, running down the day's schedule with Lori Henderson, who has now replaced Dale as the farm's veterinarian, John watches Cherry Bomb '09. She's grown into a leggy, athletic yearling, but she's also unsettled. Pacing and weaving across the front of her stall, she's in constant motion, pausing just long enough to paw the floor, which is going to wear down her soft little hooves. After hanging up, he watches her a moment longer, then asks the groom to move the Raging Apalachee filly from across the aisle to the stall next to Cherry Bomb, where the fillies can see and sniff each other through a grated window between the stalls. Cherry Bomb sniffs her companion through the grate, then drops her head and recommences her pacing. John watches her for another couple of minutes, sighs, and walks away.

Andre O'Connell, who works for Bobby Langley, the farm's far-rier, pulls up outside Dayjur. The farriers trim the yearlings' feet every few weeks, depending on how fast they're growing. Andre has been with Bobby Langley for almost a decade, having started out as an apprentice. He pulls his gear into the aisle and straps on his farrier's apron. Stocky, his head shaved, and with the strong torso and thick arms typical of many farriers, he twirls his rasp over the ball of his hand and stares down at the yearlings' little feet as the grooms walk them up and down the aisle. Quick and confident, his hand able to cup an entire hoof, he rasps down and sideways and gently puts the hoof back on the ground. It almost takes him longer to write up his notes on each horse than it does for him to shape its hooves. John is nearby; he's got one eye reading messages and the other watching Andre. He's trying to get out for the afternoon. Keeneland's October race meet is on and he has friends in from out of town, and if he can just get every-body settled here, he'll get a rare afternoon off to watch the races.

Raging Apalachee just needs to be balanced. Cherry Bomb's sole is down and she's wearing away the outsides of her feet. Stall walking, Andre explains, makes the horses flat-footed. The best he can do is shape her toe and even things up.

While Andre is finishing up, John gets a call from Jeff Hayslett, who wants to meet him at Yearling Complex C to look at the Queen filly. After a cold weekend, the day is warm and golden, the dense greenery of summer heating up to its fall colors. When John arrives at C barn, Jeff is in the doorway, all nervous energy and pressing sched-ule. Short-haired and neat, his loafers polished, his slacks and well-tailored shirt crisp and pressed, he greets John and the two men turn to look at the filly, who has just stepped into a big rectangle of sun-shine beaming in through the double doors.

"She just don't have no leg," Jeff concludes. "She's got her daddy's *hind* leg," he adds. "The Europeans will buy this kind of horse." Then he shakes his head, repeating, "She just don't have any leg on her." The Street Cry filly is Queen's fourth foal, but she has only one of racing age. "If she'd throw a runner," says Jeff, "she'd be worth a fortune."

The filly, he confirms, will go to the clinic tomorrow and have her knees stripped—a procedure in which Dr. Rolf Embertson will make a small incision over her knee, slide in a scalpel, and scrape the perios-teum away from the bone, releasing the tension and thereby allowing it to catch up with the growth on the other side of the leg. Jeff then segues into a conversation about the merits of proteins versus starches in horse feed, as if this is an ongoing topic between him and John, but when he sees John's blank stare, he stops suddenly and wonders aloud where he got that information. John says nothing.

"Probably from the damn Purina rep," Jeff concludes, and heads out to his car.

Now that Lori has replaced Dale as the farm's on-call vet, she's got her own intern to supervise. The next day, Lori meets up with Dr. Fatima Wazir at Yearling Complex C. Tall, elegant, with long dark hair that swings down her back in a sleek ponytail, Fatima brings a touch of unaccustomed glamour to the barn. John Hall, Cesar Terrazas, and Andre O'Connell are already there, checking on Folklore's bright little colt, who has an abscess.

Andre pulls the bandage off his hoof, looks at the discharge stains, and then slowly presses his fingers into the soft spot in the colt's coro-nary band, a ring at the top of the horse's hoof where it attaches to the horse's leg. The abscess, which has been bothering the colt for weeks, has finally popped out here, as John had predicted when the colt first showed up lame. But the colt also has a hole in the bottom of his hoof, a condition that the farm has been treating for so long that the ban-daging has rubbed Folklore's heel raw. John and Andre are agreeing that the "green putty" would be the best solution for protecting that heel from further damage. Lori and Fatima listen and lean over to look. Part of their clinical training is developing respect for skilled practitio-ners. Great horsemanship is as much art as training. Andre knows more about horses' hooves than most veterinarians, and John has been healing horses since before either Lori or Fatima was born. Standing up, Lori laughs. "I have no idea what this green putty is."

To John, she adds, "I think I would have bet a hundred bucks that abscess wouldn't pop out of the coronary band."

John smiles and shrugs.

Outside, it's sunny and warm, but the barn is cool and still, sparrows twittering in the rafters. The horses who don't need to be seen by the vet and the farrier are already out. A Flying Glitter colt by Forestry who is also stall-bound watches the team from the end of the aisle, his face pressed up against the stall grating, ears straining toward them, trying to see what's going on.

Lori defends herself with a smile. "There was nothing in the radiograph. No pockets. Nothing."

They put Folklore back in his stall and then retrieve the Flying Glitter colt who has a wing fracture. To get it to heal, they have to immobilize the hoof so that the little back-and-forth motion caused by walking and moving around doesn't continue to put pressure on the fracture. Andre sprays the hoof with brake-pad cleaner, getting it superclean and superdry, and takes a roll of preplastered bandage—a product that no one else has seen before—out of a bucket of water. Dropping to one knee, he lays the colt's hoof over his other knee and, keeping it completely still, wraps the bandage in a figure-eight pattern around it, the pressure perfectly even. Impressed by his skill, the others fall into deferential silence as they crowd closer.

"I would have dropped it by now," Fatima says.

Humbly, Andre responds, "The first five of these I did came off in the first six hours."

Across the aisle from Flying Glitter is Alidiva, who is also stall-bound with a wing fracture, but she's healed so well that no one can remember which foot it is. "I know it was a front one," John jokes. (Wing fractures happen only to front feet.) Lori runs out to her truck. "It's the left," she tells them.

The first bandage that Andre wraps around Alidiva's hoof is defective—a lump of plaster in the middle has made it stick to itself—and he tosses it aside. Still fascinated, Fatima, John, Cesar, and Lori all follow it, picking it up, feeling it between their fingers, poking it, squeezing it.

Alidiva goes back in her stall, and they return to Folklore. Iodine-soaked cotton, John and Andre agree, will have to be packed into the hole in his hoof to harden it up before the rest of the hoof is bandaged.

Though it's only October, the first of the yearling sale deadlines is approaching. Horses are entered at the end of January for Fasig-Tipton's sales in July and August, and May 3 is the deadline for the Keeneland September sale. Part of the strategy for getting the best price for your horse is placing it in the right sale: Fasig-Tipton's July sale for those who look like precocious runners and therefore will appeal to pinhookers; the best pedigreed and the most beautiful, who can stand up to the extended scrutiny of leisurely buyers at Fasig's "boutique" sale at Saratoga in August; and the rest for Keeneland's supersale in September, but even those need to be placed in the right "book," or section of the sale, so that they will either outshine their competitors or at least not be outshone by them. Getting the yearlings to sale sound and blemish-free, says John, "is a long, intense, grueling process." But, at the end of it, "you get to see the accomplishment of a year's worth of work."

Frank Taylor likes to do his monthly appraisals of the foals in the company of his staff. "What I'm trying to do," he says, "is see what they know and then teach 'em." It's overcast the next morning when he meets his team at Dayjur at 8:00 A.M. This morning, Frank is joined by John Hall, Scott Kintz, Cesar Terrazas, Bart Barber, who is milling around, done with rounds, and Tom Hamm. Frank assumes his customary position in the middle of the aisle, where his gaze will be centered on the horses as they walk. John Hall tucks in next to him, slipping back just behind his shoulder, and the rest of the men fan out behind, in order of height, every one of them aiming for the center spot, where they can best evaluate a horse's walk.

Frank records his impressions into a Dictaphone. "I'm looking at a good colt, a little on the small side." He signals to the grooms to walk the colt away. "Tracking good in front," he adds.

"I think the mare can really run," Scott offers.

When the grooms bring the foals out, their coats are brushed, their manes are damped down to one side, and their hooves are oiled. A foal out of the mare Hope Rising stands in front of Frank.

"This is a very nice horse here," Scott says.

"Very nice colt," Frank says into his recorder. "B plus plus."

Frank's grading system only goes down to a C. "When I'm throwing those grades on horses," he explains, "that report's going to the owner. I don't want to say, brutally, he's just a piece of crap. But I do want them to know—this is not a good horse." He gives maybe two A's out of a hundred. Maybe five out of those hundred will be A-. "I thought about just calling them very good, good, fair, poor," he says, but he has settled on a grading system.

Cherry Bomb's 2009 filly by Henny Hughes comes out of her stall. "This is a chestnut filly," Frank says into the recorder. "This is a really attractive filly. Great head, neck, and shoulder. Super profile." He turns the recorder off to watch the filly walk, pointing out that she toes out a bit in her right front. "She's got such a body on her," he says to the men with him.

"Look at the hip on her," John Hall says admiringly.

Frank developed his judgment, he says, "by watching the very best guys in the world pick them and then seeing their results over thirty years." There are a few specifics that all judges of conformation can identify—straight legs, shoulder and hip angle, feet—but the judgment is largely subjective: an impression the judge gets of the horse's balance and athleticism. In fact, the study on the heritability of conformation faults from the University of Glasgow found that one of the challenges of even figuring out what a conformation flaw is, is establishing criteria for them. "The principal disadvantage," the authors stated, "is that each attribute is assessed against an idea that is largely unique to the individual assessor."

There is no accurate measure of exactly what a horse should look like, and while there might be genetic diversity among Thoroughbreds, as a breed, they look a lot alike.

But Frank knows exactly what he's looking for. "If you take a horse's back," Frank explains later in his office, "I think a big important thing I look for is where his withers finish, where his back is, where his hip starts." He draws two dots on a piece of paper to show where first the withers and then the hip connect to the horse's back. He then draws a curved line underneath that connects and then extends beyond those two dots that represents the horse's belly, or underline.

"The more underline you can get and the more length, what that does is get your hip angle right and get your shoulder right. Just think about it. What's a horse doing when he's at full stride? If he has a straight shoulder, he might be a good horse; he's just going to have to work more. But if a horse just naturally has a short back, and he's long underneath, I think all that's really telling you is that the horse has a very good angle to his shoulder and his hip angle is right."

Frank not only judges the quality of the horse but, based on its type, knows who might like the horse. "I've done it for so long, I can look at a horse and say, 'I'll bet that guy will buy this one,' or 'He'll like this one and this guy will like that one.'" Lorraine Rodriguez, the owner of Collect Call, says that her husband, Rod, always makes the final decision when they're setting the reserves at the sale, but they always start out by asking the Taylors, "What would you value the horses at?"

Jo Pollock, Queen's owner, who made wildly unanticipated profits on one mare and then lost money on the five mares bought with those profits, doesn't see any logic to what a horse is worth. "It's all luck," she says, then adds, "I guess it's some luck. You have to look to the Taylors for the skill." The merit of Frank's and his brothers' judgment is determined by their success at the sales, and by the annual in-house betting pool on whose valuations come closest to what the yearlings actually bring at the sale. This year, Frank won, though, he says, frowning, "When I win, no one pays up."

A filly by Bluegrass Cat comes out of her stall. "This is a bay filly," Frank begins, "that's a little better than the usual Bluegrass Cat. This filly has a little bit of a plain head. I'd like to see her a little bigger."

The grooms lead the filly up the aisle as the men line themselves up behind Frank. "This filly is traveling pretty good in front." Frank pauses the recorder and asks his team if they think she's a touch wide. No, they tell him. "You think she's back at the knee?" He gets a noncommittal nod. "I'd grade this filly a B."

Once the filly is put away, Frank shares his current concern with his team. "I never thought I'd say this, but out there at the sale, I think our feet are almost too big."

John Hall laughs. "We were just talking about that," he says. They were laughing about it, actually. This is another example of Frank's fastidiousness, which borders on paranoia. Later, when he explains what he meant, even he seems aware that it sounds a little crazy. "Ummm. I was thinking . . . knowing that . . . I always wanted a big, sound, good foot." Such a foot, he explains, "is a foundation for the horse to be sound, and to be correct." No foot, no horse, as the saying goes. Because everyone is concerned about the appearance of the foot, they trim it back every time little cracks start to appear in the edges. "But, actually, in raising horses, you can overdo it," Frank says. Too frequent trimming, he says, takes the hoof down too much, and for the horse, it's like wearing the wrong size shoe. If your shoe is not the right size, Frank explains, you're not going to break over at the right place and you'll put strain on your calves and joints. In the wild, the horse's toe breaks off where it needs to. Frank went on a cattle-drive vacation in Montana once and returned with deep respect for the feet of the horses he rode. "These old horses out there, they're so damn tough, and I'm riding them through shale rock, and you'd think when I ride him through that spot, he's going to be bleeding and all torn to hell." But his horse was fine. Applying that lesson to his own horses, Frank wants their feet to grow out, to splay out as they need to, with the toes trimmed back only as much as necessary to keep them from breaking. But Frank worries that the buyer, whose eye has been trained by the overtrimmed feet of the other sale horses, won't know what he's looking at, that the horse's feet will look too big, like there's something wrong with them.

"They're *so* big, and I love it," Frank says to his team a little defensively, as if he perceives the slight irritation with all this back-and-forth about feet. "But people don't know what they're looking at. If we could just tuck them in a little."

A filly by the popular stallion Malibu Moon comes out of her stall. "This is a big, strong filly," Frank says. "A little on the coarse side. Back at the knee. This filly toes out a little in front." He pauses the recorder and says to the team, "I really don't like her," then clicks the recorder back on. "I'd give her a B minus."

A filly by Posse comes out of the stall and Frank gives her a sour look. "That mare sure has been a failure," he says of the filly's mother. Small, but with nothing major wrong with her, she ends up with a B.

Cintarosa's Unbridled's Song filly steps out of her stall.

"This was the maiden mare who could have died," Scott volunteers.

Frank wants to know what the mare is like now.

Scott says she's great. "She's just a regular mare now."

"She's big and scopey and strong. She's a nice filly," Frank says, and gives her a B++.

They work through the fillies one by one. A Glory Lane filly by Rock Hard Ten steps out of her stall.

"God, this thing's a monster," Frank says. "This is the best one we've seen so far." The filly walks up the aisle and turns around. "God! This thing is unbelievable!"

The filly stands quietly as she's admired.

"What do you all think?" Frank asks the team. "Do you like her as much as I do?"

It's all gloom and glory with Frank. He rides the hopes and fears of his industry to their heights and depths. Duncan and Mark pitch themselves to the middle of the road, and Ben tends to linger in the depths, but Frank is committed to an exhausting cycle of up and down, up and down. His team, in an effort to conserve their energy perhaps, refuse to pitch themselves to peak and lows. Yeah. Yeah. Yeah, they nod, and the filly gets an A–.

5

Christmas 2009

 IT'S THE WEEK BEFORE CHRISTMAS, 2009, AND THE foals are all about to turn one. Their actual ages range from just under a year, for those foals like Queen '09, who were born in January, to just eight months, for those born in May. Taylor Made's offices, in a converted house tucked into a hollow facing Union Mill Road, are holiday-festive, with a big tree, golden lights, and Christmas cards from all over the world taped to the fireplace, lining the window frames, and propped open on every surface.

Next to the walkway leading to an addition is a Nativity scene tucked into a memorial garden for Joe Taylor, who died in 2003, after leaving the farm's Christmas party to deliver gifts on behalf of one of his charities. On icy Tates Creek Road, a truck slid out of control and slammed into his car. "I never imagined he'd die that way," Ben Taylor says, shaking his head and smiling ruefully. "He drove so damn slow—he's moving too slow to get killed." The baby Jesus is missing from the Nativity scene. In its place in the manger is a big orange tomcat who's made the farm office his territory. "That cat," says Mark Taylor, laughing when he sees him, "is the bane of Duncan's existence." Duncan likes cats, Mark explains, but not in the house, and definitely not in the office, where this one keeps appearing, allowed inside by the female administrative staff, who feed him.

In the low forties, it's gray and cold, and the first snow of the year is predicted for later in the week. Crows yak in the trees and the voices of the grooms, bringing the horses in for breakfast, drift up through the early-morning gloom as they talk, laugh, and whistle softly to the horses. The babies plod to the barn sleepily. As the days have grown shorter, their coats have grown longer, and now they're as puffy as plush toys. Their knees have been shaved so that the poultice can get down to the horses' skin instead of just sitting on top of their fur.

John Hall has caught up with Frank and Cesar and they are finishing up evaluations at Eagle Creek C. Watching Collect Call's big bay colt by Empire Maker, Frank speaks into his Dictaphone: "Big, scopey, good-looking colt. Has a nice profile."

There's a scrape on the colt's neck, and Frank wants to know if he's been kicked. Cesar doesn't think so. "A touch parrot-mouthed," Frank continues. "Nice profile. This colt wants to be offset in his left knee." Frank pauses the recorder and looks at the colt. Cesar and John wait in silence. "He's just a big, good-looking colt," Frank concludes. "B plus." He pauses the recorder and after a moment turns it back on and adds, "Plus."

Of the horses in this barn, this one is Cesar's favorite. "He's got family," Cesar says.

A car pulls up outside and Devi Hall, John's wife, sings out, "Coffee break!" John beams. Crackling and energetic, younger than John, she bustles into the barn with a cardboard box in her arm that holds carafes of hot coffee, hot water and tea bags, a little china creamer, a sugar bowl, and a pan of brownies.

Setting everything up in the office, she points out which half of the pan are mint brownies and which are regular. "Not everyone likes mint." She shrugs.

John Hall summons the grooms into the office, but they linger in the aisle. Separated by language and station, they are unsure. Frank and John pour themselves coffee and then, skipping the brownie, Frank gazes at a dated Winner's Circle photo of himself and some clients that hangs over the desk.

John steps out the door to motion the grooms into the office again. They glance at Cesar, who nods, and they follow John, getting coffee, but most of them skip the brownies.

"I don't remember your being that trim, Frank," says Debbie, teasing him.

"I don't remember it, either," Frank replies dourly.

John's wife takes her leave with a kiss and he, Frank, and Cesar head out to the paddocks with two grooms to evaluate three colts who are outside.

Looking over the paddock, waiting for the grooms to bring the colts to the front gate, Frank explains, "I had a guy call me who can't pay thirty stud fees. So he gave me thirty horses instead. Now I'm trying to get rid of 'em. Get my money back."

As he explains this, John Hall looks down at his feet and Cesar's gaze moves off to some distant point past the tree line.

The thirty horses—mares and weanlings—that Frank didn't want came down from New York about a month ago, hungry, wormy, their tails chewed, and half wild. Since they arrived, he's been trying to unload them for whatever price he can get. What's left of the bunch will go to Keeneland's Horses of All Ages Sale in January. Unlike other products, racehorses can't be warehoused when the economy tanks. Their racing careers are short and start when they're young. Training fees, about forty thousand dollars a year, are the same whether you win or lose. Even leaving them out in a field costs around ten thousand dollars a year. Sales are down about 40 percent, leaving breeders with horses they don't have the resources to support.

As the men wait at the paddock gate for the grooms to bring up the colts, Bart Barber comes through the back door of the barn, chewing.

"Did you get a brownie?" John Hall asks.

"I did," Barber replies.

He's just returned from the American Veterinary Medical Association's annual convention in Las Vegas. Frank and John, devout Catholics, want to know if Barber, a Mormon, committed any sins while he was there.

Barber nods toward the colts and wants to know if Frank's been able to get rid of them yet.

"I'm thinking of sticking them in Archie's paddock," Frank jokes.

Coming second to last in the line of Taylor children, and six years older than Mark, Frank, like his brothers, has retained his boyish features into adulthood. But unlike them, he does not have a boyish expression. Responsible for the day-to-day management of the farm, his face bears the deep frown lines of someone who has spent his life on constant vigil—as if his face carries all of the farm's worries so that his brothers can carry the promise of future success. He has never not worked all day long. His wife, Kim, remembers that in high school Frank would arrive before class, hopping down out of a truck in a shower of straw and hay, having already been at work for a couple of hours, and then immediately head back to the farm after school—no time for sports or hanging around.

When Frank evaluates horses, he stands flat-footed, facing forward, his shoulders and hips square, as if he's expecting what he sees to give him a gut punch. The colts in front of him, he's surprised to find, look better than they did a month ago.

The other colt Frank wants to see is in a back paddock. Cesar sends the grooms on ahead and Frank and the men walk down the lane to the gate. They arrive in time to see the colts gallop up and over a rise on the far side of the paddock. The grooms come up the rise behind them—one with a bucket of grain and both with lead shanks slung over their shoulders. The colts turn and disappear down the rise, the grooms going after them. Frank and the team wait, and suddenly the colts burst onto the horizon as they gallop up the rise. The grooms meander up behind them, but before they can even get close, the colts turn and gallop back down the other side. The two grooms, in burgundy and khaki and silhouetted against the sky, go after them again. Moments later, the colts roll over the top of the hill like a wave, leaving the grooms behind again.

"They're never going to catch them," Frank says.

He leads the men up the lane that runs adjacent to the paddock. From the top of it, he'll be able to see over the rise. The walk takes a few minutes and gives Barber enough time to share the Tiger Woods jokes he's brought back from Vegas. When they get to the top of the lane, it takes just seconds for Frank to see that the New York colt hasn't gotten any more promising since he last saw him. "Okay," he says, and the men turn and head back down. The temperature has plummeted since morning, and none of the men are dressed for the sudden cold. Barber has a vest over a short-sleeved polo shirt, and there are goose bumps on his arms. Frank and John both have red, rough hands but are too manly to put on gloves until they run the risk of frostbite. Strolling down next to them, Cesar keeps his hands in his pockets, his shoulders hunched into his jacket.

Behind them, the colts have scrambled themselves into a race. Breaking from the top of the hill, they tear down toward the bottom of the paddock—all bays, in a tight pack, the New York–bred one at the back of it.

"Look at that," Frank says glumly. "He's last."

The others had already noticed. They continue trudging through the cold. The colts skid to a halt at the lower corner of the paddock, popping out their front legs and slamming on the brakes as they crowd up against one another and the gate. Sorting themselves out, they break away again, this time racing uphill, heads down, reaching from their shoulders, hooves digging in. One colt breaks away from the pack. Stretching out his body, leaping forward at each stride, the New York–bred colt opens up first one length and then another.

"Now he's first." Barber pauses in the lane to watch.

Frank stands still next to him, watching the colt run. "He's not that bad."

The colt streaks away, his mates chasing him but unable to catch him before they all disappear over the rise, their short tails waving out like pennants behind them.

Trudging on, Frank shakes his head. "You never know," he says.

Joe Taylor, says Frank, had his sons involved in everything—tobacco, cattle, farming. Duncan adds that the financial benefit of whatever project they took on often couldn't be realized unless they worked together. His dad, says Mark, "was just the master of having an end that he was trying to reach and disguising it beautifully until it had been accomplished." What Joe Taylor wanted for his sons was that they stick together. "I don't know of anybody else today," says Mark, "in modern day, who thinks like this, and I don't think that I really even think like this with my own two sons. But my dad, for whatever reason, he just preached day in and day out, our entire lives: 'You need to stick together.'"

They went to Catholic school, which, says Ben, was a sacrifice for his parents, and they worked. Up early to finish chores, they'd then go to school, and then the two oldest sisters, Mary Jo and Emily, would drive the boys from school to the farm to join their father and work until dark. When he was as young as twelve, Ben says, too young to drive, his father arranged for someone else to drive him down to Lexington's Vine Street, where he was to hire a crew from the day laborers who hung out there looking for work. Then he took them back to the farm and supervised them. "We learned how to get along with everybody," Ben says.

Duncan, the eldest surviving son—his older brother, Danny, was killed in a car accident in 1968—started the farm in 1976. When asked about the accident, Ben's first response is that it's lucky no one besides Danny was killed. Danny was a little wild, Ben remembers, and speed was a factor, and probably drinking. Mark got his name, Ben says, because it was the one that Danny had told their pregnant mother he wanted if the baby was a boy.

Using his father's contacts through his position as Gainesway's manager, Duncan began taking on clients who needed some place to board their mares before and after they were bred to Gainesway's stallions. The farm was just 120 rough acres then. Duncan housed the mares in converted cattle barns on the Nicholasville property, then leased farms throughout Lexington as the business grew. That practice continues today. The farm carries no debt. The brothers buy their real estate in cash, no mortgages. Acquiring property that way, says Ben, was "pretty damn easy." They befriended their neighbors, and when those neighbors were ready to sell, the farm was the first, and favored, offer.

The land where the stallion complex is currently located, says Ben, used to be owned by a farmer named Leroy Davis. "We were trying to buy it forever." Ben laughs. Davis kept cattle, and the farm was run-down and covered with thistles. When Ben pointed this out to him, he says, Davis responded, "Hell, Ben, what else do my cows have to do all winter but pick through thistles?" A two-hundred-acre farm about two miles outside of Nicholasville came on the market, the Taylors bought it, and Ben offered to trade it to Davis for the thistle-covered pasture where they wanted to site their stallion complex. Davis accepted, they moved to the other, bigger property, and then Davis died, leaving his wife, Geraldine, stuck on a farm far from town. Geraldine was not happy with the Taylors, says Ben. But part of the deal when they traded properties was that if the Davises ever wanted to sell, they had to offer their land to the Taylors first. Geraldine called Ben, and he paid her asking price. She moved into town, and the Taylors now lease the farm to someone who grows corn, wheat, and soybeans. The Taylors get all the straw.

Though he takes credit for starting the business, Duncan believes that if any one of his brothers had come first, they would have done the same thing because of their father's insistence that they stay together. Initially, he started the enterprise with a friend named Mike Shannon, whom the Taylors bought out years ago, but coming up behind Duncan was this line of brothers. "I was nineteen, and I had a brother Chris, who was seventeen. Ben was fifteen, Frank was thirteen, and Mark was six," Duncan explains. "It was like stair steps. It's a Catholic family, you know, so every two years."

Without those brothers, Duncan says, he doesn't think he would ever have been able to build the business. "If it had been me, and I hadn't had any brothers under me, I probably would have been too cheap to hire the right kind of person to replace me when I went into the office." The beauty of all those brothers, Duncan says, was "every time you moved somebody, you had somebody with a little different skill, but who had been trained by the same master."

Chris Taylor, who came between Duncan and Ben, was shot and killed in 1981. They were a few years into the business, says Ben, and Chris, who was managing a farm they had leased out in Bourbon County, noticed stuff was disappearing. He stayed to guard the property and one night, when he was chasing off a carload of guys, including the brother of their housekeeper, according to a 2005 article in the *Lexington Herald-Leader,* they turned and shot at him as they were driving away. "I think about that kid," Ben says of Tim Edward Wireman, the man who was eventually convicted of first-degree manslaughter for Chris's death. "He ruined his life." Ben is referring not to the lost life of his brother Chris, but to Wireman's life, wasted in jail.

In that same article in the *Lexington Herald-Leader,* Duncan lamented the lapse in judgment during the farm's early years, when they hired, as Frank explains, whoever would work cheapest. They got some of the brightest young starters in the business, many of whom have since gone on to be top trainers, managers, and breeders themselves, both in the United States and Great Britain. But Duncan admits that "We probably had some people out there working that were just sort of a rough crowd." If Chris had survived, says Ben, "he would have been right here in the middle of this. He was a great horseman. A great horseman."

And behind all of them came Mark, who says that when growing up, he wasn't sure there was going to be a place for him in the business. "I always had a lot of anxiety about . . . you know, what can I do? When you're young, you don't think of how the business might expand, or what might happen." Mark is the only one of the brothers to have finished college. Duncan went to work right out of high school. When Chris was killed, which happened in the spring, Ben just never went back for his final year. Frank didn't like school and left after a couple of semesters. But Mark went to Clemson and graduated with a B.A. in English. He went into the Thoroughbred business after graduation, but initially he worked for other people: two years in California for trainer Ron McAnally, and then a stint in Dubai with trainer Satish Seemar. Despite having doubts about whether there was going to be a place for him in the business, Mark has ended up as the company's public face. "It's true." He laughs. "I always have to do stuff that I have nothing to do with: 'You have to write this letter.' 'You have to do this interview.' . . . Whatever." Because of this skill, Mark's brothers call him the "silver-tongued devil." Frank, whose bluntness with the media has caused the brothers to put Mark in front of him when people come looking for interviews, shrugs, as if puzzled. "Yeah, people like Mark," he says.

Growing up as the youngest in a house with all those brothers, and with his two oldest sisters, who were kept separated, according to Ben, from the rough and coarse world of the farm and the breeding shed, Mark had a very different experience with his parents than his brothers did, because he was alone with them. His father was busy with his job at Gainesway, but he would get his kids to do what he wanted them to by bragging on them, emphasizing their strong points. While his sisters were "civilized," Mark explains, his brothers were all wild. ("*I* was civilized," Ben says when he hears this description.) "You know, they would trash the house and break things and fight and do all these things." His father, he says, would reinforce in Mark that behavior he wanted. "'Oh, you're the good diplomat. You're good to your mom. You make them do better. You help your mother keep all this sanity,'" his father told him. "If they were about to get in big trouble—they had smashed something in the house or my mom discovered that they had stolen a bottle of my dad's liquor—I would always try to cover up for them. I would try to keep the peace because I wouldn't want the violent episode of my mom going crazy. I was always covering up for them. That was my role in the house, and how I endeared myself to them," he says, adding with a smile, "and then I would want reciprocity." Today, he says, he still plays that role, balancing the strong personalities, filling in the gaps of what needs to get done. "It's on the verge of dysfunction at all times," he explains. "Maybe I can provide just a little bit of encouragement to get it to work."

Working with his brothers, Frank says, is a blessing. "You go look at most families, and they'll have somebody living in Washington, and one living in New York, and they're scattered, and their business has just dispersed them. Well, our business has held us all; it gave us jobs. We all work together."

🐎

It's midmorning on a cold, hard, and bright December day and half of the office staff, including all the Taylors but Ben, heads out to the barns to evaluate the horses going to the January sale. They start off at Mackey Pike, where Lindsey shows them the mares who've just been retired from racing and are going straight to the sale. Then they head to Bona Terra B, and then off to the Yearling Complex to look at some of the farm's weanlings whose owners want to sell, and the horses from New York. Each of them—Duncan, Frank, Mark, Mark's assistant, Patrick Mahan, Pat Payne, the only partner who isn't a Taylor, account managers Jeff Hayslett and Wally Burleson, the latter of whom arrived late, dressed in full camouflage, Teresa Little, Shannon Potter, Stuart Angus, Scott Kintz, Bart Barber, and John Hall—drives a separate vehicle. In single file, phones to their ears, their motorcade rolls over the smooth roads to Yearling Complex C, where Tom Hamm is waiting for them.

The grooms are waiting at the intersection of the barn aisles. One weanling is ready to go, and another stands behind him, on deck. Jacob says the horses were half wild when they got to the farm, though John Hall shakes his head and smiles. "They weren't that bad." They had worms and had been chewing one anothers' tails, and though they've been wormed, fed, groomed, and tamed, there's nothing that can be done about their conformation or their pedigree.

Everyone arranges themselves into a burgundy-and-tan amoeba that surrounds the lollipop-shaped path of crushed stone on which the horses will be shown. Mark and Frank stand closest, Mark in front because he's shorter. John Hall is next to them, as is Tom Hamm. Duncan lingers by the door, watching the horses as they go in and out. Scott and Barber lean up against the wall of the barn, where Wally Burleson is telling them something that's making them laugh, and everyone else is filling in the spaces in between.

Each of the grooms waits for a nod from Mark, or a signal from Tom or John, and then escorts a weanling into the walkway, making sure never to get his body in between the horse and the observers. When horse and groom walk the path, everyone crowds in behind Mark, trying to get closest to the center position, which will allow them to see how straight the horse is walking, whether the hinges of the joints are opening straight up and down, or whether that motion is a number of degrees off in either direction—suggesting that the wear on those joints is going to be uneven. This straightness is an obsession with buyers, especially those looking for horses to race and breed. It's the reason for the ankle and knee surgeries, and the most likely reason that a buyer, faced with an abundance of nearly identical horses and looking for things not to like, will reject a horse at the sale. "The leg is the landing gear is all it is." Frank shrugs. "A straight leg doesn't make a horse run fast; that's just what they land on." Crooked horses may have a harder time staying sound, but some crooked horses, Frank says, "when they run, they just kind of skip over the ground."

Finished with his walk, the first weanling—a colt—stands quietly as the team moves in for a final look, curling away in one direction, crowding together in another, stepping in to peer, crouching close and then backing away. They reach out their hands to touch, to feel, to calm, to know this horse just a little better.

"Okay, that's good," says Mark. "That's a pretty nice baby."

No animal, writes Elaine Walker in her book *Horse,* has served humans in so many ways: food and warmth, transportation and warfare, imperialism, evangelism, colonization, hunting, honor, status, labor and energy, object of desire, and, finally, companion. "In return for domestication," she says, "the horse loses its freedom. But it loses too the constant anxiety of the prey animal, the relentless walking from one grazing ground to another and seeing its young starve to death during a hard winter, or being left behind to be eaten alive because of an injury."

The trade-off suggests that the horse was complicit somehow in its own domestication, and the fossil record suggests that it was domestication that saved the species from extinction. Evolving from the little Eohippus, or the "Dawn Horse," in North America, the animal became extinct here, but it survived on the Eurasian steppes. In a 2009 article in *Science,* a team of archaeologists found three strands of evidence suggesting that the horse was domesticated around 3500 B.C.E., a millennium earlier than previous estimates: the first was metacarpal bones that bear a stronger resemblance to Bronze Age domestic horses than to Paleolithic wild ones; there's evidence that horses there were bridled and possibly ridden; and evidence of fatty acids most likely from mare's milk. Knowing when horses were domesticated is important, says Dr. Sandra Olsen, curator at the Carnegie Museum of Natural History, because in addition to providing food, transportation, social status, and being central to the development of religious and mythological symbols to more cultures than can be easily counted, the horse has been crucial to empire building all over the world. "Every political boundary would be different," she says, had the horse not been involved. Writing in the May 2008 issue of *Natural History Magazine,* Olsen explains: "But you need only recite a short list of empire builders—Alexander the Great, Attila the Hun, Genghis Khan, Charlemagne, and Napolean Bonaparte—to realize they all relied mightily on their cavalries." Indeed, the scope of the horse's contribution to human history is almost impossible to measure. "You cannot pull the horse out of human history," Olsen says.

Once horses were domesticated, humans quickly adapted them for whatever their bodies and their temperaments made possible. "Through the process of domestication," writes Ann Norton Greene in *Horses at Work,* "horses became living machines. For five millennia, humans have been modifying horses by breeding them for size, strength, speed and temperament and appearance so that they would be more useful in transportation, work, warfare and sport. In addition, humans create the devices that make it possible to access horses' physical power and apply it to their purposes."

The Thoroughbred racehorse has resulted from crossing the hairy, heavy, slow breeds that evolved in northern Europe with the thin-skinned, light-boned, and swift desert horses of Arabia and North Africa. The Arabian was settled on in part because of its speed, explains Walker, but more because of its genetic prepotency—its ability to pass on its stamp consistently through generations. For a breeder who is looking for a particular result, that consistency is more valuable than inconsistent superiority. To this day, a stallion's value is determined by his ability to replicate himself.

All Thoroughbreds come from three founding sires: the Godolphin Barb, the Byerly Turk, and the Darley Arabian. The stallions were in Great Britain by 1730, and the Jockey Club was established around 1750. In 1791, the first Stud Book was published—offering protection against fraud, guaranteeing consistency, and also closing down the genetic pool of available DNA. Under the auspices of protecting horse owners, the Jockey Club also, neatly, seized control of the breed by restricting the supply. "Their actions," explains Greene, "drew a line around a specific group of horses and declared them a breed."

Organized in 1894, the North American Jockey Club took over publishing the North American Stud Book from a private publisher. (In familiar American fashion, this was followed by litigation a few years later as the original publisher attempted to regain control of his enterprise.) So when the Taylors talk about a horse not having any pedigree, they're speaking relatively—the Thoroughbred racehorse has the most well-documented and carefully controlled pedigree of any species on the planet.

In a history of the American turf published by Scribner's for the Jockey Club in 1944, *Racing in America,* John Hervey wrote that turf history began in America in 1665, when the first racetrack was built in Hempstead, Long Island. Racing, he said, had been revived by Charles II: ". . . one of the first measures of Charles II after ascending the English throne in 1660 was to repair the fortunes of racing, to which he was passionately addicted. Under the Puritan regime it had been rigidly repressed, though Cromwell favored it personally and imported Oriental horses for his private stud. During the first years of his reign Charles II began the systematic support and patronage of the sport which continued unabated until his death in 1685." Thus, in cavalier tradition, the various Colonial governors pursued the sport, most notably Col. Richard Nicolls, governor of New York, who, according to Hervey, took over when "horseflesh in New Amsterdam was more or less a rarity."

New England, controlled by Puritans, disapproved of racing, as did the Quakers in Pennsylvania. The first days of Thoroughbred breeding occurred either in or near those states whose governors emulated the Cavalier tradition supported by Charles II: New York and New Jersey, and Virginia and Maryland, where the sport took shape. During the Colonial period, there were multiple Jockey Clubs, Hervey wrote, and eventually, due to popularity and prosperity, racing took hold in Pennsylvania.

Daniel Boone brought eastern horses west, where racing became popular with Kentucky's frontiersmen and the breeding industry evolved around Lexington, Kentucky. After the Civil War, according to former turf writer and historian Maryjean Wall, Kentuckians, fearful of losing the industry, began a major marketing campaign that connected horse racing with southern chivalrous traditions, and resulted in investments from New York absentee breeders like August Belmont.

By 1935, Keeneland had been incorporated, and it held its first sale in 1938. In the twentieth century, the industry was largely dominated by a handful of families—the Whitneys, the Vanderbilts, the Hancocks, the Phippses, the Wideners—who owned the farms, put trainers on their payrolls, and bred their own horses to race. Tax incentives that allowed owners to claim losses on racing investments encouraged passive ownership by doctors, lawyers, and others, Duncan says, who did it "initially for the tax thing, and they started to learn about it, and then they said, 'Well, this is entertaining; it's fun. It's a real market. I might buy a mare or two and breed to my stallion.'" That went on, creating what's generally accepted as the last Thoroughbred bubble of the 1980s, which ended in 1986, when the tax code was rewritten under the Reagan administration.

Writing about the fall of Calumet, one of America's great racing dynasties, in her book, *Wild Ride,* Ann Hagerdorn Auerbach, a former *Wall Street Journal* reporter, explains the change in the tax code. Horses get lumped in with all other agricultural products, which makes sense from a production end but not from an investment end, because the horse as a product won't be able to realize any profit from that investment for two to four years. The changes in the tax code meant that owners could no longer offset losses in their passive investments (racing and breeding partnerships), with gains in their active income. The loss of the capital gains exclusion also meant that horsemen could no longer exclude 60 percent of the profit on the sale of their horses. After 1986, they could claim zero. And while the reduction of the income tax rate from 50 percent to 28 percent meant that everyone initially had more money, it also meant that the maximum tax savings from a loss was also 28 percent. In Duncan's shorthand, the changes meant that "somebody had to be in the business to get the deductions."

That classic sign that the industry was in a bubble in 1985 was when a syndicate, including the principals from Coolmore, beat out a group that included D. Wayne Lukas, Eugene Klein, and Mel Hatley to buy a half brother to Seattle Slew for $13.1 million. The colt, eventually named Seattle Dancer, had a less than stellar racing career and died at aged twenty-three at the German stud farm where he had ended up. His record for highest-priced yearling held until 2007, the eve of the next bubble burst, when a two-year-old colt named The Green Monkey, out of a mare named Magical Masquerade and by Taylor Made's stallion Forestry, sold for $16 million, again to a Coolmore syndicate. He failed to break his maiden after three starts and was retired, at four, to a Florida stud farm.

Examples like Seattle Dancer and The Green Monkey may make it seem like the Thoroughbred industry is comprised *entirely* of very wealthy and seemingly shortsighted people. But a 2005 Deloitte Consulting study commissioned by a handful of equine organizations, including the American Horse Council and the Jockey Club, among others, placed the total impact on GDP of the horse industry in the United States at $101.5 billion. The horse industry, which includes not only racehorses but also recreation and performance horses, creates a total of 1.4 million jobs. There are 9.2 million horses in the country and 4.7 million people participate in the horse industry in some form. And even though Thoroughbreds, according to the Jockey Club's Web site summary of the study, account for only 14 percent of the total population of horses, they are responsible for 33 percent of the industry's total economic impact.

There are just over 840,000 Thoroughbreds in the business, according to the report, more or less evenly divided between horses used for racing and horses used for breeding. The Thoroughbred industry provides about 146,000 full-time jobs and generates an additional 383,000 jobs in related industries.

The industry's impact on the state of Kentucky is even more substantial. The Kentucky Equine Education Project estimates that the impact of all horses on the state's economy is four billion dollars, which includes between 80,000 and 100,000 jobs. The state has built its tourism industry around the horse, and that decision, according to the Equine Education Project, means that horses have had an $8.8 million impact on the tourism industry and have provided over fourteen thousand Kentuckians with jobs. Researcher Craig Infanger of the University of Kentucky indicates that receipts from the equine industry totaled $805 million in 2010.

And those jobs are real jobs, many of them for people whose main talent—excellent horsemanship—has no economic value anywhere else. The Kentucky accounting firm Dean, Dorton & Ford annually surveys its Thoroughbred industry clients. In 2009, the farm's Equine Industry Survey tallied data from 75 of the 456 surveys that were mailed out. Of the farms surveyed, the majority employed fewer than five people and had six to ten horses per employee. Most grooms' wages start between $7.65 and $8.64 per hour, and can go as high as $15.65 to $18.64 per hour. Foremen make a few dollars more. Watchmen make slightly higher wages—most of them clock in at $9.65 to $11.64 per hour. Agricultural workers on the farms make slightly less, and seasonal sales help make more, with a portion of the respondents paying that help between $18.65 and $21.65 per hour. Office help make around $13.65 to $15.64 per hour, with bookkeepers and booking secretaries making slightly more.

There are opportunities for advancement in the Thoroughbred industry, and that is one of the ways in which it differs from its peers in showing and recreation. Divisional managers like Steve Avery and Lindsey Terrazas can start at a salary of around $30,000 and can go as high as $69,000, and the majority of farms add free housing to that salary. Stallion managers also start at around $30,000 but can make as much as $100,000. Farm managers may start as low as $25,000, but working their way up is worth the effort because at the top end they can make more than $160,000. The majority of the farms provide life insurance, which the employer pays, and a little under half of them also offer some kind of dental coverage. That majority of the farms surveyed provide health-insurance coverage for both individuals and families. Most of the farms offer their full-time employees paid time off, and most of the farms provide vacation days for full-time employees, as well.

The big commercial farms like Taylor Made are also the jumping-off point for nonfarm jobs, such as positions as veterinarians, farriers, equine health practitioners; retail, racetrack, and auction management positions; and corporate positions, like being an accountant who specializes in the equine industry at Dean, Dorton & Ford. The industry respects horsemanship, and it's the last place on earth where those skills, which may have made the difference between life and death for those tribes from whom we are all descended, still matter.

The well-managed commercial farms will probably be able to ride out the recession, though some experts predict that as many as 40 percent of Kentucky's farms will fold. But there's a bigger problem. Even after the recession passes and the market corrects itself, the fact will remain that racing is losing its fan base.

According to the Jockey Club *Fact Book,* in 1975, the year that Affirmed, the last winner of the Triple Crown, was bred, the North American foal crop numbered 28,271 horses. That number doubled over the ensuing decade, until dropping to about forty thousand in the 1990s, and the current crop is slightly below that.

During that same time period, when the foal crop was doubling, racing in America *fell* from 74,000 to 51,000 races in 2007. So the industry is breeding horses for races that don't exist. Since 1974, writes Bennett Liebman, who blogs for the *New York Times'* the Rail, the handle (the pool of money generated by bets) is just 20 percent of what it was in 1974. Legalizing slot machines at the racetracks (now called "racinos") has bought the industry time, but this hasn't solved the problem, and it has resulted in managers at racetracks who don't know anything about horses or about Thoroughbred racing.

One of the recommendations the American Association of Equine Practitioners makes in its white paper entitled "Putting the Horse First" is that this new generation of racino executives needs to learn about horses. "We believe it is imperative," the report says, "that senior racetrack management become knowledgeable about the issues and business practices that affect the welfare and safety of the horses that race at their tracks."

Critics of the industry, and they are legion, are all trying to point to the one thing that, if changed, would solve the problem of wastage—the growing number of career-ending and sometimes fatal injures to the horses. Some object to racing horses as two-year-olds, while their bones are still forming, but research shows horses who race as two-year-olds actually have longer and more successful careers, because, researchers believe, early racing actually shapes the horses' developing bodies for the job that they'll be expected to do.

Many people, especially those within the industry, point to the failure to establish consistent national regulations both about licensing and drug use. Now, each state has its own licensing process, which makes it difficult not only to ship your horses to advantageous races but also to regulate drug usage—even for drugs that are considered therapeutic. Says Niall Brennan, one of the industry's more successful pinhookers, "For crying out loud, you can't even get the states to give you one license." They won't, he says, because they don't want to give up the income from licensing fees.

The problem of not enough fans contributes directly to hardship on the horses when racetrack management starts pressuring trainers to enter their horses in small races, which typically produce small handles. The AAEP white paper has singled out this practice as one that needs to stop if the industry is going to put the welfare of the horse first. Speaking at a 2010 Jockey Club–sponsored Roundtable Conference on the Welfare of the Horse, trainer Neil Howard said he dreads it when his phone rings at 9:15 and he sees that it's the racing secretary, because he knows he is going to be pressured into putting his horse in a race that only has five or six horses in it. "Usually when you fill a race, you shouldn't have been at that race," he says.

The plight of Thoroughbred racehorses is not necessarily much worse than it was fifty years ago, but what has changed is the public's willingness to tolerate it. Less than 15 percent of the population, the

AAEP report states, has any kind of contact with horses, and as a result, a horse is no longer perceived as a "beast of burden," but as a companion animal, akin to a cat or a dog. "In this societal context," the report warns, "welfare issues affecting the horse resonate with the public like never before."

Part of this concern is reflected by the incoherent drug policies, in which there is very little consistency among breeders, trainers, and veterinarians. The AAEP does not have a problem with the commonly used drug called Lasix, which controls bleeding in the horses' lungs. But trainer Ken McPeek would like to see it banned. "I don't think the Triple Crown can be won as long as Lasix is used in all the races," he says. In his experience, it dehydrates the horses too badly for them to rebound in time for the next race. He goes even further: "I think we need to eliminate all medication in graded races." But a trainer can't do it on his own, because the owners can simply move to a trainer who does use the substance.

Track surfaces, especially after the much-publicized breakdowns of Barbaro and Eight Belles, have come under scrutiny, but even there the research isn't conclusive. Keeneland has had good luck with Poly-track, but McPeek thinks that might be because Keeneland made the decision to dig down and replace all the old dirt in the track before putting down the Polytrack. Santa Anita is actually replacing its synthetic track with dirt after seeing an increase in fatalities.

Trainers like McPeek, Howard, and Hall of Famer Jonathan Sheppard, who also spoke at the symposium, would like to see American trainers with more training methods available to them, like their Japanese and European counterparts. Being able to vary the horses' training would make them fitter and less prone to injury, says Sheppard. At the Miho Training Center in Japan, for instance, trainers have access to multiple tracks with different surfaces, are able to train uphill, in either direction, and swim their horses in a pool. In North America, says McPeek, "our hands are tied." Unless trainers can afford their own private facilities, they must use those at the racetracks where the horses are housed—forcing everyone on the grounds to share one or two tracks, and finish their training before the start of the day's races.

Although there has always been criticism of the industry, in 2008, that criticism became an uproar when, after crossing the wire behind Big Brown in the Kentucky Derby, the filly Eight Belles, who was sired by Unbridled's Song, snapped both of her front ankles as she galloped out just after the wire. The fans in Louisville and those following the NBC broadcast watched in horror as the game filly, who had just been blazing down the track moments before, pitched forward, fell, and never again got up. And this was just two years after Barbaro, who broke down at the start of the 2006 Preakness, held the country's attention for a *year* as he fought to come back from his injury before finally succumbing to laminitis. But the industry is reluctant to draw conclusions from a single tragedy.

"We had a lot of that family," says Mark Taylor about Eight Belles. "It was a very good, very brilliant family." Mark was on the backside the day before that Kentucky Derby. The filly was in the barn of Larry Jones, universally acknowledged as one of the good guys in racing, known and sometimes lampooned for his tender and sometimes unconventional care of his animals.

The day before the race, says Mark, Eight Belles was standing naked in her stall. "Every single horse in that barn," Mark recalls, "is done up to their elbows in bandages, poultice. They got four-foot piles of straw. They are wrapped in cotton. Eight Belles is standing there and does not have a single bandage on—you can see all four legs." The day before the biggest race of her life, and she was so fit, so sound, she needed nothing. "I can tell you that filly had to be training like a monster," says Mark. "I've *never* seen a Grade One winner standing there the day before they're running in a Grade One and not have bandages on."

Eight Belles, he says, "wanted it too much. . . . She gave it everything she had and she left it all out there on the track. That was her day." That desire, that willingness to run, is what breeders *want* to breed into the horse. "A horse with great courage and heart really are what you want to breed. You want a horse that has a huge pain threshold, that wants to win so bad, it will run through a brick wall. That's what we're trying to breed."

A November 2010 *Thoroughbred Daily News* report entitled "Do We Need A Sturdier Racehorse?" considers all of the reasons why racehorses start in so many fewer races than they did fifty years ago a more useful measure of the health and fitness of the breed. Many in the business, like Arthur Hancock of Stone Farm, believe that the industry relies too heavily on drugs and is breeding a "chemical horse." The breeders may be producing weaker horses, but genetic changes don't occur over a fifty-year period, and they don't occur suddenly.

What did occur suddenly, the report found, was a change in training practices brought on by the ease of creating and distributing complex statistics. Handicappers like Len Ragozin, who was the first to pioneer the use of statistical "sheets," which rate a horse's performance based on multiple factors, not just on whether or not they won, have heavily influenced how trainers prepare their horses, the report claims. When Ragozin identified that horses are more likely to win after a big race if they have time to rest in between, leading them to "bounce" back with a strong performance, that information was so influential that trainers started adopting the practice, and once they became successful with it, other trainers copied it.

A trainer's percentage of winning starters is also easily accessible. Todd Pletcher has the customer base he does, says the report, because he "typically wins with about 25% of his starters." But other horsemen wonder if horses are starting in fewer races not because they're too fragile to hold up to frequent racing, but because they're simply not trained enough. The report cites an equine exercise physiologist and racing blogger Bill Pressey, who studies both equine fitness and the workout schedules of past Triple Crown winners and has found that they trained and raced much more often than their contemporary counterparts. Horses are not training *enough*, he claims, and everyone is coming to the same conclusions because they're all following the very same training regimen. "I don't need to go into training regimens of the top 3 year old contenders," Pressey writes about the preparation for the 2010 Triple Crown races on his ThoroEdge blog, "because they are all essentially the same; gallop 1.5 miles a few times a week, never breeze further than 6F [furlong] on dirt, no speed work 2 weeks after a race, breeze 0–1 times between the Derby and the Preakness, etc. . . ."

The trainers face risks for being innovative, though. Not only do they run the risk of losing clients, who will switch their horses to a different trainer who has a higher percentage of wins; the "primary goal with some horses," the *Thoroughbred Daily News* report claims, for top trainers like Pletcher, "is to turn them into valuable stallions and broodmares."

Owner Jeff Lewis explains the economics of managing a horse like Folklore or Resplendency. To keep a horse in training, he says, costs about fifty thousand dollars a year. For all the horses he has, he's spending about three million dollars a year for operational expenses and, at best, can expect to cover only half those expenses with winnings.

Given the population of racehorses, says Lewis, about two billion dollars a year is spent on training, but there's only about a billion available in purses. The 20 percent commission that's split between the jockey and the trainer comes off the top of that, bringing down the total available take for all owners to $800 million in winnings against $2 billion in investment. That equation is going to be more or less the same for every horse owner. And nobody paying those kinds of bills can justify that type of financial imbalance. "The thought of success doesn't outweigh the agony of defeat when it comes to large sums of money," he says. To stay in the game, you need to sell the bloodstock. His plan, he says, is to "sell the colts and enough fillies to cover the deficit of the racing operation and come out with a few dollars at the end of the day."

According to Steve Crist, turf writer and publisher of the *Daily Racing Form* and the author of the 1986 book *The Horse Traders,* the contemporary commercial breeding industry really began in 1973, when Secretariat's owner, Christopher Chenery, died, leaving his daughter Penny Chenery Tweedy his farm, along with a bill for about $6 million in estate taxes. Riva Ridge and Secretariat, who hadn't yet raced as a three-year-old, were her most valuable assets and so she and her advisers arranged to syndicate the colt through Claiborne Farm. Claiborne had long been run by Bull Hancock, who had also recently died, leaving behind two sons, Seth and Arthur. Claiborne's board of directors put Seth in charge of the farm. To save her farm and the other horses, Penny Tweedy and her lawyers, according to Crist, had come up with a plan to sell shares for between $175,000 and $200,000. Seth Hancock, just twenty-three, and about to make the biggest stallion syndication deal in history up to that point, settled on $190,000 and sold Secretariat as a breeding stallion, in shares, *as a two-year-old.*

The syndication deal required that Secretariat enter the breeding shed the following year, at the end of his three-year-old season. "The equation between racing and breeding had changed overnight," Crist wrote. "A horse who had not even raced as a three-year-old was worth over $6 million, almost three times what any horse had ever earned by racing."

That was the beginning of the commercial breeding industry, where racing became the way you established the value of your breeding stock, with the ultimate payoff coming not from great racehorses, but from valuable breeding animals—creating an industry in which the focus was on breeding profitable horses, leaving the racing to others. This also means that every time a Thoroughbred appears before the public, either training or racing, it either adds to or detracts from the horse's value. If a top trainer puts a horse in a race for some other reason than winning—say to test him against older and stronger horses, or to push him into running a longer distance, or to see if another track surface would be easier on his legs—he or she runs the risk of undermining the horse's value in the breeding shed.

The Taylors, the trainers, and many in the industry are nostalgic for a time when racing mattered more than profits. The business end of it, says Duncan, is what has undermined plain old horsemanship. "Like the Phippses with Shug," says Duncan, pointing out the long relationship that Hall of Fame trainer Shug McGaughey has had with the Phipps family. "Shug's been training out of the same mares forever. He knows a lot about that family and what they do and what their tendencies are and what their weaknesses are."

Matings now, says Mark, "are done with someone getting on the computer and checking the nick. A lot of the people making the decisions, honestly, have never seen the mare herself, and they may not have seen the stallion. . . . You compare that to John Nerud"—another Hall of Fame trainer—"of Tartan Farms. He trained the mother and the grandmother and the great-grandmother. He trained this whole group of stallions. What he'd do, he'd say, 'You know the mare's got ankles. Always had to fight her ankles. I'm not going to breed her to this horse over here who always had to fight ankles. I'm going to breed her to this horse over here who was like hickory,'" he explains. "They try to balance flaws with strengths that mitigate the problem on the other side."

Frank, who concedes that he and his brothers and other consignors like them have had a hand in creating the current market, explains the opposite process—the career sales horse: "A mare comes off the track; they breed her to a horse. She goes to the sale in foal. Somebody buys her, gets the foal out, and sells it as a weanling. That weanling is bought by a pinhooker; he sells it as a yearling. Then the guy that buys it as a yearling is a two-year-old pinhooker, so he rolls it into the two-year-old sale. Then a guy buys it at the two-year-old sale. Know what I'm saying? How much different a scenario is that than a guy who's just owned all these horses, bred the horses, knows all the details and knows all the idiosyncrasies of that family and knows how to breed 'em."

What they don't have enough of now, Frank, and almost everybody else, says are the people who are in the business because they have a dream, who want to win the Kentucky Derby or a Breeders' Cup race, or just want to have a big horse. It's market breeding. "We need more people who can come in and enjoy it," he says. "That want to race, enjoy the racing, and want to do it as a sport, and not be so driven to make money."

But those are not the people who are the most profitable customers. "Uh, those actually are the customers we did not want in the past," Frank concedes. The farm's profitability is in selling, not boarding. But Frank thinks there could be a balance with an owner who wants to breed "but isn't afraid to race one."

And successful breeding animals are just a fraction of the 30 percent of horses that compete at the top end of the sport, in the allowance and stakes races. Seventy percent of Thoroughbreds, says the AAEP, end up in claiming races—races in which horses can be bought or "claimed" by anyone paying the claiming price. American trainers sometimes use the races to build a horse's confidence by letting him win one against lesser peers, but mostly they're used to move horses into someone else's hands, and almost always farther down the food chain. The rules around claiming races, says the AAEP, need to be changed to protect those horses who are at the bottom of the barrel. Among other things, it recommends that postrace testing be required and that tracks be allowed to rescind claims at their discretion for horses who test positive for performance enhancing drugs. Purses and claiming prices should be close to equal. Avoid running horses into the ground by forbidding them to run in a claiming race until thirty days after their sale, the AAEP advocates. And if they break down, the claim is voided. This is a recommendation with which trainer Ken McPeek wholeheartedly agrees.

Diana Pikulski of the Thoroughbred Retirement Foundation points to claiming races as one of the places where she would like to see more industry accountability. "The industry's got to be more responsible for the horses at the low end whose owners don't have a pot to piss in," she counters. "Those horses were once owned by somebody more substantial who put them in a claiming race. If you're going to have claiming, then it's the industry's responsibility." It's not just the right thing to do, says Pikulski; it's necessary if the industry wants the sport to survive. "If they're going to get new fans, and modern fans," she says, the industry is going to have to "think about the horse for its whole life, rather than a couple of years."

Out at the farm on this cold December day, what everyone is looking at in Yearling Complex C is overproduction. One of the best advantages a horse may have starting out is whether or not it's bred in Kentucky. According to the Kentucky Horse Council, there are 350 stallions in Kentucky, and Kentucky-bred horses have won 76 percent of all the Kentucky Derbies and 74 percent of the Breeder's Cup races. Eight out of eleven Triple Crown winners have been Kentucky-bred horses. Many other states have tried to compete with Kentucky by offering incentives to breeders who stay in state, but the best Thoroughbreds in North America come from a handful of counties in Kentucky. During breeding season, there are twenty thousand mares in Kentucky, some native, but the rest are shipped in to be bred to the state's stallions. The industry created by those mares and stallions, the Horse Council claims, generates, directly and indirectly, about sixty thousand full-time jobs in the state. Thirty percent of the state's income is from agricultural products, and between 1999 and 2009, the number-one cash crop in Kentucky was horses.

The next filly out of the barn is by Dixieland Band, one of Kentucky's great sires, who's recently been retired. She's a good-looking filly, and Tom and Mark do a fist bump.

"Hell," calls out Pat Payne, scanning the sire list. "It's the last of the Dixieland Bands and the last of the Forest Wildcats."

Duncan asks Tom if there's any plan to blood-type the New York horses, in case they haven't been correctly identified.

Mark thinks the weanlings look better than expected. "Did you call anyone?" he says to Frank.

Another bay filly is less promising. "She's not too good up front," Pat Payne observes.

"Her pasterns were on the ground when she got here," Frank says.

Mark tells Tom to vacuum the horses because they're dirty underneath their coats, and then Tom assures Duncan that the horses were tagged before they left New York and they've had their neck straps on since they arrived.

Looking at the filly, they settle on fifty thousand dollars. "If she continues to grow," Frank observes, "that filly might be worth a hundred, a hundred and fifty thousand."

Mark has his hands on the filly's legs. "She feels a little juicy up front, and that's a little suspicious."

Frank and Duncan price her at $100,000, Mark at $125,000.

The next horse, they value at ten thousand dollars.

"I can't believe there weren't people in here trying to buy these things." Mark shakes his head.

Frank reports that he sold some of them, and Mark wants to know how they did.

"I made the critical mistake of naming the price before he made the offer," Frank confesses, shaking his head. "I sold those horses too cheap."

Frank speaks into the Dictaphone: "This is an attractive filly. Good head and shoulder."

Duncan thinks she's parrot-mouthed. He reaches out to check her mouth, letting her sniff his hand before he touches her.

"Put some ShowSheen in their tails and really comb them out," Mark tells Tom. "Might bring another hundred." (He means $100, not $100,000.)

Fatima pulls up in her truck and unloads her portable X-ray machine. Seeing her with the heavy equipment, Barber walks out to carry it for her.

The team lets him know that he's very nice.

When they're not hassling one another, those on the team are largely closemouthed—a quiet chorus to the leads played by the Taylor brothers. When the horses are led out, Tom Hamm announces who they are, getting irritated with requests to repeat himself because no one was paying attention to him the first time around. Patrick Mahan's job is to write down the estimates. If they decide to tote them up for the betting pool later, that will also be his job. Before he trotted off to help Fatima, Barber was hanging around with Scott near the fence, Wally Burleson nearby. Jeff Hayslett is watching the foals, taking notes on a clipboard. He wants to know what everyone thinks of the idea of moving the Breeders' Cup permanently to Churchill Downs.

Frank's head is tilted as he looks at the weanling in front of him. "That hock don't look too good," he says, stepping forward to look more closely. "But I think it's hair poofed up."

Frank lets his brothers know that he's not x-raying anything that's priced below five thousand dollars.

Mark looks at his watch. "We gotta pick up the pace," he tells everyone. "That's one thing we gotta do."

The weanling, they decide, will bring two grand.

"That one there's a little squirrelly," Mark says about the next little horse, who steps out into the bright light of the December day and sees the team assembled before him.

"The queen in New York is Linda Rice," Mark tells Frank. "Bring her down and see if she'll buy them as a package."

Frank puts a price of thirty thousand dollars on the squirrelly weanling.

As they cross the lane to barn B, Mark takes a last look at barn A, tilting his head back. The new paint, he tells Frank, looks nice.

"I just painted the fronts," Frank tells him.

It takes a moment for this information to sink in, and when it does, a broad smile spreads across Mark's face.

The team crosses the lane to B barn, where a Speightstown filly who's part of the farm's regular roster is the first to step out.

"She's got a fast body," Mark says.

"Awesome body," Frank agrees. "Fast. Short leg."

Mark wants $25,000, but Pat Payne thinks $45,000 to $50,000. They start picking up the pace. They are getting tired; the rest of the day's commitments are bearing down, and they look quickly at hip number 313. "Put me down for twelve," Mark says. "I say fifteen," Pat Payne replies. They continue pricing: $40,000, $50,000, $7,000, $8,000, $5,000, $25,000.

Mark offers an over/under bet on who's going to be closest on the prices.

Done with the X-ray, Fatima lingers by the fence rail with Scott and Bart. When they are bored, Scott and Barber complain.

They're down to the last few. John Hall notes that the colt in front of him is "one screw away from perfection." But it's too late for surgery, and he's got no pedigree—five thousand. The last horse comes out of the barn, and Duncan pulls his buzzing phone out of his pocket and turns away. "Hi, Mom," he says.

The day after they set the prices on the New York breds, the weather takes a hard turn into winter. The sky is steel gray, and it's cold. At Dayjur, the grooms are slipping out into the dim light to bring the babies up from the paddock. Inside the barn, the stalls are clean and laid with fresh bedding. The grooms have already filled the water and grain buckets. The babies are sleepy, their heads low as they plod up the hill behind the grooms. Once they're inside the aisle, the grooms stop to look carefully at their legs, moving methodically from one side to the other and then stepping back to look at their hind legs. By now, the horses have learned to stand patiently for these daily inspections. A barn kitten that Lori and Fatima have named Beyoncé, because she's fierce, meows out a greeting to the grooms each time they walk past.

Cherry Bomb '09 quickly finishes her breakfast. She's settled down since October and is calmer in her stall. As the grooms work their way down the aisle, getting the horses ready for Frank's evaluations, she presses her head against the stall grating, ears pricked, watching them.

Both Frank and John Hall arrive around 8:00 A.M. Their first horse is a filly by Unbridled's Song. The last time Frank evaluated her, he called her a rat. This time, he says, "She's grown up, gotten stronger." He peers at her, steps closer to see her legs, stands back and evaluates her whole body. "God, I can't believe this is the same horse."

"One of the things about the Unbridled's Songs," the ever-positive John Hall says, "you know they're going to get better."

A Closing Argument filly, Frank decides, has a good shoulder, and a good profile.

"You oughtta see the mare," he says to John Hall. "Skinny, old, hopping around. You can't believe she can have a horse like this." That filly is put away and Cherry Bomb '09 is pulled out.

"God, these horses look good over here," Frank says.

He turns on the recorder. "This filly is a long-bodied filly," he says. "Very strong, though. Pretty neck and head. Just a strong filly that profiles well." Pausing the recorder, he comments to John: "Man, this is a nice filly."

Cesar arrives in time to hear Frank compliment the grooms on how sharp their barn looks, and how well-groomed their horses are. "These are two guys who get the job done," he says.

The Cintarosa filly steps out of her stall. "Aah, the champion," Cesar says.

"She's good through the hocks," Frank says. "Better than most Unbridled's Songs."

Another Unbridled's Song filly comes out of her stall and John Hall jokes that she's got the "Unbridled's Song shuffle." Frank grades her a B to B+ and wants to know why her tail is chewed off.

Holding up his hands, deflecting responsibility, John says the filly just came over to his side of the farm. "That's Stevie Avery," he says.

"Blame it on Steve," Frank says.

On a second and more careful look, the men realize the tail isn't chewed; it's just short.

🐎

Over at Yearling Complex B, Fatima is meeting with Dr. Raul Bras, one of Rood and Riddle's podiatrists. Bras is both a veterinarian and a farrier, and, lucky for him, he's in one of the few places in the country where horse owners need and will pay for his level of expertise. Folklore's '09 colt is not getting over his abscess. Despite the good care, he's got an infection that has moved into the bone.

They're treating the wound aggressively, and the colt has already been sedated. His weight distributed between just three of his feet, and his head cradled in the arms of his groom, he stands quietly while Bras peers into a hole in the colt's hoof that's big enough for an index finger. When they cleaned the wound, blood ran down the colt's leg, and the red stain on his bright white sock makes everything look worse than it already is. The wound was debrided on Tuesday. Now, peering up into it with a flashlight, Bras can see that the sides are clean, but it's still infected at the top. Today, he's going to administer antibiotics and pack the hoof with sterile maggots.

Bras's colleague at Rood and Riddle, Dr. Scott Morrison, first thought about using maggots on racehorses after he saw a documentary about their use on humans. They've been standard practice at Rood and Riddle for about the last five years, according to Bart Barber.

In addition to the sedative, Bras has also injected a nerve blocker so the Folklore colt won't feel all the scrubbing they have to do to get his wound clean, or the catheter they have to insert to get the antibiotics into his foot. There's a tourniquet around Folklore '09's ankle, applying pressure so that the antibiotics will head down into his hoof instead of rushing up into his body and away from where they need to go. Bras and Fatima are on their knees and Bras is talking Fatima through the process of getting the tiny catheter into the very small vein just above the colt's coronary band. "Just get under the skin and feel the vein," he advises.

Blood drips out the end of it and Fatima pushes in the needle. Bras tells her to hold the catheter down with her thumb, or the force of the fluid being injected will pop it back out.

He also points out that she needs to get this done before the colt moves. "Fatima's taking forever," he says, teasing.

As soon as the catheter is out and before the leg has a chance to get dirty, he cleans and bandages the leg. After plunging the colt's hoof into a plasma bag that's full of oxyclorosine, he tapes the top down securely, then lifts up the foot with the bag on it and swishes it around.

His assistant, Tristan, has made a big square out of strips of duct tape and is standing by, ready to secure the bandage once it's on.

"Wet and dry, wet and dry, wet and dry," Bras says, explaining why the farm is seeing so many abscesses this year. Fatima wants to know if there was anything they could have done with this one to have kept it from getting worse. Every farm he's been to, Bras says, has had the same problem. And now, with winter close, those soft hooves are going to start cracking against the hard ground.

After the plasma bag comes off, Bras needs to get an X-ray of the hoof. He also stops to take a tracing, in case he needs to make a special shoe for the colt, as well. They place the colt's hoof onto the flat wooden box that holds the X-ray plates, but the screen of Bras's portable scanner is fuzzy.

"C'mon, please work," he begs the machine.

Tristan goes over the connection while Fatima heads out to her truck to retrieve hers. Once it's plugged in, they're able to see the big hole that tunnels all the way up into the colt's bone. While they're looking at the screen, the colt camps out his back legs and has a nice long pee. The vets sigh as the puddle seeps toward tens of thousands of dollars' worth of electrical technology, then quickly shut the machinery down, moving the scanners out of the way.

Bras needs to move even more quickly now to get the maggots in and the hoof bandaged before the colt steps down into the puddle of urine.

The maggots are smaller than fleas and cost about two hundred dollars per application. To get the maggots out, Bras rinses the container with saline solution and pours it and the maggots back out onto gauze, which he stuffs up into the colt's wound. The maggots will nibble away at the dead tissue until they're stuffed with blood and then somehow wriggle out of the bandaged hoof. Once they're in, Bras quickly and extravagantly wraps tape around the hoof and releases the tourniquet. A thick, padded quilt goes over the colt's leg. Over that goes a stretchy bandage and over that more duct tape to lock everything into place. Still groggy and unable to feel his foot, Folklore '09 rocks forward and lets his groom lift his foot and place it down where it needs to go. Like this, Folklore and his groom make their way to his stall.

Once he's in, the grooms help Fatima carry her X-ray machine back to her truck.

Abandoned in the middle of his own disarrayed gear, Bras calls out, "Well, that's nice!" He and Tristan pack up and leave, and five minutes later the only sign that the barn's aisle was used as an impromptu operating room are the drips of blood on the floor.

Winter descends for real on the farm the week before Christmas. On a cold and gray Friday afternoon, snow starts to fly. The January horses are appraised and ready to go. The mares with the earliest due dates have now been moved into the barn overnight. A concern with those early January due dates is that the mare might deliver too early, and if her foal hits the ground in December, he's already a year old on January 1, essentially ruining his racing career. A few years ago, says Bob White, section manager of Bona Terra, the Jockey Club started inspecting barns right before January first to see those mares with the early due dates. They confirm that they are still pregnant, and then return with some regularity until January first, to make sure that no one tries to cheat the incredible bad luck of ending up with a December foal. Bob Curran, Vice President of Corporate Communications for the Jockey Club, explains that this would be consistent with Jockey Club rules, citing Section V, Rule 1-C and 21-1 of *The Principal Rules and Requirements of the American Stud Book*: "The Jockey Club may require any party who seeks to register a foal or who submits information related in any way to registration of a foal to make the horse(s) involved available for inspection." This is not a problem that Taylor Made has had, but the evidence suggests that some other farms did. For the record, the Jockey Club does not disclose information about inspections.

The brothers are still relentlessly busy. Annie Padron welcomes holiday visitors to the office, inviting them to help themselves to the counter full of holiday treats in the office. "What's ours is yours," she says warmly. She has a right to feel proprietary—she's a second-generation Taylor Made employee, the daughter of one of the farm's first broodmare managers. The guest book, filled with signatures from practically every state, many countries, and almost every continent, lies open next to a chair. Even this time of year, not many days go by without visitors to the farm. They pop into the office and ask if they can visit the horses, and with graciousness, the Taylors comply, interrupting someone's day to provide an escort to an unscheduled visitor who may be a customer, or who may just be a fan in love with one of the farm's rock stars, like Farda Amiga, Alidiva, or maybe even little Folklore. Or maybe the visitor is someone who's just in love with horses and who wanders into Lexington, knowing that it's one of the rare places in the world where horses are as central to the existence of the humans around them as they were on the Eurasian Steppes four thousand years ago.

Mark bustles out the door for a meeting. He shares his brothers' feelings about working together, but he also says that there's a lot of pressure. If he was an independent bloodstock agent, he says, and wanted to take some time, do some other things, he could "ratchet it down" if he wanted to. "But when you have three other brothers you're working with who are all working extremely hard and extremely focused, and you've got a big team that you've built around you that's depending on you to keep the thing moving forward, *especially* during tough times . . . you feel like you have to pull your own weight."

When he thinks he's working hard and coming in at 6:00 A.M., Mark says, he sees Duncan's car already in the lot. Late for his meeting, he hustles past the cat in the crèche, shaking his head. He has no idea what happened to the baby Jesus that's supposed to be there.

6

March 2010

THE ONLY PART OF THE THOROUGHBRED BUSINESS that's doing well right now, jokes Michael Blowen, who runs Old Friends, a Thoroughbred retirement farm in Georgetown, Kentucky, is his part of it. Public scrutiny and the closing down of the last American slaughterhouse for horses have all increased the demand for some kind of program for the Thoroughbreds once they're done racing. The demand for accountability from the public has also led to an increase in industry dollars for long-term care. The Jockey Club has a check-off donation program; at the time that you register your horse, you can check off a donation, which the Jockey Club will match for up to $250. That money goes to the Thoroughbred Charities of America, which funds, among other groups, the Thorough-bred Retirement Foundation, which both retrains horses at their Maker's Mark Secretariat Center for use as recreational horses and supports prison programs where the retired horses are part of a rehab program for inmates.

Philadelphia Park has created a program, Turning for Home, that's located right on the track, where an unwanted horse can be gotten out of its stall in thirty minutes—faster than the slaughterhouse buyers could do it—and has taken over four hundred horses out of the park in just its first two years, says Barbara Luna, director of The Communication Alliance to Network Thoroughbred Ex-Racehorses. For this, they get fifty thousand dollars a year from the Pennsylvania Horsemen's Association. Horse owners have added their support by pledging ten dollars per start, and the jockeys have ponied up ten dollars for every win and five dollars for every second place. There are organizations like CANTER, which, since it first opened in Michigan in 1997, function as a clearinghouse, connecting potential adopters with horses who need a home. Michael Blowen, onetime COO of the Thoroughbred Retirement Foundation, started Old Friends when he saw that there was a need for someone to take the retired stallions, who are often more challenging to handle. In the process, he ended up with many of the industry's rock stars. Some organizations, like the Thoroughbred Retirement Foundation, receive a part of their funding directly from the industry.

On a cold and overcast March morning, Linda Dyer of Kentucky's Blackburn Correctional Complex heads out to the prison's paddocks in her truck. She's in lined overalls, her jacket zipped up, and has a radio clipped to her belt. A small woman, she makes it look like the steering wheel is a long way from the truck's seat.

There are a handful of Blackburn inmates milling around the old barn, sweeping slowly, raking. Dyer explains that the facility was once an orphanage and then a reform school and the barn was used by both those facilities to keep cattle. Once the state took it over as a correctional institute, the barn fell into disrepair, but it was restored when they started the equine program. Still, there's little to no budget for her program—the state pays her, and provides the facility, such as it is. And the state's partner in this program, the Thoroughbred Retirement Foundation, pays for everything else. Fortunately, she says, smiling, she's had a few carpenters come through and, happily for *her*, one electrician who was serving a few months for writing bad checks.

The men who aren't lingering by the barn head out to the paddocks with brushes in their hands. The horses live outside, coming into the stalls only if they're sick or injured. The ground has thawed, and heaves of black dirt have chucked up under the horses' feet. The men trudge up and over them. When it's warmer, Dyer will assign horses to the men, but in the winter and early spring, when it's cold, she doesn't bother. Their prison overalls are not warm enough for them to be outside for long.

Drivers on Interstate 64 can see the facility from the road, and there's a huge sign advertising the partnership between TRF and the state of Kentucky in this endeavor. The paddocks are rough—crowded squares of wood and wire. The horses ruin the grass, and so they need to be fed hay year-round. Dyer tries to rotate them to keep the paddocks in better shape, but she's got too many in too small a space. There's one larger paddock for horses who still run around, but for the most part, they pass their days in the company of their friends, look forward to their interactions with the inmates, and hobble about slowly and carefully. "Most of these horses are lame for life," Dyer says.

The prison program at Blackburn is replicated in New York, Virginia, Massachusetts, Florida, Indiana, Maryland, and South Carolina. It was the bright idea of a former director, says Diana Pikulski, TRF's current executive director of external affairs. TRF distinguishes itself from many of its peers not only because it's one of the oldest programs, and one of the most corporate, but also because when it takes possession of a horse, it does so for the animal's lifetime. In addition to their Jockey Club check-off donation program, TRF is known for its partnerships with racetracks, even when those partnerships aren't particularly lucrative. Suffolk Downs in Boston, says Pikulski, gives TRF about forty thousand dollars a year, and in return, TRF takes fifty horses. The ones who can't be retrained for anything end up with the prisoners.

"I run it like any other farm," says Dyer. She parks the truck and locks it up. Everything needs to be locked. "Guys come in and you clean stalls." Before coming to Blackburn, Dyer worked in the industry for thirty-five years, including running her own farm. But she needed insurance and a retirement plan, so she took a job with the state, working first for the state police, and when the job at Blackburn opened up, she applied.

She teaches the men stable management and horsemanship. They sign up for different reasons—to get outside, or because they like horses. Some of them grew up in the country or had a relative with a horse or two. Every once in a while, Dyer says, she gets lucky. "I get a real horseman. Someone who grew up around here." Within a mile of the facility are three of Kentucky's premiere farms: Dromoland; Hill 'n' Dale; and Vinery Stud; whose president, Tom Ludt, is also the chairman of the TRF board.

Dyer spends a fair amount of time maintaining the old gambrel-roofed barn, and this morning she's inspecting the year-old paint job that's already bubbling up on the siding. The paint was a donation, but now, she says, she's going to have to phone the company that donated the paint and find out how to fix it.

In addition to their hands-on work, Dyer also prepares the inmates for an exam that she administers. She takes them to Three Chimneys so they can see how the professionals handle the mares and the babies. They go in the spring and fall to watch the farm prep for the sales.

While the program would prepare the men to take jobs in the industry, for most of them, that's unrealistic, says Dyer. The farms and even the big clinics like Rood and Riddle have indicated their willingness to hire the former inmates who've come through the program, but most of them have some kind of child support to pay, Dyer says. Entry-level pay in the industry can't compete with what men can make as laborers, or in construction. But, says Pikulski, the job-training aspect isn't the program's biggest selling point. The benefits to the inmates, she says, are many: They learn to overcome their fears. They build self-esteem. They develop empathy and victim recognition. By using natural horsemanship methods—to which the program is committed—they learn anger management and develop leadership abilities. "They learn to lead by strength and caring," says Pikulski, "and not by being an asshole." TRF can demonstrate that inmates in the program benefit, and that acting-out episodes go way down. "The truth is," Pikulski says, "we don't have a hard time selling this."

With the appointment of Tom Ludt as president of their board of directors, the Thoroughbred Retirement Foundation strengthened its ties to the industry. The foundation has twelve hundred horses on its "payroll," says Ludt, and to find the support needed to take care of them, he says, "You do the most unsexy thing out there—grassroots campaigning." Like many of the problems in the industry, many of TRF's challenges come from the absence of national oversight in the industry. "If we could mandate a dollar a horse per start," he says, "we'd be healthy. You think we're going to be able to sell that to all thirty-eight states?"

As part of the commercial end of the business, Ludt has an interesting role with TRF, which hasn't been able to convince all the owners that they should be responsible for the horses for more than just their racing careers. "I want people to understand that if you get into the business, you're responsible for the horse. But not everyone agrees with that." And it's not even clear what taking responsibility for the horse means. "It's important for the industry to care for the product," says Ludt. "Now, defining care for the product is very vague." But like his colleague Pikulski and the AAEP, Ludt sees claiming races as part of the problem, because they invite trainers to pass a horse down the line like a "junked car."

The commitments they do get from the industry include contributions from trainers and jockeys, who donate a percentage of their winnings to TRF; a stallion's season and individual donations. "You know who gives a lot of money? The grooms," Ludt says. Once TRF takes a horse off the track, if it's lame, the foundation finds a lifelong home for it, like Blackburn, or one of their other prison programs, or they are sent for retraining at places like the Maker's Mark Secretariat Center, housed at the Kentucky Horse Park. Susanna Thomas, who is the director and chief trainer at the facility, relies almost entirely on volunteer help to retrain the horses. She makes sure that the volunteers get to "lay hands" on the horses—patting and grooming and bathing them. "People have it in their hearts to support the animals and the animals have it in their constitution to be in relationship with us." In the two years that she's been running the center, she's re-schooled and placed between eighty and ninety horses.

Even though Linda Dyer's horses are all lame, right now she has only one who's stall-bound. A gelding named Clever Book has laminitis—a painful hoof injury in which the walls of the hoof separate. His head is hanging over the door of this stall and every time someone passes him, the person reaches out to pat his face. "This horse is getting attention all day long," says Dyer, laughing. Clever Book lost his inmate just two days ago when he was sent to a work-release program. Dyer suggests to the inmates patting the horse that he needs to be groomed, and three men step up, clipping him to the cross-ties and scouring him with their brushes. Clever Book closes his eyes and takes a deep breath. About 150 men have been through the program in Kentucky, says Dyer, and she's lost only two, at most, who simply weren't able to get over their fear of the horses. And the program is a strong incentive for the men in prison. They want to be at the barn because working with the horses is therapeutic. "You hear them talking to the horses all the time," Dyer says. "They miss their families, so they really give the horses a lot of affection."

Out at Taylor Made, by March the big beautiful redheaded filly out of Cherry Bomb has been moved from Dayjur to Yearling Complex A. She's been injured, and outside her stall hangs the clipboard with the veterinarian's diagnosis. "RF medial collateral ligament injury of the elbow joint." About a month ago, says her groom, Tanner Tracey, she came up lame from the paddock, and an exam revealed the injury.

John Fort, who's very excited about Cherry Bomb's 2009 filly, has already named her—Sasanqua—after a type of camellia in his home state of South Carolina. Because he breeds horses to race them, she will be shipped down to Florida in July to begin training.

Her mother has already left the farm. After breeding her to Midnight Lute, Fort had her shipped to Eisaman Equine in Florida, and she has already aborted her foal. Of three pregnancies, Cherry Bomb has lost two. According to the autopsy reports says Fort, the foal died of a twisted umbilical cord, though Fort thinks it could also have been the result of an infection. They found one after the mare aborted, but, he says, they don't know when it started. In Florida, Cherry Bomb is being treated by Dr. Michelle LeBlanc—Rood and Riddle's head of reproduction. Cherry Bomb is getting, Fort says, more than the normal treatment, so they can make sure she's absolutely free of infection, and then she'll ship back to Kentucky to be bred to Red Giant, who stands at Three Chimneys.

The grooms at Taylor Made don't know that the filly has been named, so they still call her Cherry Bomb. She'll be hand-walked up and down the aisle until she can jog soundly, and then for thirty days, her turnout will be in the round pen. She's been moved from Dayjur because there's another lame foal in this barn, so she's not alone. To help keep her calm, John Hall has put a miniature horse in the stall with her.

Named Star, the dun-colored pony used to belong to Bart Barber's children, until the pony's irritability with them made Barber worry about their safety. He moved the pony to Taylor Made, where his job is to travel from stall to stall, keeping the young horses company. He is thick-coated and bushy-maned, and his dorsal stripe is an evolutionary remnant that links horses, donkeys, and zebras to a common pre-historic ancestor. The pony pins his ears at people, but he seems to get along well with Sasanqua.

It's a sunny and lazy morning in March, and the yearlings in Cherry Bomb's barn have already been turned out. The grooms are busy elsewhere, and Sasanqua and Star stand pressed against each other in the stall. Sparrows shoot in and out of the big doors and twitter in the rafters. It's the season of preparation, and outside the barns, tractors grind in the background, their chain harrows jingling behind them as they harrow the paddocks.

Coming only halfway up her neck, Star stands between Sasanqua and the door. When the filly nudges him, he obligingly moves in the direction that he's pushed. She dozes in the warmth of the barn and his company, her chin resting on his neck, her eyes drooping. She sighs deeply. Tucked up against her, Star is square on his tiny little feet, his ears pricked and on alert as he stands guard.

There are minis in almost all the yearling barns. They live outside, moving into stalls when they're needed to keep a yearling company. Cesar loves them not because they're cute but because they do a good job. He doesn't know where they come from; they just appear at the barn when they're needed. Frank used to breed them as a project with his kids, so they have some from there. Bart sent one. The others, lame, old, end up at the farm because it's the only job available for them.

Pointing to a little brown pony in the field outside Eagle Creek B the next morning, Cesar says his name is John Hall. Last fall, the yearling with the pony had to be shipped to Rood and Riddle and the farm sent the pony with her to keep her calm. Lori needed a name for the paperwork, and Cesar blurted out John Hall. Laughing, Lori wrote it down, and it became the official name of the aged, lame, and miniature gelding. "I could kill her for that," John Hall says ruefully.

Cesar watches the grooms bring up the yearlings for their breakfast. John Hall will stay out, hobbling around on his misshapen feet, eating grass. Folklore, relaxed and strong, comes up from his paddock. His abscess has finally healed, though they've got a shoe with a steel plate screwed over the bottom of it just to be sure. The colt, says Cesar, is one of the best in this barn. The other one is Resplendency's colt by Unbridled's Song.

Cesar sends the grooms out to retrieve Alidiva's filly by Giant's Causeway. Charles Wacker died several months ago, and he left his Thoroughbreds in partnership to the people who worked for him. Duncan has just arrived to show the filly to an English woman who is visiting the bluegrass and looking at a couple of horses on behalf of a friend. Alidiva '09 has been scrubbed clean, her hooves have been polished, and her mane has been damped down so that it lies tidily on one side of her neck.

Duncan is outside with his visitor, and John Hall is with him. Sheri Pitzer, the farm's photographer, is here coincidentally. She takes the photographs that the farm sends to the horses' owners once a month. Cesar is inside with the grooms.

"She wants to toe in," Duncan says, pointing this out to his visitor as the chestnut filly with the bright white stockings walks down the lane. "But that's the case with the entire family," he adds. According to John Hall, Duncan's knowledge of Thoroughbred pedigrees goes back six generations. Even though they're in the business, most people, Hall included, can keep track of only a generation or two. Duncan tells his visitor that the filly's feet look rough because they're just coming out of winter. For the past several months, the ground has either been muddy or frozen.

Alidiva '09 walks up and back, up and back. No one has anything else to do today but watch this filly walk up and back. John and Duncan offer bits of useful information as it occurs to them: Her legs are shaved, John says, so the poultice can get down to her skin and do its work. The filly has had her knees stripped, Duncan volunteers.

The grooms can't get Alidiva '09 to behave. She's snatched her hooves out of the woman's hands. She won't stand still, twisting her body first one way and then the other to see what's going on down the lane or down the road. From the front pocket of her overalls, Sheri pulls out her phone and plays a recording of horses whinnying and galloping. Alidiva '09 plants her feet, pricks her ears, and stands perfectly still, listening for the invisible herd that sounds like it's about to clatter into view at any moment.

"Thank you," the visitor says. "That's perfect."

Alidiva '09 is not fooled a second time, and the visitor never gets a good second look.

Duncan has sent the grooms to retrieve a colt out of Oonagh Maccool, who shares a family with Alidiva '09. She didn't ask to see this horse, but Duncan pulled him out anyway, "because she's from Europe and she might do some free advertising for me."

The colt's walk piques the visitors' interest, and she teases Duncan for playing her. "It's the European thing," she jokes. "We all love a walk." Duncan and John smile as if to say, Of course you do.

She pats the Oonagh Maccool colt before sending him back into the barn, and all of them watch him, his stride long-legged and far-reaching, his head hanging low and just below his groom's shoulder. John Hall and Duncan are silent, waiting for their visitor to speak.

"They're quite a family," she finally says. "Aren't they?"

Sold!

7

July 2010

THE HEAT IS HEAVY, WET, AND SOUTHERN. IT'S THE end of July and Frank is up and out early, on the broodmare side, evaluating weanlings. Scott Kintz, who would normally be evaluating them as well, is no longer with Taylor Made. One of the Taylors' clients has started her own farm in Bourbon County and has hired Scott as her farm manager. It's a loss for the farm, but Frank is optimistic: "He's still in the family. We just don't need to pay him."

Jacob West, who's been transferred over to the broodmares as part of his continuing education, is pulling out weanlings for Frank to evaluate. Frank's youngest son, Chris, is with him this morning, and Frank keeps his hand on his son's back, steering him close to his side and away from the unpredictable weanlings. Hands in his pockets, shifting his weight from foot to foot, Chris watches for as long as he can, then heads to the truck to wait.

Standing in the aisle, Frank steps forward to look more closely at a weanling whose coat is too heavy for this time of year. "This foal's *hair* is not right," Frank says, and then directs Bob to have the horse's thyroid checked. That foal goes back, and the next colt, who's been waiting in the corner stall with Jacob, rears up as Jacob walks him forward, his head dangerously close to smashing into the top of the door. Jacob heaves him back down to the ground, but he blows up again, this time leaping forward and out of the stall toward Bob and Frank. Both men throw up their arms and growl.

"Let him walk down and back," Frank tells Jacob, "before he commits suicide." Frank grins. "That's the Storm Cat jumping out of him." Storm Cat, who was pensioned in 2008, at age twenty-five, was one of Kentucky's most successful modern sires. At his peak, he commanded a $500,000 stud fee. He's known for his temper, and when his children and grandchildren act up, it's blamed on him.

After walking the colt for Frank, Jacob returns him to his stall, but he balks, giving the enclosed space the stink eye. "Fifty to one you can't get him back in the stall," Frank says. The colt lowers his head and follows Jacob quietly and obediently. Frank shrugs.

Over at Whitehouse, Bobby Langley and Andre O'Connell are trimming up the mares and foals while Steve Avery watches. The farm has offered him Scott's position, and Steve has accepted it, but he's hemming and hawing about it. They're not going to hire anyone to take over Whitehouse, which means that Steve will essentially do both jobs. "We'll see," he says.

Steve's relationship with Scott and his family goes back twenty-five years. At different points in their lives, when they were trying to get established in their careers, both Scott and his brother stayed with Steve when he worked at Gainesway. "Scott has always been an impressive young man," Steve says. "I'm gonna miss him."

Then he says, "You know what I'm gonna miss the most?" Both Bobby and Andre, doubled over under the teeny little foals, are dripping with sweat, their shirts soaked through, their hair wet in the July heat. They wipe their sweaty hands on their pants before they pick up their tools. "He tells the best story of anyone around."

Trying to look on the bright side, Steve adds that the vet work will probably go faster in the morning without Scott and Barber telling stories. Steve walks over to a column of hatch marks on the outside of a stall, where he and Scott were measuring the growth of Scott's son, Nick. Pointing to the bottom mark, just feet off the ground, Steve says they started when he was five. The most recent one is at Steve's shoulder. "I'll still go to Nick's baseball games," Steve says. But then he adds, "When you're not on the same farm, you're like a million miles away."

The farm has come through the first yearling sale of the season, Fasig-Tipton's small July sale. Popular with pinhookers who are interested in precocious yearlings at the midlevel of the market, who may not have a first-class pedigree but whom they can train and resell as two-year-olds, the sale, says two-year-old trainer Niall Brennan, came out okay. Overall, there was a 9 percent drop in the median and a 2 percent drop in the average for the first sale of the season, but that's what everyone expected. Analyzing the sale for *The Blood-Horse,* reporter Lenny Shulman wrote, "The breeze you feel against your face is the collective sigh of relief that the Fasig-Tipton sale averted having the bottom drop out of the market." What people forget, says Brennan, is that "the horse business has proven time and time again that it's resilient."

On Tuesday morning, the week before the horses leave for Saratoga and the August select sale, a low ceiling of smooth, dark clouds sits over the farm, covering the sky from one side of the horizon to the other. Not far away, white-hot jags of lightning crack down to the ground. It's been a few years since they've lost a horse to a lightning strike, says John Hall, but it's always a worry. When it's stormy, the horses cluster together, standing nose-to-tail, often under trees. A single strike can take out several of them.

Overhead, the thunder sounds like tumbling boulders as the rain starts to fall. In Dayjur, where the grooms are getting ready to show horses to John and Frank, the rain on the roof has drowned out all other sounds. Even though they're standing face-to-face, they have to shout to be heard. In their stalls, the yearlings are quiet. They've come in, eaten their breakfast, and are settling in for a morning nap. It's all about the routine for them. As long as they're following their routine, they're settled and calm.

Cherry Bomb '09 never came back to her stall mates at Dayjur for the summer. Returning from lunch one day about a month ago, Tanner Tracey, who just took over as the Yearling Complex manager after Tom Hamm was moved into the office, found her lying dead, though still warm, next to the paddock fence. Spooked or rowdy, she apparently tried to go over or through it, fell, and cracked her skull.

At 7:30, Frank pulls up outside the barn but stays in the car, making calls. John arrives about fifteen minutes later and gets completely drenched jogging the twenty feet from his truck to the barn. The rain is blowing in through the open doors at the ends of the aisle, and Tanner heads down to close them. A trickle of water is seeping in through a leak in the roof and running down the ceiling, where it drips off a light fixture. Frank notices it as soon as he walks in the door.

The heat and moisture make the barn smell sour even though it's clean. Holding his Dictaphone over his face so that Audra Tackett, the young woman in the office responsible for transcribing the tape, can hear him over the sound of the rain, Frank starts his evaluations. Cesar arrives and stands close behind him and Tanner, who's now part of management and has been given the job of reading out loud the notes from Frank's last evaluations.

Frank is not happy with anything the way it is. For him, the farm is a canvas that's always one or two brushstrokes away from perfection. No sooner does he mention one problem than he notices one somewhere else. While they wait for a yearling to come out of its stall, Frank watches the hard rain saturate the paddock and run down gullies that have been cut into the dirt by the runoff. He wants them filled with topsoil, he tells Tanner and John. And someone needs to go out there and pick up every single rock in the places where the horses gather, like under the hayrack. A second gate over here—he points to the section of fence closest to the barn—would mean less walking for the grooms, and would give them a chance to seed and add topsoil to the beaten-down patch under the existing gate. Using his hands, he demonstrates how he wants the topsoil spread, how the grader should smooth it out, how the seed should be broadcast, how the muck should be laid over the seed, and how the driller should be used to press the muck into the ground. Tanner and John respond affably, but John knows this already, suggesting that Frank's detailed instructions are for Tanner's benefit. If no one has time to do the job, Frank will get on the tractor and do it himself.

The yearlings are now taller than the grooms—their nostrils at eye level. Looking at a horse who's had knee surgery, Frank uses his own leg to explain how the growth plate stabilizes as the horse grows, and how the surgeries have to be well timed so they don't overcorrect. John and Cesar know this, and Tanner might, too, at least in theory. They all watch as Frank curves his khaki-covered leg to the outside, describing the undesirable arc.

He reminds the grooms to keep a rag with mineral oil on it with them all the time, and every time they groom, they can wipe the horses' manes down to one side, training them to lie flat. No braiding. Frank hates braided manes. He brags about Cesar, who's come up with the innovation of putting the mineral oil in spray bottles. Frank tells the grooms to use it on manes, tails, bridle paths. He instructs them to clean the sheaths of the colts whenever they can get them to let down, and to wipe the udders of the fillies. Frank wants the horses ready to show every day, which both eliminates extra work before the sale and has the horses ready for buyers who stop by the farm early.

Looking at his watch, Frank decides he has time to squeeze in another set of evaluations at Eagle Creek B. Before he has even confirmed that this is what he'll do, Cesar has called ahead to the grooms at B barn to let them know that they're coming.

Standing in the aisle at B barn, Frank takes a deep breath. Everything is right about this barn, he says. Cesar's management is impeccable. The first horse was already in the aisle when they pulled up—his coat glossy, tail silky, eyes and nostrils wiped clear, mane lying neatly to one side, hooves polished. Frank's son Joe, who's just graduated from the University of Arizona's racetrack-management program and is working as a groom this summer, joins them.

"How's it going, Joe?" Frank asks.

"Good," Joe replies, stepping quietly to his father's side. They look alike, though Joe is a little taller than his father, and not quite as tidy: His khakis are slung a little low, and his shirt poofs out the waistband.

There are also two interns at Eagle Creek, who get college credit from their institutions for the time they spend working on the farm: Dominic Corbin, who's from New Zealand and whose father, the brothers found out after Dominic got here, used to drink beer with Joe senior, and Noelle Duff, from Ireland, who's been working with show jumpers as a rider and trainer. Petite, blond, and competent, she's exactly who the farm wants to show the yearlings at the sale because she makes them look bigger. She's in a more stylish version of the Taylor Made khakis as she leads out a filly by Unbridled's Song.

The filly's not very tall, though Frank observes that being thin will make her look taller. "Make sure she doesn't gain too much weight," he says, "or she'll look like a butterball." Watching her walk away, Frank comments that her owner hasn't yet paid the stud fee on her. "I'm thinking he'll get seventy-five percent of his stud fee back," he says.

Bigger, stronger, and mouthier, the horses now wear Chifney bits, brass rings that circle through their mouths and under their jaws. The grooms aren't allowed to hit the horses, less out a concern for the horses' welfare than because it makes them head-shy and unwilling to walk along smartly with their grooms. When the colts nip and bite at them, which they do constantly now that they're getting older and more aggressive, the grooms can only employ defensive measures. Noelle sets the Folklore colt up for Frank, her elbow popping up to keep the colt from biting her arm.

"God." Frank's amazement rocks him back on his feet. "This horse is looking good!" Staring, unable to criticize, he adds, "Man, this is a good-looking horse." It's impossible to tell now which one of Folklore's hooves had the abscess. "Man, you all did a good job on those feet," he says. Looking toward Cesar and John, he says, "This is probably the highest-value horse we got." Using the Dictaphone, he assigns the colt an A.

"Tell you what," Frank says. Noelle is trying to keep the colt standing square while also trying not to get bitten by the colt, who's aiming for her arm with his big grade-A teeth. "We oughta switch that horse into Drosselmeyer's stall." The 2010 winner of the Belmont Stakes lived in this building as a yearling. Folklore's colt is so good, Frank wonders aloud if it would be worth it to scan his heart—the latest diagnostic technology and one that the farm thinks could actually be useful. "That foot could have ruined this horse," Frank says. Instead, he might be the next Drosselmeyer.

Frank's preferred mode of declaration is the superlative. He "loves" the new rubber mats on the floor of the barn. And he "hates" braided manes. "Don't braid another mane on Taylor Made," he tells the grooms.

The next colt by Tale of the Cat looks exactly like his father, down to the white striping on his face. "That's a typical Tale of the Cat," Frank says to Joe.

Alidiva's filly has grown up and has a nice neck, Frank says, though her head is a little plain. Typical of her sire, Giant's Causeway, she's a touch soft in the pasterns. She's got an abscess and is stall-bound for the time being, a little dun pony at her side. The screws in her fetlocks straightened her right up, but there are tiny white hairs left behind by the wound that "need to be worked on" so that the scar tissue isn't the first thing the buyer notices.

Every horse going to the sales at Keeneland and Fasig has a set of X-rays in the repository. After an initial inspection of a horse, buyers send their vets in to examine the radiographs. The terms of the sale require sellers to disclose invasive joint surgery, but the screws and wires procedure commonly used to fix toeing in and toeing out does not require the surgeon to go into the joint, nor does the knee-stripping procedure. Removing chips, ossifications, and bone fragments does require disclosure and is considered joint surgery. Mark Taylor's estimate, with which Frank concurs, is that 20 percent of all yearlings have joint surgery and he says that maybe 40 percent have had either joint or corrective conformation surgery. Mark calls this estimate a "WAGNER—wild-ass guess, not enough research." Dr. Embertson, at Rood and Riddle, doesn't feel confident making a guess, and Geoffrey Russell, Keeneland's director of sales, says that they ask about the cosmetic surgeries for the horses they inspect, but because they don't inspect all of the horses in the sale, he's not confident at all about an estimate. But, he adds, Taylor Made is a "microcosm" of Keeneland, and Mark and Frank might know better than anyone.

Picking up Alidiva '09's lower leg, Frank calls Tanner and Joe to his side. He tells them that when they're looking at a horse's feet, they shouldn't hold on to the hoof, but on to the leg, so the hoof can flop down into its natural position. A hoof can be remodeled to make the leg look straight when the horse is standing on it, but when you pick it up and let it hang, its natural angle will reveal itself. Frank points to the frog, a thick V-shaped cushion of tissue in the middle of the horse's hoof. If that's pointing off to one side or the other, he says, it's a sign that the hoof has been too extensively remodeled—shaved away so the horse's leg looks straighter than it is. Alidiva's frog is centered in the middle of her hoof, but if they're looking at a horse whose frog points in one direction or the other, he says, "that's a horse you don't want to buy."

Frank asks John if a colt who's been wearing a liquid-titanium hood has calmed down. The Taylors are also known for being open to new ideas in an industry that is defined by its adherence to tradition. Susan Rodgers, an equine massage therapist, says that when she started, Taylor Made was the first barn to "throw open its doors" to unconventional treatments. The inventor of the liquid-titanium hoods approached them at the July sale, and they agreed to try one. John Hall says he can't be sure it's the hood, but the colt wearing it has certainly calmed down. Frank wants to take if off and see what happens, but a note of panic creeps into John's voice as he tells Frank no. The colt is finally calm, John says; he doesn't want to change a thing.

Frank wants to repeat the experiment with multiple horses to see "if the damn things work." If they do, he says, "I'm gonna buy one for *me* to wear at the sale," which conjures an image of Frank and his horses standing around in tinfoil hats.

Glenarcy's filly by Master Command comes down the aisle. She's back at the knees and a little sickle-hocked, though getting straighter as she fills out, Frank observes. She'll be one of just a few Master Command foals in existence. One of Taylor Made's own, Master Command was euthanized after a breeding-shed accident last year. Frank thinks this filly would do better waiting until she's three to go to the track.

Grooms in Yearling Complex A wrapping the legs of a recently retired race mare who is headed to the November 2009 bloodstock sale. "That's what I like," Frank Taylor said about her. "Put that into words, and that's what I like." [*Susan Nusser*]

Angela's Love's 2009 filly by Forestry. She was born in the wee hours of February 15 and in this photo is less than thirty minutes old. This was the mare's second foal. Night-watch staff member Terry Pellin noticed that this baby was very careful when she first started to walk around her stall. [*Susan Nusser*]

Cherry Bomb's 2009 filly by Henny Hughes at one month old. After a couple of lost pregnancies, Cherry Bomb finally delivered a healthy filly on the evening of February 13. The filly was feisty and a little wary, not unlike her mother. [*Susan Nusser*]

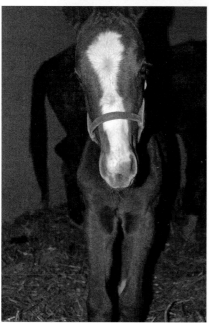

Mare and her foal in Whitehouse lower paddocks, spring 2009. Taylor Made, says Mark Taylor, believes that foals need to be raised outside, in natural conditions. In their paddocks, they fight and play with the other horses in their band, and, most often, with their mothers. [*Susan Nusser*]

New foal. At 11:00 P.M., the night-watch staff turn off the lights in the stalls, but until then, the foals are playful. Even at just a few weeks, like this foal, their personalities— curious, shy, feisty—are apparent. [*Susan Nusser*]

Collect Call with her days-old colt by Empire Maker. Of his crop, he was one of the colts those at the farm were most excited about, estimating his sale price as high as $1.3 million at one point. [*TMSA, Sheri Pitzer*]

Mares and foals in the Bona Terra B paddock, summer 2009. When the grooms feed the mares in the paddock, they toss the hay out of the tractor as it drives in a straight line, then pour a scoop of grain on top of it. From a distance, it looks like all the horses have lined up to graze. [*Susan Nusser*]

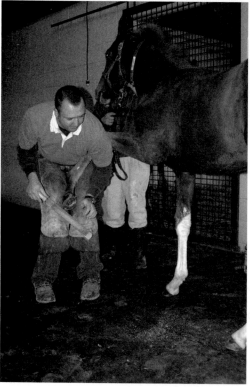

Farrier Andre O'Connell shaping the hooves of Folklore's 2009 colt by Distorted Humor. Shaping foals' feet every few weeks helps maintain their confirmation and can improve it. It also helps foals develop their manners as they get accustomed to being handled by a farrier. [*Susan Nusser*]

The Taylors at the 1990 Keeneland September sale. From left to right: Duncan Taylor, Ben Taylor, Satish Seemar, Mark Taylor, Frank Taylor, and Joe Lannon Taylor. In 1990, Joe Taylor, Sr., retired as Gainesway's farm manager and joined his sons at Taylor Made, helping to launch their stallion division, which opened in 1997. Mark Taylor would go on to work for Sateesh Seemar in Dubai for a year before returning to manage yearlings at Taylor Made. [*Joy A. Gilbert*]

Conducting evaluations in preparation for the 2009 Keeneland November bloodstock sale. Left to right: John Hall, Scott Kintz, Frank Taylor, Jacob West, Tom Hamm, and groom Rosalino Domingo. Every horse on the farm gets evaluated once a month, and Frank's notes get sent to the horses' owners. This weanling had been shipped in as a consignment in the fall of 2010, and Frank and his team are evaluating him before he goes to the November sale. [*Susan Nusser*]

Frank Taylor briefing the staff at the Keeneland September sale. Every day of the sale begins and ends with a staff meeting. The quad leaders—in this case, Frank Taylor—summon their teams together to review what worked, what didn't work, and what should have worked better. Like those at the other top farms, Taylor Made's staff is disciplined, focused, and supremely professional. [*Lee P. Thomas*]

Mare and foal in Bona Terra A's paddock, winter 2010. A mare and foal get out to stretch their legs, even in the snow and cold. [*Susan Nusser*]

Even though he's a baby, Collect Call's '09 colt by Empire Maker already has good confirmation in his hind end and through his legs. "That mare," says Collect Call's owner, Lorraine Rodriguez, "has a tendency to put pretty into all her offspring." [*TMSA, Sheri Pitzer*]

Though tiny, fuzzy, and adorable here, just a few weeks after his birth, Resplendency '09 will grow into a monster of a colt. By the time he's a year old, he'll be bigger than his dam and have the size and substance of his sire, Unbridled's Song. [*TMSA, Sheri Pitzer*]

This is Queen's 2009 filly by the Irish stallion Street Cry in one of her more awkward stages. Her baby coat hasn't yet grown out. Her hind end is way above her shoulders, though that evens out as foals get older. Her biggest problem is going to be those front knees, which are offset, or tilted to one side. [*TMSA, Sheri Pitzer*]

Taylor Made yearlings, October 2010. These are three fillies who had just moved over from the mares' side of the barn during the previous month. These fillies are waiting for the grooms to arrive with hay and grain and are the most curious of the fillies in their pasture. [*Susan Nusser*]

She'll need that time just to grow into her massive body. Turning her around, Noelle gets crowded up against the wall. "She's so damn big, we can't even turn her around in the barn," Frank says. He asks Cesar what the filly is like in the field.

"She doesn't run," Cesar says. "She never runs."

"This is going to be a hard horse to sell," Frank concludes.

Maizelle's A.P. Indy filly gets a better evaluation. "How's she in the field?" Frank asks Cesar. "She runs good," Cesar replies.

Jo Pollock thinks Frank should pay someone to stand at the fence rail and keep track of those horses who outrun their peers at the farm to see if they do better as racehorses.

Frank offers to start up the ten-dollar betting pool on which horses in the barn end up being the best racehorses. But everyone blows the odds by picking the same three horses: Maizelle, Officiate, and Folklore.

Oonagh Maccool's Street Cry colt has a beautiful head and neck but stifles that are too prominent. Frank wants to start the horse in some light training, working him on long lines to build up the muscle mass in his hind end. If you can do it safely, Frank says to John, he would like the horse to get started.

It's time for lunch and a nap. The horses stretch out in their stalls, snoring gently. The grooms pull off their boots and sprawl out over chairs in the office, or lie down on the floor, using their boots as a pillow. They gather in the barn's intersection, drowsing where the breezes meet. Even the birds are too hot to twitter. At noon, the entire farm lapses into the stillness of sleep. After siesta, everyone slowly rouses themselves. In her stall in Yearling Complex C, the Queen filly lifts her head and sighs. She's been sleeping all morning but looks like she'd like to sleep just a little longer. She blinks, blows dust out of her nostrils, flings her feet out in front of her, and, with a groan, pushes herself up. She lowers her head and gives her whole body a hard shake, casting off the wood shavings clinging to her coat. Most of the horses sleep on straw beds, but those, like Queen, who eat the straw—which has no nutritional value but will cause the horses to gain weight—get switched to wood shavings.

Miguel, Queen's groom, slips in through the door and puts the Chifney in her mouth. She jingles it in a distracted way, relaxed, the lead shank attached to her halter dropped on the floor while Miguel starts on her hooves, picking out her feet and painting them with mineral oil. He's unhurried, as if he's got nothing to do today but groom this one horse. The farm assigns each groom a fixed number of horses—around five—and how they get them done is up to them. Some of the guys, Cesar says, fill up their entire day with grooming, moving slowly, meticulously. Others work more quickly, and if they get done early, they can take an extra break.

Miguel rubs Queen's coat with the currycomb. If there was actually any dirt on her, this would bring it to the surface, but the yearlings are bathed every day. The currycomb stimulates the oils in her skin and gives the horse a good overall scratch. The filly is big enough now that Miguel has to push up on his tiptoes to curry and brush her back. She's half-asleep in the corner of her stall, and Miguel tugs at her, trying to get her to move away from the wall so he can groom her other side. Queen lets him tug out her head and neck, but she never moves her feet. He squeezes between the wall and her body and gives her a shove. She wakes up and walks to the other side of the stall, Miguel trailing her, currycomb in hand.

After currying her, Miguel rubs her down with a pimpled rubber mitt that he uses all over her body and on the bony parts of her face and legs, where the big comb would hurt. She closes her eyes and leans into his hand. He follows the mitt with a brush, and by the time he's done, every inch of her body has been gone over twice.

Standing behind her, he spritzes her tail with conditioner and uses just his fingers to gently brush out the shavings. The farm never uses combs on the horses' tails because they pull out too much hair. Queen's mane already falls tidily to one side, so he just needs to flatten the hairs a bit with the brush. His chin lifted a bit so he can see above her eyes, he uses his fingers, which have oil on them, to brush her forelock over to one side. Stroking gently, he lays the forelock flat and tucks the edges in neatly, like a mother who's curling her daughter's hair behind her ear. When he's done, he takes a towel dampened with rubbing alcohol and runs it over her coat, pulling up any last bits of dust.

Three stalls down from Miguel, Duncan Taylor's son Danny is speeding along. After working with Lindsey over at the Casey division last winter, he's switched to the yearlings. Mario Ramirez, the foreman in this barn, is teaching Danny to pull a mane—yanking out the long hairs so that it lies flat and even. Mario is holding the shank of a roan colt named River Drive '09 and coaching Danny in Spanish. As instructed, Danny grabs a few long hairs with his fingers, pushes the rest of the mane away with a comb, and yanks. The crest of River Drive '09's neck bounces down and back, but he doesn't respond. There are little to no nerve endings along his crest. River Drive '09 looks ready to sleep.

When the mane is done, it's shorter, and Mario offers Danny some encouraging words. Then, quickly, stretching upward, he works his way back down the horse's neck. In two minutes, the colt's mane is perfectly even, looks thicker, and is lying smooth and flat. Danny bursts out laughing, telling Mario he's got a lot to learn. He's majoring in business at the University of Kentucky right now, but he hasn't yet decided if he'll follow in the family business. "I don't really like horses." He shrugs and then smiles at the irony.

It's early afternoon and eight members of the administrative team—Frank and Mark, account managers Wally Burleson and Jeff Hayslett, John Hall, Tom Hamm, Sue Egan, and Patrick Mahan—join veterinarian Deborah Spike-Pierce in the farm's big conference room to go over the radiographs before the Saratoga sale. On the walls, painted the conservative green popular with banks, are posters of the farm's winning horses. Taylor Made is consigning twenty-three horses in all. Six of them are at Eagle Creek A right now, and a few more will be shipped in from their owners' barns right before the truck leaves. The truck will pick up a barnload from a nearby farm on its way to Saratoga, and another client is shipping his via plane. In front of everyone are the medical reports on the horses for which Dr. Spike-Pierce is providing an assessment.

Looking fresh and cool in a crisp white shirt, Duncan pops his head in the door. "Y'all giving us all A's today?" he asks her.

Of all the problems—sesamoiditis, a spur, OCD (a joint disorder), a small slab fracture that should heal with time—only one horse, the one with the spur, has a problem about which she's concerned. Mark grimaces as she assigns the horse a B. The sesamoiditis is more of a problem for American buyers than for European ones, and the Saratoga sale, now that Sheikh Mohammed has bought a controlling share of Fasig-Tipton, draws in European buyers. Jeff Hayslett points out that the radiographs are being read by American vets. The grades that the farm gives the horses will no longer go on the vet reports—that information will be just for the buyers. There's nothing, says Dr. Spike-Pierce, that should damage the horses' value too badly. In the past at Saratoga, she explains, "there was a lot of pathology that sold well."

Frank tells everyone how much he likes Resplendency's big bay colt. He looks exactly like his sire, Unbridled's Song, did when he was a yearling. To quell concern over his size, Frank wants to put side-by-side photos of the horses at the same age in the sales books. The photos, Frank thinks, would help buyers overlook any conformational flaws. For another horse who's knee spur is healing, Frank wants to include older scans with the current ones, so that buyers can see that the condition is resolving itself.

Dr. Spike-Pierce takes her leave and the meeting ends twenty minutes early, leaving some of the team members hanging around, waiting for the sales meeting, which is next. They reminisce about past Saratogas. It's the social event of the year for an industry that has the means to throw itself a hell of a party. The men are stumbling over themselves to be the one to tell the story of staggering home to their shared house, only to find that one of the early-to-bed types had moved the furniture and unscrewed the lightbulbs.

The women who work in the office, none of whom attend Saratoga, exchange looks and press their lips together in disapproval. "How old are you?" chides Susan Ballard, the farm's public sales manager.

Frank returns to the room and everyone stops laughing. By 3:10 P.M., Mark is seated at the head of the table and the meeting begins.

The horses leave Wednesday and the humans leave Thursday.

"Signs and ring stakes," Mark says. He wants to know what are they doing for new signs. The new banners don't match the old valances. "We're taking the old banners with new logos," Patrick tells him. Mark wants to be sure that there will be individual posters of Drosselmeyer, and not just one where he's part of a group.

"What'd they get all pissed about last year?" Mark is trying to remember why they got in trouble with Fasig-Tipton.

Tom grimaces. "We drilled holes in the entrance they had just painted."

Frank wants to start the fillies on Regu-Mate—the hormone supplement used to regulate the mares' ovulation cycles—to keep them from coming into heat during the sale, and he tells Patrick to make sure there's plenty of Vicks. They wipe it in the colt's noses so they can't smell the fillies. Mark says he'll tell his account managers to check with the owners to see if it's okay to get the fillies on Regu-Mate.

Tom Hamm, the grand marshal of the traveling encampment, distributes an eight-and-a-half-by-sixteen-inch chart that maps out the stabling area. Stalls run on three sides around the perimeter, and there are consignments on either side of them. They're across the residential road from the main sales area and the entire grounds are enclosed by a black iron fence. In the center of the stabling area is the showing area, divided up into "rings," separate show areas that are marked off by small white stakes in the ground. Frank Taylor is listed as "Zone Captain" on the chart.

They're traveling with as small a team as they think they can manage, so everyone needs to do more than one job. Mark says to make sure that the girls who are showing horses are assigned to the fillies if they're not comfortable with the colts. He also tells them to make sure that even if the girls want to handle the colts, they're able to.

The housing assignments are also on the charts. Mark's house has six people. Barrett Midkiff, the driver, is head of one with eight. They've got sixteen people assigned to the racetrack's bunkhouse, and Finn Green, the farm's recently hired business developer, is stashed in the Comfort Inn, whose nightly rate Tom Hamm has negotiated down to ninety-nine dollars from the three hundred that the economy hotels get during race season. Frank wants Finn moved into his house.

Most of the help is driving up—the grooms will ride in the back of the truck with the horses for a long, straight seventeen-hour shot. The account managers are flying, as is the recently promoted Tom Hamm.

"How did you convince me you're flying?" Mark asks Tom.

Hunter Houlihan, the research assistant who works with marketing director Mark Brooking, points out that paying mileage if Tom were to drive would only save about fifty dollars.

Telling them to check temperatures on any horses coming back to the farm after the sale, so they don't bring Potomac horse fever back to the barn with them, Frank gets back to the business angle.

Catering, says Tom, is down to $2,100 this year. It was $5,500 last year. Barrett is in charge of making breakfast.

Frank, who's been staring at the chart, renumbers the zones, though no one understands why. And he wants designated showmen—showmen who are assigned to specific horses. John Hall, who's been largely silent, jumps into the conversation, pointing out that having designated showmen means that you need more help in the barn.

Frank wants to know why they need more help. "We've got twenty-three horses and thirty-one humans," he says.

They go through the list of help again: Cordell, Mario, Freddy, and Leandro can handle anything. Ron can be good. Frank's son Joe is too big to show the small horses, and Noelle is great with the fillies, but the colts at the July sale walked all over her, Mark says. One of their bigger clients is sending along a groom from his farm, and though she's reputed to be very good, no one's seen her show yearlings yet.

"All I know," says John Hall, "when I was over there yesterday, she was the only one sweating while twelve guys stood around."

"Maybe being in the barn with twelve guys was what was making her sweat," Mark quips.

Dean, whose job it is to help the vets who won't be around during those first few days, can do a little more than wait for them to arrive, Mark says. "Put him somewhere where he's not laying on a twitch for three days, waiting for the vets to show up."

For one week's worth of work, only two days of which are the actual sale, Taylor Made's payroll for the temporary help is twenty thousand dollars.

The meeting ends, leaving behind just Frank, Mark, and Tom Hamm. Frank missed an earlier meeting, and Mark wants to make sure that he knows that the farm's marketing consultant is preparing responses that will be distributed to the frontmen and anyone else who might end up responding to the media. "Just so you know," Mark says, smiling, knowing that Frank is the person most likely to look at a horse in front of a journalist, frown, and say, "Yeah, I like it okay."

The next morning is hot and muggy, the skies already bleached out and hazy by 9:00 A.M. At Eagle Creek C, six horses are trotting around the mechanical free walker—a circular pen, sectioned like an orange, in which gates hang in between the horses so that they can trot freely but can't get to one another. Like carnies packing fairgoers onto a ride, the grooms load the horses into their space, turn the central spindle, using a control panel by the gate, and load the next horse. Once everyone is in, they turn the walker on and the horses begin to trot, or walk fast, or stop and go, stop and go, cantering to catch up, stopping to sniff the ground and then trotting off.

They get up to forty minutes, says Cesar, depending on how fat they are. Frank, he jokes, "needs, like, two hours."

"I'm getting ready for a hard winter," Frank calls back from the paddock, where he's doubled over, digging up a sharp-edged stone with his fingers.

Young Joe brings up Collect Call '09, puts him in the walker, and then reverses direction. The horses sigh, swing their heads around slowly, and jog off the other way. Their hooves land softly in the shredded rubber, their Chifneys jingle. Some of the colts bite at the dividers. Watching them, Frank asks Cesar if he ever turns the electric on to keep the colts away from the gates. Cesar shakes his head.

"Does it work?" Frank asks.

"Maybe that's why I never used it," Cesar replies. "Because it doesn't work."

Frank notices that they're surrounded by wasps, and the men quickly back up, looking for the source of them. Pointing at a hole in the instrument panel, Frank says, "That's where the sons of bitches are living." Cesar pokes at the panel, trying to figure out how to get it open. John and Frank back away.

"You're going to get them all pissed off," Frank says.

Frank and John head back to the tack room, trailed by a groom whom Cesar's sent to retrieve some wasp spray. The groom returns empty-handed. "*No haya* spray?" Cesar asks. The groom shakes his head.

Inside the walker, Collect Call '09 is full of energy. His full, big, bounding stride pushes him right up against the front of the gate. The colts who've been jogging longer are getting tired, but Collect Call '09 is fired up. As he passes the gate where Joe is standing, he looks at him, banging his nose on the gatepost as he jogs past. Every time he passes Joe, he bangs his nose in the same way. As he jogs, he drops his head to the ground, his nose traveling in front of his hooves. He snorts, blows out the dust, relaxes, his legs swinging loose and free from his hips and shoulder.

"He's definitely an athlete," says Joe. "He moves better than any of them."

Collect Call '09 was the last to go into the walker. It's 9:30 and exercise is done. The sky is already a washed-out blue and the whir of the cicadas pierces the heavy air. Once the colt is done trotting in the other direction, Joe leads him to the wash stall—a three-sided enclosure closed off by a single heavy rail—where the horses stand on a rubber mat to be bathed after their daily workout. Leandro, Collect Call '09's groom, is waiting with the hose, and while Joe holds him, Leandro sprays the colt down and scrubs him sudsy with a giant sponge. Collect Call '09 leans his head against Joe's arm, rubs his face against him, his eyes closed, and then tries to bite him. Expecting to be bitten, Joe pops up his elbow, and the colt flings up his head before making contact. Joe leaves his hand on the colt's muzzle while the horse flicks his ears.

He's scrubbed top to bottom, starting with a conditioning shampoo for his coat. Since May, the horses have been turned out at night and kept in during the day so their coats won't get bleached out by the sun. His tail is soaped and rinsed, Leandro snapping it like a whip to flick out the water. His face is washed, and when Leandro sprays it off, the colt lifts his head, turns his ears back, closes his eyes, and presses his lips together, trying to keep the water out of his nose. Before they're finished, a bluing shampoo is used on the white socks on the colt's hind legs. When Joe and Leandro take him back to his stall, the skin under those socks is an electric pink.

By 10:00 A.M., each colt has been returned to his stall. Eagle Creek C houses all colts this year. Some of them stand directly in front of the box fans that are strapped to the stall doors, letting the breeze from them lift their forelocks and cool their faces. Joe puts Collect Call '09 in his stall and takes out the colt's water bucket. The horse has pooped in it and Joe needs to scrub it out.

"I don't know why he does that," Joe says tiredly.

Outside, the barn cats have gifted the grooms with a headless bird that has already started to rot in the heat. Inside the barn, Collect Call '09 has his nose pressed up against the stall grate and he's watching the grooms as they go about their work, tilting his head from side to side, flicking his ears. He whinnies softly and another colt whinnies back.

By afternoon, Frank is back at Eagle Creek C for evaluations. The weatherman has recommended that everyone stay inside with fans or air-conditioning because the heat index will be around 102 degrees. Every fan on the farm is blowing at top speed.

Instead of watching his father evaluate horses, this time Joe is showing them to him.

"Joe," says Cesar, who is standing behind Frank signaling to Joe that he needs to lift up the hand that holds the shank of the colt he's showing. When holding the horses, the grooms keep one hand where the chain meets the leather, and the other holds the long end. Joe has let the hand holding the long end drop to his thigh instead of holding it up, ready and at attention.

Looking at a bay colt by Tiznow, Frank runs a hand over his loins. He's too thin on top and has too big a belly below. They need to get his gut up over his loins, Frank says, and recommends swimming. On the other side of Lexington is a therapeutic facility where the horses can swim or use a treadmill to get fit.

Frank has a visitor with him today. The visitor's husband, after getting lucky with the first racehorse he bought, quickly built up a sixty-horse band. She's here because she's trying to learn everything she can, and Frank has agreed to let her tag along. Frank and John Hall are teaching her how to evaluate conformation. "The closer the joint is to the ground," John Hall says, "the sooner the growth plates grow." That's why there's a small window in which to fix ankles that's followed by a small window in which to fix knees.

"God, he looks like a Tiznow," Frank says, giving the colt a B++.

"This horse wasn't raised here," Frank says defensively as a skinny colt comes out of a stall. "He was starving to death when we got him." Watching him walk, Frank points out that his hocks are a little high, but he's not back at the knee.

Another horse who looks a little light in the bone steps up. Decent head, neck, and shoulder, Frank comments, but he's a little soft in the pasterns and wants to paddle slightly as he walks. The visitor wants to know if he also came from off the farm and Frank pauses. "No," he says. "But I can see why you think that. I'm not too proud of him."

Collect Call '09's stall is right next to the intersection of the aisle and he's had his nose pressed against his stall door through all the evaluations, just watching. Impatient, wanting attention, he starts kicking his door, and John Hall growls at him. The colt pauses and then does it again. Cesar, the enforcer, slides open his door and shoos him away from it.

An Unbridled's Song colt comes out and Frank stares at it, silent and frowning. "We had a five-million-dollar offer for this mare," Frank says, referring to the colt's dam. "And the owner didn't take it. Now we have an ugly little Unbridled's Song."

An A.P. Indy colt comes out. He's got a little bit of a clubbed foot—one that's too steep and straight. "Comes straight from A.P. Indy," Frank says, referring to Kentucky's most valuable stallion.

Collect Call '09 finally gets his turn. "This is a hell of a horse," Frank says. "If I had to pick a runner out of the whole farm right now, it'd be him."

Andre O'Connell is in Yearling Complex C when the team gets there. Say It with Feelin '09 is getting a special shoe for her clubby foot. Her custom shoe is made of aluminum and at its peak is a rivet, which allows the sides of the shoe to swing back and forth. On the inside edge of the shoe is a V-shaped bar spring. Once Andre glues the shoe to her hoof, that spring will apply moderate and constant pressure to the heels of her hoof. As she walks, the heel will slowly spread out.

"You see Scott's new F Two fifty?" Andre asks Cesar. Cesar nods.

"He came in to see those horses," Cesar says.

"Did he now?" Andre laughs.

Scott's new employers will be keeping their horses at Taylor Made, which will continue to be their consignor, until after the September sale, when repairs and upgrades are finished. Scott now keeps track of the horses by visiting the farm and requesting showings—just like an owner.

Cesar is holding the silicone gun for Andre.

"You're sweating already," Andre says. "And you're not even doing anything." While Andre holds the hoof still, the shoe in place, Cesar squirts in clear silicone packing material that will protect the site.

At the barn's intersection, Frank is watching River Drive's colt by Unbridled's Song walk down the aisle. Thanks to Mario and Danny, his mane is beautiful, but he paddles when he walks; his right hoof flips out.

"He's walking like he's dealing cards," Frank says, mimicking the motion. He lifts the colt's right front knee and pulls its straight forward from the shoulder. The colt doesn't resist. Frank's hoping that maybe it's just a tightness in the muscle, because they can't find any reason why he walks the way he does. The difference between the colt's current walk and a correct walk could be worth $100,000 to $200,000.

"When you get to the sale and they say walk him," Frank jokes with Mario, "say no."

John thinks it would be more effective if they just put a cast on Mario.

Danny brings out a "studish" colt—one who's already feeling the surge of his hormones. He nickers throatily to the fillies at the other end of the barn. He's challenging and aggressive.

The Queen filly, who has had her fetlocks fixed and her knees stripped and stabilized by screws, stands for her inspection.

"This is a horse, you could have gave it away before we started working on her." Frank likes her body, and really likes her deep heart girth, though her hocks are set out a bit. "I'm starting to kind of like her," Frank says.

Evaluating another filly with a great body, Frank comments, "Her mother had a body like that." But the filly is a little back at the knee and clubby on her left foot. When you see a horse with a clubfoot, Frank tells his visitor and young Joe, "nine out of ten times, they're also back at the knee."

Patty Seattle's '09 filly comes out of the stall. Her mother is known for throwing bad-tempered fillies, and the team takes a minute to congratulate John Hall on the one-year anniversary of having his ribs broken when this filly's half sister kicked him last year.

On hot, still days like today, the breeze rolls down the hill and cuts through the middle of the barn, meeting up with the breezes coming in from the long sides. In the intersection, the air is moving, even though it's hot. The birds are silent. In their stalls, the horses are still, shuffling only to flick away flies or slop a drink out of their buckets. The team members are laboring in the heat. They've sweated through their shirts, even though they're standing still. John Hall has pressed his knuckles into the small of his back, as if it's sore. Cesar is standing squarely over his feet but is leaning back just a bit, as if he's trying to give them a break by shifting his weight on them. Even young Joe looks spent, his damp shirt sagging over his waistband. But Frank is attacking every evaluation with the same energy as the first. He carries on without the input from his team members, who are now looking at the horses from where they stand, making little effort to walk around them, but John and Cesar see these horses every day. The grooms wait silently until it's their turn to walk up. Finally, Frank is on the last horse. It's almost a hundred degrees outside, and the grass crackles in the slow, hot breeze that brushes up against it. A van pulls up and disgorges a hot, rumpled, sweaty driver, who heaves a cardboard box holding a 5-gallon jug of corn oil to his shoulder. He walks up behind Frank, who's still in the aisle, and says, "You want to know who taught me about horses?" he asks.

"Who?" Frank says.

"Joe Taylor."

Frank smiles slowly. "He taught me a few things, too."

The driver takes the corn oil into the feed room and everyone heads out to their cars. Frank starts to get in; then, leaving his visitor waiting, he walks back toward the driver as he gets into his truck. He leans toward him, talking quietly, and then, smiling, leans away and extends his hand. "I'm Frank," he says.

It's Saturday, 6:30 A.M., and Cesar is standing outside the door of Eagle Creek C, watching the grooms bring up the colts. Everyone starts work at Yearling Complex C, because that's where one of the two time clocks is located. They punch in, bring up the horses, chuck them in their stalls, leave behind the barn's foreman to feed them, and then they hop into the back of Cesar's truck and head to the next barn, repeating the procedure. After the last barn, they pile back into the truck and Cesar returns them to their assigned barns for chores. The routine is military in its precision and uniformity. The grooms are dressed the same—burgundy polo shirts, khaki pants. They move quickly and efficiently, their boots hitting the ground hard when they jump out of the back of the truck. Almost all of them are Mexican or Guatemalan, and are about the same size. Dominic, the intern from New Zealand, stands out because he's over six feet. Although not that tall, Joe stands out, too, but Danny, thin and quick-moving, melts right into the group. Noelle, with her blond ponytail and mascara, is the only woman.

One behind the other, ten colts are coming up the tarmac lane between the paddocks.

"Op! Op! Op! Op!" Cesar calls out. Noelle has lost the Winterberry colt. Cesar jogs to the head of the parade, and the rest of the grooms halt, keeping hold of their charges while the loose colt jigs in among them. No one moves as he breaks out of the line and starts to canter up the lane. Cesar steps in to block him, gets hold of the lead shank, and hands him back to a red-faced Noelle.

"He's a tough horse," he says. He's gotten away from a few of the grooms. There's no point in getting mad about it, Cesar explains. It happens. Once the horses are in, a chestnut colt is led out of his stall and put in a paddock. Cesar doesn't have quite enough room for all his horses—the colts can't be dumped into their paddocks in herds like the fillies can, because they fight. They have to be very carefully grouped, and Cesar has one more horse than he has room for in his paddocks. When he has to put horses out during the day, Cesar says, he chooses the chestnuts because their coats don't bleach out as badly as the darker horses.

At Eagle Creek B, Cesar watches the grooms retrieve the yearlings from their fields. The pony named John Hall stays out. "We got another one," Cesar says. "Little chestnut pony, fat. We're trying to call him Frank."

Cesar has been at Taylor Made for twelve years. He comes from Chihuahua, Mexico, and followed his cousin, Gilberto, who is Taylor Made's stallion manager. There were horses around when he was growing up, but he learned how to handle and care for them at Taylor Made.

Once the horses are in, the first sets of them are marched up to the walker that the two Eagle Creek barns share. It sits on top of a hill, where there's always at least a little bit of a breeze and the view is nice. But for the grooms who have to walk as many as ten horses up and back, says Cesar, it's a long haul.

From the walker, the entire yearling side of the farm is visible, swooping downhill and away; the trees that border the yearling complex barns are visible to the southwest. It's sunny and warm, the skies a bright blue, the haze of the day not yet settled in.

Outside the walker are two side-by-side wash stalls, partitioned off by steel rails painted black. In between them, a shelf is covered with quart- and gallon-sized bottles, holding three different kinds of shampoo—a regular conditioning one, one for sensitive skin, and an antifungal. There's bluing shampoo for the horses with white parts, as well as conditioner to make their tails sleek. There are also buckets, sponges, sweat scrapers, and a tub of yellow sweating gel, which they use with neoprene wraps to sweat down necks that are too heavily crested.

For now, it's breezy and comfortable by the walker, though the weather people are predicting the hottest day of the summer. The birds are still cool enough to twitter, and dragonflies zip and hover, zip and hover. Deputy of Wood has arrived early for her workout and stands patiently at her groom's side, lifting her muzzle and placing it gently against his cheek. He tilts his head toward her, turning it so that her hot, grassy breath blows across his ear.

There are six of last winter's New York horses left. They've been living outside since May. When the horses come over to the yearling side, those who are going straight to racing live outside. The grooms check on them every day, and they get their feet trimmed and they're wormed, but they're not "pampered," as John Hall puts it. No cosmetic surgeries, daily bathing, mineral oil in their manes and tails, or baby oil around their eyes. They live and play rough—like normal baby horses. "They are being raised the way they should be," John Hall says.

They're being bathed this morning because Raul Reyes, a trainer of two-year-olds in Florida, has agreed to take them on for the farm. It's some kind of share, but John Hall says he doesn't know the details. Since they're shipping out, they're getting baths. Their coats have been bleached by the sun and are all the same faded tannish orange color. They're covered with bumps and scrapes and their manes are willy-nilly on both sides of their neck. They have whiskers.

And they don't want baths.

A dust-colored colt refuses to go into the wash stall. Noelle stands outside of it, turning the colt into the stall and getting dragged away when he refuses to enter. The two grooms bathing a horse in the next stall glance over their shoulders but make no move to help. The colt doesn't like the wash stall; he doesn't like the smell of the soap, the rubber mat. He's having none of it.

John Hall arrives on scene. Cars are parked on the other side of the walker, and he appears quietly. He helps Noelle get the horse in the wash stall, where the colt stands with his back humped up, tense, preparing for the onslaught of cold water. John turns the pressure down, backs away, and slowly moves the hose up and down the colt's body. He relaxes and John starts with a sudsy sponge, moving from ears to tail, down the legs, under the belly. The colt fidgets and stamps, pushing at Noelle but not fighting too much. John keeps up a steady conversation with Noelle and the horse as he is bathed. The colt tosses up his head when John comes at him with the sponge. Noelle keeps hold of the lead shank and John talks the horse into lowering his head. The colt squeezes his eyes shut as the suds slide down his face. By the time John rinses off his body, he's standing quietly, but he still has a soapy face, and John doesn't think he's going to put up with having it sprayed. He turns the pressure way down and slowly trickles the suds away. The colt snorts the water out of his nose and pricks his ears, clean and refreshed but still dinged up and faded. He's led back to the barn.

Alidiva's chestnut filly is led into the walker. Her three white socks are quickly blackened by the wet, shredded rubber. She's got an abscess on her left front hoof, which is packed and taped up. She trots out, her face right up against the gate. The other horses have settled into the groove that's been worn away on the inside of the track, but the Alidiva filly trots all over the place, moving from side to side, looking at the outside of the fence, at the other horses, at the inside of the fence. Even after ten minutes, when most of the horses settle into a steady rhythm or slow to a walk-trot combination, she's still tracking back and forth.

John Hall has left and the grooms are struggling to get another colt into the stall. The colt has planted his feet, and on the other end of the lead shank, a groom named Mario has planted his. The colt's neck is stretched out as Mario leans back against the lead shank. Both stretched as far as they go, they are at an impasse. The colt tosses his head and Mario is yanked off his feet. They circle and approach again; the other groom uses the hose to spray the horse's heels, and when he picks them up, they quickly pull him into the stall. He's in, but he doesn't like the hose and bolts back out again, dragging Mario with him.

"*No bueno*," Mario says, laughing.

They turn the pressure down on the hose and try again, getting him into the stall and running the water over his legs. "Good boy," Mario croons.

Cesar arrives.

"We've got a scared one," Noelle tells him.

The colt has backed out of the stall again. Cesar takes the hose, clicks the sprayer to a new setting, and backs far away, misting the horse with almost no pressure. The horse lowers his head and walks into the stall. Cesar follows. While Mario holds on to the colt, Cesar wordlessly and with awesome authority soaps him from head to foot. Cesar is tall, and with his feet squarely planted, he presses into the horse with one hand while soaping with the other. He keeps his body close to the horse, his hands reassuring him. In five minutes, the colt who was just dragging two grooms across the asphalt is calm enough for Cesar to take a phone call. Phone in one hand, hose in the other, he rinses off the colt, who sighs deeply and lowers his head. Done with the call, Cesar closes his phone, turns the pressure down on the spray, and lifts the hose to the colt's face. He stands still even for this, closing his eyes and curling up his lip to keep water from running into his nostrils. When he's done, the grooms lead him away, and Noelle shakes her head, awestruck.

Cesar looks in on the horses in the walker. The Alidiva filly is nice enough, he says, but she's nervous in her stall, and the back-and-forth business in the walker wastes energy.

He steps away to the lane and watches the next batch of horses come up the narrow chute in between the paddocks. The groom in front is getting banged around by the colt he's leading. Struggling for control, trying to keep the horse from climbing up over his back, the groom is snapping the lead shank, banging the Chifney around the horse's mouth. The horse starts to trot away from him.

"The horse is always going to win," Cesar explains after the colt is safely inside the walker. Holding the Folklore colt, who's waiting his turn, Cesar jiggles the shank. Agitated even by just a gentle shaking, Folklore lifts his nose into the air. "You slow down," Cesar explains. He pats Folklore's neck, turning the colt into him, and Folklore lowers his head, pricking his ears in Cesar's direction. "You keep hitting him, he's going to get mad."

Opening up the tub of sweating gel, Cesar rubs it over Folklore's crest and straps on his neoprene hood. He leaves two grooms behind and heads off to the rest of his barns. Resplendency's big colt arrives from Eagle Creek A. Massive, strong, he's right on the edge of being too big—like Glenarcy's filly. He stands squarely over his four hooves while the groom applies the sweating gel.

"Hot!" the groom says, laughing and shaking his hands.

Resplendency is climbing all over them as they strap on his hood. He strikes out with his left front hoof, fidgets, tries to push them out of the way with his big body. They growl at him and snap his lead shank. He drops his head and stands still, mouthing his Chifney, and looks out from under his forelock. Thirty seconds later, still bored, he starts up again. Once they get him in the walker, he trots right up against his front gate—he seems almost too big for the space. Three trot strides and he's up against the gate and slows to a walk. When the rear gate threatens to bounce off his big butt, he trots away. He's fifteen minutes into his workout before he settles into a steady jog.

By 9:30, the last of the horses is in the walker and the grooms are finishing up. There's still a breeze on top of the hill, but the heat is building. Grasshoppers *tsk tsk* in the grass, but the birds are silent. In their rubber boots, the grooms finish up the last of the horses' baths. There are three of them left at the top of the hill, two bathing and one holding the horse on deck. Relieved to have the sweat washed off their bodies and accustomed to being bathed, the horses stand quietly as the cool water washes over them, lifting their noses to rest on their grooms' shoulders. With no one around who understands Spanish well enough to eavesdrop, the grooms' storytelling gets louder and funnier, their laughter forthright. A bubble of language builds around them, separating them from the farm, from Lexington, from America. Inside, it's just them, their story, and their horses, who understand English and Spanish equally well.

The farm's new marketing initiative has been thought out a little more completely than Duncan's idea, several years ago, to buzz Keeneland with a plane trailing a banner that advertised one of their yearlings. To that end, they've hired business developer Finn Green.

Like everyone else's at Taylor Made, Finn Green's bio on the farm's Web page lists his years in the business and where he's worked; it also adds that he's a fourth-generation horseman. But untypically, Finn Green's bio also tells the site's visitors that he graduated from the University of Kentucky with a B.A. in English at age forty-four. Summa Cum Laude, Phi Beta Kappa, he was a Gaines Fellow and a recipient of the Algernon Sydney Sullivan Award. He grew up down the road from the Taylors, a "humble country boy"; tall, leaning in to talk, he describes himself as "a fallen soul."

It's midafternoon on possibly the hottest day of the summer, and Finn and the events director from Centre College are trailing around after Frank, who's evaluating horses in Yearling Complex B, pressed for time because he leaves for Saratoga soon.

The 2010 World Equestrian Games are coming to Lexington in September. Preparations for the event have been going on for two years and have built to a frenzy around Lexington. Hotels have been booked up for months. Craigslist is full of houses renting for thousands of dollars a night as the world of horse people prepare to descend on the little city. As part of the festivities, Centre College is hosting the Vienna Symphony, and Taylor Made is sponsoring the event. Once he's done evaluating horses, Frank is going to tour the events director around the farm to see if there's a good place to host an outdoor party.

"We're trying to identify like-minded people," Finn Green drawls. He is crisply dressed in neatly ironed slacks and a bright white dress shirt. Neatly barbered, he does not look like he's been standing in one-hundred-degree heat. Duncan's other ideas include partnering with yacht brokers. He'll take their clients to the races, and they can take his boating.

At 1:00 P.M., after everyone has finished siesta, Cesar arrives at Eagle Creek A; his house is just across the lane, a stone's throw from the barn. Between 3:00 and 3:30, the truck is arriving to take the New York horses to Florida, where they'll start their careers as racehorses. There's also a buyer coming by this afternoon to look at the Saratoga horses, but Cesar's not sure when. Before they are shipped out, Cesar needs to take photos—every horses has its photo taken when it arrives and leaves. A groom named Freddy brings out the yearlings one by one and Cesar snaps their photos with his phone. Less accustomed to posing than their peers, the horses won't square up or stand still, and Cesar swears as one picture after another is ruined by a fidgeting horse.

After photos, Cesar measures their height and girth, and all that information is texted to the office. He's got paper tags with the horses' vaccination information and he attaches those to the horses' halters, rolling the tags into tight cylinders and tucking them into the buckles of the halters. If their papers get misplaced, the tags have all the information that the new farm needs.

John Hall pulls up and lets Cesar know that the trainer who was coming to look at the horses has postponed his visit by an hour. Everyone is at loose ends, waiting, reading phone messages, looking in at the horses. The farm is almost perfectly still. The dark green leaves on the maples are so heavy with the humidity that the breeze can barely lift them. The sun glints off the windshields of the cars traveling down East Hickman Road. On the other side of the yearling division, a line of cars pulls up in front of the Yearling Complex barns, suggesting that elsewhere on the farm, people are busy. In Eagle Creek, the floors are blown clean, the feed room's been swept, and the supplies are neatly stacked on the shelves. Light pours down through the barn's skylights and in through the arched windows over the barn's double doors. The crew is standing around, waiting. When they're bored, they twirl the lead shanks, whip-cracking the leather ends against the floor.

"Where is this guy?" John Hall asks. He calls the man and cheerfully asks him where he is. He's actually on the other end of the lane—by the Yearling Complex barns. John tells him just to follow the lane to the end and that will bring him to the right barn. He slips his phone into his holder and peers into a stall that has two horses in it because they're out of room. "Hi, buddy," he says to one of the New York horses.

"I bathed that one," Hall jokes to the grooms. "That's why he looks the best."

John manages all the yearling showings at the barn. They have so many people who want to see the horses early that after Saratoga they restrict showings to just four days, sometimes fewer.

It's twenty minutes since John spoke to the buyer who was on the other side of the farm and he's still not here. "What happened to that guy?" John says in frustration. It's almost three o'clock. While he's waiting for him, John can't get anything else done. He calls again. "Are you lost again?" he asks warmly, no sign of irritation in his voice.

The buyer is on his way, and Freddy, the groom, will handle all the showings. He's changed into his blue shirt and burgundy tie, and John has his notes ready. Once the buyer arrives, he looks at the horse first in the shade of the barn, and then Freddy leads him out into the harsh sunlight, standing patiently while John shows the buyer the colt's catalog page, which lists his pedigree and the important members of his dam's family.

"I think he's a hell of a Gone West," John says as Freddy leads hip number seventy-six out and back. The buyer has a legal pad in one hand and he's half watching the horse and half talking to John. He's got some complaints about the business that need to be aired, and John's a sympathetic listener. The buyer doesn't fully focus on the horse until the third time that Freddy's walked him.

Hip number 198 comes out, and John points out her catalog page. "This is her family," he says. The buyer has some questions about horses going to Keeneland. Freddy and the filly wait patiently.

"One more time," the buyer says to Freddy as he turns back to John.

Resplendency's colt comes out, but John and the buyer are talking about past sales. Freddy skillfully walks the restless and fidgety colt up and back on a loose lead, his head low, his walk loose and powerful, but the buyer doesn't see it. Freddy waits. "One more time," the buyer says, sending Freddy and Resplendency out and back again.

Sam and Jo Pollock's Critical Cat yearling comes out, followed by a filly out of a mare named Teenage Temper. John holds the clipboard in his left hand; his right rests in the small of his back.

Watching from where he sits on a straw bale inside the barn, Cesar mutters, "Just focus on the horse." He's looking at Freddy and Resplendency as they wait patiently while the buyer chats with John. "I hate that shit," he says. "It's easy for him to say 'One more time.'"

When Frank looks at horses, Cesar points out, he's totally focused on them; that's why he can get half the farm done in an afternoon. Cesar is glowering. For obvious reasons, he doesn't work the sales. He hates them. They're too busy, too crowded. He's happy on the farm, and the farm is happy to keep him here.

The buyer finally leaves. John Hall heads off somewhere, and the grooms can get their afternoon chores done. The New York horses don't get any dinner. They've got a long drive and a full belly increases the risk of colic. They look hurt as their stablemates get their piles of hay and tubs of grain. Baked by the heat, the barn smells like straw and molasses. The grooms slap poultice, or "mud," onto the horses' knees, an every-other-day routine that keeps them from filling with fluid, and keeps the flies off so they don't stamp their feet, risking injury. The landscapers who've been running their mowers all day have finally reached Eagle Creek and they grind by noisily.

Because he's a big boy, Resplendency '09 has licked his tub clean. There's not a single kernel of grain left behind by his tongue and he looks out of the stall eagerly, as if he's hoping for more.

The six-horse slant-load trailer that will take the yearlings to Florida pulls up at 4:00 P.M. The driver steps out of the truck, shakes hands with everyone, and picks up the paperwork from John while Cesar and Freddy unlatch the rear doors and let down the ramp. The grooms walk quickly as they lead the colts up the ramp, not giving them any time to think about it. The first colt gives the van a healthy look and marches in. The second one plants his feet, but before his weight is completely settled, Freddy and Cesar give him a shove from behind and up he goes. Colts three and four both plant their feet, not budging. Cesar and Freddy reach behind the colts' butts, clasp each other's wrists, and haul the colts forward, their arms literally lifting the horses' hind ends off the ground. Not wanting to be left behind, colt number five whinnies for his buddies and practically runs up the ramp. Once they're in, they're calm. John signs the papers. Cesar hands the driver the envelope with the horses' complete records. Freddy and the other groom lift and close the ramp and throw the latches. In less than ten minutes, they're done. Another handshake all around and John tells the driver to have a good trip. He'll drive about thirteen hours straight through the night and will arrive at the training barn of Raul Reyes tomorrow morning. The men watch the van as it pulls away. Freddy grins and lifts up his hand. "Bye-bye!" he says, and waves.

Turning back into the barn, John calls Reyes on the phone to let him know the colts have just left. "They loaded like champions," he says.

Noelle, Dominic, Joe and Danny Taylor, and everyone else whom Cesar and the grooms call "the gringos" go home at 4:00 P.M. They've ceded the overtime hours needed for mucking and nighttime chores to the grooms who want them. Joe Taylor thought about sticking it out, but he was too slow and held everyone up. "They were always yelling at me," he says. Between four and five o'clock, they take a break for dinner. "They eat really fast," Noelle says. "And have a nap." They've been working in ninety-degree heat since 6:00 A.M.

At 5:00 P.M., the tractors rumble to life and slowly roll down the lanes and into the first barn's aisles. In the barn, the grooms strip out the soiled straw, or shavings, tossing the piles directly into the tractors. Every few minutes, someone hops into the driver's seat and pulls the tractor forward, its engine coughing to life throatily.

Once the stalls are clean, they shake out fresh straw, or fresh shavings for the horses who are on a diet. When they're done, they head to the next barn, leaving behind one groom to pick up loose baling twine, blow the aisle, and rake. They retrieve the grooming totes and brushes that were washed and left to dry in the sun all afternoon. Then they all meet back at Eagle Creek C, where the tractors are returned to the equipment shed and everyone has another short break until it's time to turn the horses out at seven.

The horses settle down for a nap, too. Normally, says Cesar, when someone walks into a barn with sleeping horses, all the horses get up. But at Eagle Creek C, where the grooms always take their break because that's where the time clock is, the horses know that when the grooms are lying down, they get a one-hour break, too. As long as the grooms are lying down, says Cesar, the horses stay lying down, too.

Down in Eagle Creek A, the last groom finishes up the raking and heads out of the barn. The yearlings on the driveway side poke their heads over their outside doors and watch him go, ears pricked, until he disappears around the bend in the driveway. Then they all lie down, except for Folklore, who's staring at where the groom disappeared from view, and the sweet-tempered Glenarcy, who looks like she's hoping for one more pat.

Cesar is not hopeful about Glenarcy's future as a racehorse. She's too big, he thinks, and too weak in the hocks. Of his bunch, he thinks

Folklore is the most promising. As much as he likes Collect Call's colt, he thinks Folklore is going to be the best runner. Folklore is more compact than the Collect Call colt, and Cesar thinks he's more powerful.

With everyone gone, the barn slips into silence and the orange barn cat appears. His food is behind the feed room door, which has been closed for the night, and he sits in front of it hopefully.

Just before seven, the horses rouse themselves, getting to their feet with groans, shaking off the straw bits stuck to their coats, having a last pee or poop in the stall, nibbling around their feed tubs for the last bit of grain. They know they're about to go out. Grasshoppers whir, and the evening birds start their songs, but it's so quiet, you can hear the box fans from the driveway. The only other sound is the clink of metal on metal as the buckles on the horses' halters brush against their outside doors when they lift their heads over them. Yellow-and-orange butterflies flitter up and down in the haze.

Up the hill, one of the colts in Eagle Creek C whinnies, signaling the beginning of turnout. At Eagle Creek B, all the horses whinny in return. In a long parade, the colts from C barn head out to the paddocks with their grooms. The grooms make them wait until everyone is inside the gate, and then they unclip them together. Some colts amble off; others wheel and snort, farting as their energy explodes and sends them racing down the hill. The sound of the blower drifts down to the lower barn from the groom who was left behind, and moments later, a three-car caravan, led by Cesar in the truck, pulls into the lane outside B barn. Eight pairs of boots hit the ground almost at once as the burgundy-shirted grooms jump out of the pickup and march into the barn, followed by the grooms from the two SUVs. *Bam, bam, bam*—a dozen doors slide open simultaneously and the horses are clipped to their leads and led out. The grooms dump the water buckets over the stalls' outside doors, and as soon as the last horse has stepped out the door, the blower starts.

Standing in the doorway, Cesar watches his team turn out the horses. Minutes later, they're racing off to Eagle Creek C. It takes his team less than half an hour to turn out eighty horses spread over four barns. Once the grooms are gone, from two to six per compact and banged-up car, Cesar drives a final loop. He rolls along the lanes slowly, looking out at the paddocks, watching his horses. When friends and family visit him in the evenings, they walk down the lanes in the gathering dusk, kids running ahead or being pushed in strollers. Cesar doesn't have children, but, he says, "I love kids."

It's Tuesday morning, the day before the Saratoga horses ship out, and they're getting their first pair of shoes right after they're done with their workouts. At the top of the hill between Eagle Creek A and C, Cesar is watching the horses in the walker. Folklore is trotting right along, head up, face near the front gate. Drosselmeyer, Cesar remembers, never jogged out in the walker. "He always had to be pushed by the gate."

In A barn, the farriers have arrived in three trucks. Andre O'Connell stations himself at one end, Bobby is at the other, and Logan and Ben move into the middle and start pulling horses out of their stalls.

John and Cesar are both leaning against the wall, texting. It's hard to remember running the barns without this technology, though John thinks he probably did a better job because he was paying more attention to the horses.

Frank has already left for Saratoga, but if he were here, he'd be loving these horses' hooves. Big, spread out, a solid base of support for the horses standing on top of them.

Shortly after Bobby arrives, he drives away again. The younger Langleys start pulling horses out of the stalls.

"Right now," Ben explains, "we're just cleaning them up, lining everything up." The younger Langleys prep everything in the barn by cleaning and trimming. "Then the older guys shoe them," Ben says. Once the shoes are on, the younger Langleys clinch the hooves—turn and press down the nail heads with a special tool. Then they use a drill sander to buff the hoof smooth, spray on some mineral oil so any flaws are easy to see—and repair—and then they're done.

Andre is working on a colt out of Teenage Temper and has shooed everyone forward so he can see the colt walk. Since Vadahilla is blocking the end of the aisle, that leaves the Resplendency colt in the middle, distracted by Vadahilla and climbing all over poor Ben, who's underneath him, despite Joe's efforts to keep the horse still.

"C'mon, son," Ben says to the colt in irritation.

"Hey," Logan yells at Vadahilla, who just jigged forward and crashed into him.

Ben is upright while Joe tries to get Resplendency to stand still. "I'd like to bust him," Ben says. "I don't think it would affect him much. I'd hurt my hand more than the horse, but he's just being a butthead right now."

Doubled over under him, Ben almost gets his foot smashed by the colt, who yanks his hoof out of the farrier's hand and stamps it down, while he is leaning on Ben for support.

"Get off me, son."

They move Resplendency into the stall and Cesar goes with him, watching Joe's work in handling the big colt. The farriers use first a coarse and then a fine rasp, and Cesar holds the one they're not using.

One-handed because the other hand is always holding onto a hoof, the farriers position their tools by spinning, flipping, or bouncing them off the floor's rubber mats. Rasps and hammers spin blurrily, their wooden ends thunk the rubber mat, and the metal slaps into their hands as they turn their tools into whirligigs. If they think about it, Ben says, laughing, they can't do it. A filmmaker shooting a documentary asked them once to repeat what they were doing so he could get a close-up, and they all dropped their tools.

At the end of the aisle, Andre is done looking at Teenage Temper. "I think I'm gonna spread the inside heel on that left one," he tells John.

This is the last chance to use the horses' shoes to make them even more perfect. It's also possible to overcorrect, or bang a tiny little nail into the sensitive part of the horse's hoof, laming him and dropping his price by tens, if not hundreds, of thousands of dollars. That's why Bobby's apprentices work for him for five years before Bobby will even let them shape a front hoof on a yearling, much less bang a nail in one or two days before they go to auction.

Bobby returns and straps on his apron. He's tall, broad-shouldered, and the sun behind him throws him into silhouette at the end of the aisle, where he stands with his hands on his hips.

"See that right foot?" he calls to Andre as a horse walks up and down the aisle. "You just need to let him walk like he's walking."

"Yes, sir," says Andre.

Ben is finishing off Teenage Temper in the stall, clinching down the nails and buffing the hoof with the sander. Teenage Temper is quiet and still. "You're doing a good job," he tells Noelle. This will be as much flirting as he gets to do with his uncle around.

It's Bobby's turn to get under Resplendency. Joe Taylor is wrestling with the colt's head, trying to keep him from sinking his teeth playfully into the middle of Bobby's back. Because they've been friends a long time, John Hall acts as Bobby's assistant and he's down on one knee, handing Bobby nails. When Bobby is done and lets the foot fall, his son, Logan, has it in hand, finishing it off, almost before it hits the ground. When Logan has finished, Bobby then picks up the right foot, dancing Resplendency back and forth. The colt is momentarily amused by this, and he drops his head to look at his own feet, then tires of the game, using Bobby to prop himself up.

"Awww, quit!" Bobby stands up and elbows the horse in the ribs.

"Did you hurt yourself?" John jokes.

"My elbow went numb." Bobby laughs.

"He's a beast, isn't he?" Ben says to Noelle.

Noelle is still holding Teenage Temper. "All right, young lady," Bobby calls to her. "Let me see a few steps."

Teenage Temper turns and walks, then plants his front feet and bucks. Cesar, who's behind him, rears back, and the hooves whiffle the air in front of him. Noelle walks the colt one more time.

"You good with that?" Bobby asks John.

At the other end of the aisle, Bobby looks down at Critical Cat's feet. "Good job. Good job," he tells Andre.

Bobby calls to Noelle, "You want to hook on another one, young lady?"

Everyone in the barn is happier in the presence of a pretty girl.

Vadahilla is leaning backward. Cesar, on the end of the lead shank, is leaning backward in the opposite direction. "Quit, quit," he growls.

"Did he have a bad abscess at one time?" Bobby asks Cesar as he rasps away.

"Yeah."

Like John, Bobby moves with the stiffness that comes from a sore back. When he stands up after crouching over, he squares back his shoulders and pauses, his first steps away from the horse small ones, as if he's gauging how sore he is. As he bends down under Vadahilla again, the colt strikes at him and gets a smack on the neck.

"Motherfucker," Bobby says.

In solidarity, John calls the horse an asshole and then slips a second shank under his lip before he hands the horse back to Cesar. Like the twitch, the lip shanks lie over an acupressure point and the horses usually relax once they're applied. Vadahilla drops his head, relaxes, and stands quietly enough for Cesar to take a call with the other hand.

Still tied to Resplendency, who is in his stall, Joe Taylor has cleverly slid the door closed between them, leaving just a few inches open for the lead shank to pass through. It's the first unmolested moment he's had since he clipped it onto the horse's halter.

Ben has squatted down next to Andre and is handing him nails for the shoe he's tacking onto Critical Crew. "Don't drive 'em like fence nails," Ben says, teasing Andre.

Bobby calls to Ben, who looks up toward him at the other end of the barn. "Yes, sir," he responds. But he's made the critical error of leaving his fingers resting on the anvil, and in revenge for the crack about the fence nails, Andre taps those fingers with his hammer.

"Ow." Ben snatches them to his chest, laughing.

"For an A.P. Indy, he's got damn good feet." Bobby is looking down at Vadahilla. After he watches him walk, Logan moves in to finish him off. Holding the edge of the rasp in the thread of space between the bottom of the colt's hoof and the top of his shoe, Logan rasps back and forth just once, smoothing out the hoof and taking the coating off the metal of the shoe. When he's done, the hoof looks like it has been machined.

And then they're done. Tools clatter into wooden totes. The anvils thump down into the backs of the trucks; doors bang. Bobby and John exchange a hug and a manly pat on the back. They shake hands all around. "Good-bye. Good luck. Travel safe," John says, and they're gone, leaving behind swirls of straw and bits of hoof.

After two hours, four farriers, three grooms, two managers, one kick, one extra lip shank, one elbow in the ribs, one smack on the neck, and one "Motherfucker," the Taylor Made yearlings are back in their stalls in time for lunch, their first pair of shoes still shiny on their feet.

🐎

Wednesday morning, 10:30 A.M.: The horses are shipping out this afternoon and Lori Henderson drops by to oil them. To help prevent colic, the horses are dosed with mineral oil that contains electrolytes and a sedative. Before she puts the feeding tube down their noses, she also gives them a shot of Banamine. While she's working, Steve Avery wanders over from the mare's side and peers through the stall grating at Resplendency, who's calm and sleepy looking. "I love this one," Steve says.

"He's the man," John Hall agrees, adding that he thinks the colt will bring $450,000. Two years ago, the last time they held a betting pool on actual prices at the sale, John came in second, behind Frank. He likes to point this out.

The barn's office is full of gear—suitcases, sleeping bags, a brightly colored fleece blanket (it gets cold on the truck), folding chairs (or they'd have to stand or sit on the floor for seventeen hours), coolers, and bags of snacks. Noelle is dragging along her laptop. The office is sending up boxes of sales notebooks and office supplies.

The grooms are taking a two-hour lunch today, which will give them a chance to get home for a shower and to change before their overnight trip. Before they go, they flick away the last of the stray whiskers, buzz off the last bits of ear hair, oil manes one more time, and daub at the horses with their tips of their brushes, smoothing down out-of-place hairs here and there. In his stall, Resplendency has lain down for a nap. On his side, he nibbles at some bits of hay in front of his nose. With a groan, he lets his eyes flutter closed and he drifts off to sleep.

🐎

The grooms are back by 2:00 P.M., as tidy in their street clothes as they are in their uniforms: polo shirts tucked into jeans, hair combed, boots clean. Showered, freshly shaved, they look and smell fresh and are milling around in the aisle, waiting for the truck. Cesar is using the hose to fill plastic jugs with sprayer attachments—one for each horse. The grooms will use these to mist the horses down for their long trip. Joe Taylor is the last to arrive, wearing pajama pants and carrying a loaf of sandwich bread. He's brought extra folding chairs, and Noelle is quick to grab the sturdier of the two. Mario, arriving last, grabs the other.

One behind the other, two tractor-trailers pull into the lane, dwarfing Cesar's little house. The first of them rumbles up to the chute—a grass-covered ramp with fenced sides that they use to load the horses. This truck stretches almost half the length of the barn, darkening the windows on that side. The truck in the rear is closer to the front of the barn, where the grooms now scurry out with their suitcases and boxes and gear. From a small flatbed they've backed up to the semi, Noelle and Mario—the two smallest people in the crew—heave fifty-pound grain sacks onto their shoulders and toss them up into the truck's storage area. Dominic and Joe—the two biggest people in the crew—hold on to the hose and watch water gather in the containers.

Once the gear is on board, they get ready to load the horses. Cesar starts giving directions in Spanish. Fillies load first; Mario leads. Cesar and Freddy come behind the first one, their hands on her hips, prodding her in. The moment she hesitates, Cesar and Freddy lock their arms behind her bum, pushing and lifting. She has to keep going forward.

"Keep her head up. Keep her head up," John reminds Mario, and the filly is loaded. Dominic is ready with the next one. "Right to the back," John reminds him.

There are five horses per truck. The trailers the trucks pull are fifty-three feet long and could carry three times that many horses, but everyone in the industry generally uses a box-stall arrangement, which allows the horses to move around freely. Once the drivers leave this farm, they'll swing by another one to pick up more horses, and the remainder will be flown out tomorrow.

The horses follow their grooms up the ramp and into the confined space of the truck, giving it a second look but mostly trusting their grooms. For those who resist, Cesar and Freddy are right behind, arms locked, lifting up their butts and pushing them forward. From inside, the horses can hear the other members of their herd and move forward to join them.

Once the horses are on board, the grooms grab their chairs and march up the ramps behind them. They've already loaded the drivers' cell phone numbers into their own phones, and there's a closed-circuit TV on the trailers. Isidro, whom everyone call Chilo, is riding in the front of the first van. He's got a giant bucket chair with a heavy cushion, and he sits down in it, facing the open door. He looks like a pearl in an oyster as he waves at John and Cesar. The drivers of the two trucks bang the doors shut and fire the latches. John steps forward to shake their hands. "All right, guys," he says. "Treat 'em like you own 'em."

The drivers pull themselves into their cabs, wave, and the big diesels rumble to life. From the barn, those staying behind watch the trucks make their way down the long lane, disappearing in a hollow just past C barn, then reappearing by the Yearling Complex. They disappear again and finally reappear in the distance on the other side of the paddock, as they pull out the other entrance and start their long haul to Saratoga.

John Hall is seeing Taylor Made's customers' horses off at the airport—not so much because he's concerned there'll be problems getting off, but because he's worried that the members of the Saratoga crew who are flying with the horses are going to miss the plane. When he pulls up at the airport at 6:30 A.M., it is just starting to get light, and on the walkways to the transportation company's office, he sees a pile of gear that he recognizes as Cordell Anderson's, one of Taylor Made's showmen.

He presses the door buzzer, which brings two big dogs scrambling to the door. They're followed by a big guy carrying a Chihuahua. In the office are two more big guys, one sprawled on a sofa and the other at a computer, but no more dogs. Outside at the side door is the hangar, and John heads out to the tarmac. Moments later, Tammy Frasier and Iris Ziegler arrive, dispensing hugs and kisses for John Hall. Cordell has not yet arrived, though Iris reassures John that she saw him last night and he said he was coming.

Iris and Tammy have dumped their gear on the ground—an assortment that would prompt a call to security if they were traveling on a commercial airline: suitcases, blankets, duffel bags, clothes on hangers and in zipped plastic compression bags. There's a soft cooler, a grocery bag, a purse, and a blanket. "It gets cold on the plane," Iris says. A forklift chugs over with a pallet, and Iris and Tammy and the handful of other people on their way to Saratoga with the horses toss their gear on it and head for the plane. The pilot marches up to a small group of people waiting to say good-bye and signals them onto the plane. But they're not going. Irritated, he looks around. "Where are my passengers?" he asks, wondering where everyone is.

The shipping company is a little less forgiving about federal regulations than they are about sloppy packing, and a groom named Ellen, who works for one of the Taylor Made clients and will be part of the staff in New York, has forgotten her license. She's got the number, she tells them. They can look it up and scan it. The shipping company is unmoved. John asks if there's anything that can be close and is told that the company would be shut down for letting someone fly without ID. Ellen waits nervously. Her roommate is on the way with the license, but if the horses get loaded first, she'll miss her flight.

Now that Tammy and Iris have picked up the last of their bags and are making their way to the plane, the others follow—airline staff, grooms, the farrier who travels with Funny Cide, who will be making a celebrity visit to Saratoga from his home at the Kentucky Horse Park. They're lining up and disappearing into the bowels of the plane. Cordell has not shown up. Iris turns back and gives John another hug and kiss, which he looks very pleased to receive.

The outside gate opens and Cordell ambles through it in a Taylor Made cap, carrying a Kroger bag of snacks. Relaxed, unflappable, stress-free—the very qualities that make him such a good handler of horses—he greets John and strolls across the tarmac to the plane. John doesn't know where he's been or why he's late. "He's here. That's all I can say."

One by one, the vans pull up at the loading ramp. Tall wooden boards slide onto its sides so the horses can't see over. As the vans pull up, the crew disassembles and reassembles the base of the ramp so that the horses step right onto it from the van without ever seeing the ground. From the ground, the only thing you can see are the very tips of their ears, and sometimes a nose from a horse who's lifted it up to sniff the air.

The horses loaded, John heads back to Taylor Made. He doesn't often go to Saratoga anymore—too much to do on the farm—but he'll be at Keeneland. He likes the same horses that everyone else does, but he doesn't follow his favorites from year to year. "They come and go so fast. It's hard to keep track of them," he says. But he does keep his paperwork. This year, when Drosselmeyer won the Belmont, John looked back at his records and was pleased to discover that he'd given the horse an A–.

8

Saratoga, July 31, 2010

WHEN THE TENS OF THOUSANDS OF PEOPLE WHO descend on Saratoga for its August meet gather for the racing, it's for reasons that might not be obvious. There's the immediate draw of the horses because of their beauty, their athleticism, the desire to win that they *appear* to express, the threat of tragedy signaled by the clanging open of the gate that suggests that this desire, and ours, might cost them their lives.

"The serviceability of the racehorse," wrote Thorstein Veblen, the Norwegian-born economist and author of *The Theory of the Leisure Class*, widely considered to be the first economic analysis of consumerism, "is in his efficiency as a means of emulation. It gratifies the owner's sense of aggression and dominance to have his own horse outstrip his neighbors." Social rank, Veblen argued, comes not from work, but through the liberation of personal time—freedom from the drudgery of daily toil, so that time can be spent on the pursuit of quasi-scholarly activities, the study of pedigrees and past performances, for example, and to acquire possessions. The less useful and more beautiful these possessions are, the higher their status.

Gambling on horses makes the achieving of that social rank possible for anyone who places a two-dollar bet—first by allowing them to demonstrate their achievement in the quasi-scholarly activity of handicapping, and then by giving them an ownership stake in the horse.

But it would be inadequate to see the horse in just this modern context. Art historian and social critic John Berger argues in his essay "Why Look at Animals?" that to ascribe the beginning of the human-animal relationship to the need for food would be inaccurate. Animals, he says, first came into our lives as symbols and messengers, mapping our world, allowing us to explain it to ourselves. We used them for the symbols of our zodiac, to delineate the passage of time. They are part of our creation myths. So at the same time that we were eating them, we were also coveting them. And the first animal that drew our attention, the one that shows up in all of our Judeo-Christian texts, the myths of Eastern and Western culture and was the first figure drawn by Ice Age artists on the walls of their caves when they felt the urge to depict their world, was the horse.

For those fans of racing who decide that they need to go to the next level, that they actually need to own a horse, it is only necessary to stroll across the street from Saratoga's historic racetrack and see the ones for sale. And if they want to buy one, the Taylors have one to sell them.

This year, the signage at Taylor Made has taken a new tack toward getting a potential buyer to see himself in the Winner's Circle with a Taylor Made horse. While those consignors at every barn on the sale grounds are savvy enough to put up posters of their winning horses, the Taylor Made team's special canniness has been to feature the horses' connections—their owners and trainers and agents. In the center of the posters are pictures of horses blazing over the finish line, nosing out the competition, standing proud in the Winner's Circle, just like everybody else's photos. But around the perimeter of the photo of each horse, Taylor Made has arranged photos of the horse's trainer and owner. MIKE RYAN FOUND THORN SONG AT TAYLOR MADE, the signs say. WHAT WILL YOU FIND?

What Mark Taylor says the farm is doing is creating a "positive filter." In their younger days, Mark says, they were more likely to sell the horses hard, but now Mark thinks that's counterproductive. Most horsemen, he explains, pride themselves on being good judges of horses. "You start telling them what to do, how to evaluate," he says, laughing, "immediately, they want to do the opposite."

Selling horses is a "finesse sale." Mark says that when he's standing there, his bound and laminated sales book in hand, "I like to talk about horses they've done well with in the past and that they've bought from us."

He also likes to volunteer information, which his brothers, he says, think is crazy. "If you can show them that you're being honest with them . . . Let's say we've got a horse that's gotten sick at the sale," he says. If that's the case, then he'll volunteer that information. Even if it doesn't sell the horse, it creates a sense of trust. "You're looking for reciprocity," he explains. The posters, he says, are part of that positive filter, not only inviting others to find their winners at Taylor Made but reminding those who already have how successful they've been with the brothers in the past. "You see the bloodstock agents there staring at the poster for like ten minutes and you know they're just thinking, God, that was a great experience."

When the Taylors train the sales staff, they focus on teaching them to create that positive filter. Mark explains what he instructs his staff to do if a buyer comes in who's bought a horse from them in the past. "If you haven't read about it, it's not a winner. Don't bring it up," he tells them.

It's Saturday, July 31, and the Resplendency colt and the other sale horses have been on the Fasig-Tipton grounds since Thursday morning. Every morning, the team arrives at 5:00 A.M. to feed, muck out stalls, and bathe the horses before the buyers arrive to look at them. Saratoga is what everyone calls a "boutique" sale—exclusive, limited, and somewhat idiosyncratic.

"You have to survive in advance," Mark explains. There are only two hundred horses at Saratoga and four days to look at them before the sale starts. People have short lists and plenty of time to find a reason *not* to buy your horse. Only about 10 to 20 percent of the first-round lookers will come back for a second look, he says, but at that point, their list is shorter and now they're looking for reasons to like the horse. Then come the vet grades—a system that everyone selling regards as subjective— with some vets rejecting and some passing the same horse. Sometimes the same vet rejects the horse for one client and passes it for another.

But the biggest part of getting the horses sold is up to the horses. Well-bred, conformationally correct, fit, prepared—that's all been taken care of. But at the sale, the horses have to figure out what's expected of them. Hip number forty-seven, a bay colt by Street Cry and out of a mare named Don't Tacha Me, seems to understand his job. His walk is loose and powerful, and every time he stands still, his head comes up, ears pricked, as if he's listening for the sound of his ancestors pounding over the finish line.

The Resplendency colt, on the other hand, is not doing himself any favors. Jeff Hayslett, the account manager for Beverly Lewis and her son, Jeff, shakes his head. "The lightbulb just hasn't gone off." He's already big, and they've assigned him to his own groom, Nacho, who is especially skilled at keeping him in line. Still, the colt has already gotten his hoof over his own lead shank. Jacob West reports that the response to him is fifty-fifty. Half the people really like him; half think he's just too big. He hasn't drawn a crowd, Frank says, and "he hasn't missed a meal." He cocks his hoof and lists to the side, as if he's just so very tired. "He's like a panther walking," Frank says, but he so rarely does it with energy and focus that no one has seen that walk yet. He swings his big head from side to side, his big butt sashaying lazily over his hooves. He yawns, bored and tired, and his tongue is sticking out of the side of his mouth. He gets extra baths during the day in the hopes that they'll perk him up, and the farm has also arranged for him to have massages. Something may have happened on the truck and he's sore, or maybe he's getting hit with a growth spurt, but the colt is not the $400,000 animal that left the farm on Wednesday.

It's a perfect Adirondack summer day, the weather cool, the skies blue, a breeze ruffling the trees, exactly what New Yorkers were looking for, along with the mineral springs, when they first began flocking to Saratoga Springs in the early nineteenth century. The racetrack was built in 1864, because all those people needed entertainment, and it has been one of the highlights of the racing year since then. Fasig-Tipton arrived in 1917, when they made arrangements for race owners attending the races to see young horses from the Kentucky breeders. In 1918, they made their first big sale when Man o' War went through the auction ring as a yearling.

Fasig-Tipton completed a major overhaul to the stabling area last year—hence the tension around Taylor Made screwing their Taylor Made plaques into the entrance to the stabling area, making it look from outside like the barns were Taylor Made's and not Fasig's. This year, they've screwed the sign to the *inside* of the shingled gate columns.

A neighborhood of postcard-perfect Victorians has sprung up around the sales grounds, which has nine barns, a residential street cutting through the middle of them. From the porches of the houses that border the stabling area, you can see horses just a few feet away. The barns are spotless, with both Fasig-Tipton's and the consignors' crews scrupulous about their neatness. Walking by them, you smell pine cleaner, not manure.

The grooms are busy. This is a social event for them and the beginning of their selling season together. Some of Taylor Made's sales staff members have been working together for a decade.

Standing in front of the stall, the rake over her arm, Iris is looking at photos with an older German woman, who vacations in Saratoga every year and takes pictures of the grooms and the horses. She passes the day on the benches at the edge of the quad, under the awning, coming and going as she photographs the other consignments. Taylor Made's barn she says, is the nicest of all the ones she goes to. The others, she declares, poking her chin in the direction of the barn next door, not so much. She has horses in Germany, but not like this. No, not like this. Iris and Cordell are the grooms whom she most admires. "Iris and Cordell are quiet *inside,* and the horse feels that." She takes her photographs at the summer sale and either sends them to Iris and Cordell and the other grooms at Christmastime or holds on to them until the following summer. Iris has seen her every year that she's worked this sale.

Iris is fifty-four, and she first put her hand on a horse just ten years ago. "My son was grown and I was sick of my boyfriend and I said, I'm out of here." She started as a hot walker at a track in Iowa and then went to Oklahoma. At first, she says, "I was scared." But she got over it and is now more comfortable with horses than with people. "They relax me more than people do," she says. "They're honest."

Nine years ago, she showed up at Keeneland during the September sale, looking for work, and John Hall hired her. Watching her with the yearlings, Mark asked her which farms she'd worked for and she had to tell him just that track in Oklahoma. Now she's part of the international traveling class of professional sales help. For Taylor Made, she works sales in July, August, September, November, and January. She works the sales of two-year-olds, though not for Taylor Made, because they don't sell at those. Iris works regularly in England and Ireland, but she has also worked in France, and went to Russia once.

It's late morning and the grooms are filtering to the back of the barn, where Barrett has set up a makeshift kitchen, where he prepared breakfast, and where the caterers bring lunch. When they come back from the other side, the grooms are still chewing as they take up another lead shank, or a rake, or the hose to water down the crushed stone, which gets dusty.

Finn Green is here as well, looking crisp and tailored in his slacks and sport coat. He's got appointments all week, visiting prospective buyers in the area. Finn is optimistic about the interest in horse racing, but, like everyone else, he doesn't think the industry does enough to welcome new owners. He likes to tell the story of the 1991 Kentucky Oaks, when rapper M. C. Hammer's filly, Lite Light, won, beating out the filly of perhaps the most established breeder and owner in the industry, Ogden Phipps. Excited, celebratory, and sitting right next to Phipps, Hammer ripped off his shirt and spun it over his head when his filly won. Phipps, in the next box, glared, says Green. "That's not good," says Finn, who characterizes Phipps's expression and laughs. "You can't invite people to the party," he says, "and not let them in."

Most of the trouble in the yard is coming from two fillies: hip number 126, a filly by Awesome Again, and hip number 153, the last of the Storm Cat offspring, a filly whose owner has already named her: The Last Meow. Their stalls are next to each other, and they come out of them with their heads up, ears pricked, bodies tense, and nostrils flared, as if they're looking for a fight. On her way back to her stall after a showing, the Storm Cat filly plunges her head to the ground and kicks. Ellen pulls her head in and the filly goes scrambling backward. At first, Ellen is pulling, trying to get the filly's head down, and then all her concentration is focused on keeping hold of the lead shank as the filly gallops backward, head up, hooves skittering through the stones, scattering the buyers, who are diving for cover.

Red-faced, head down, arm hanging on desperately to the lead shank, Ellen stares down, focused on keeping up, and in the opposite corner of the yard, right in front of the welcome desk, the filly finally stops. Ellen pulls her head around to her side and marches her back to her stall. "Good job, Ellen," Mark calls out.

When the action slows in the yard, Cordell Anderson wanders over to the benches for a rest. Ellen, he says, "is a good hand," hardworking and eager to learn. He helps himself to a bottle of cold water from one of the coolers that Fasig-Tipton keeps stocked in each of the stabling areas. Nacho, the groom who's been assigned to the Resplendency colt, is eating a Popsicle with one hand and hosing down the walkways with the other. Jeff and Beverly Lewis stand near the edge of the tent, conferring with Jeff Hayslett, and Sam Pollock has settled into the seat on the benches, where he will pass the afternoon.

"I stay calm," Cordell says, explaining his approach to handling the horses. "I don't have any tension in me. I give up all my fears."

Like Iris, Cordell is fifty-four. He and Iris were born in the same year and the same month, but he started handling horses when he was just seventeen. Born in Jamaica, he worked for an English family from whom New Yorker Mary Monroe bought a filly named Distinctly Restless. Cordell accompanied the filly when she was shipped to the States, staying with her for three weeks while she was in quarantine. The filly got attached to him during that time and Mrs. Monroe did not want them to be separated. She kept Cordell on, and when the filly won her first race four months later, Cordell became her permanent groom. In 1975, he says, he was making a pound a week in Jamaica, so when the opportunity arose to go to New York, he never looked back.

It took him two years to get his visa, and by then, the filly had been retired from racing and was sent to Taylor Made as a broodmare in 1981. He followed the filly and stayed on to work at Taylor Made, where the late Dr. DeWitt Owen, Jr., Keeneland's veterinarian, introduced Cordell to the then president of Keeneland, Ted Bassett. By 1999, Cordell explains, he was working yearling sales for Taylor Made and the two-year-old sales for Murray Smith. He also works for Keeneland, as one of the few people who handle the horses in the show ring.

At Keeneland, when he takes the lead shank from a yearling's groom and walks the horse into the ring, Cordell says, "I just walk him in and stand him. I don't try to force this horse to step up. I try to walk him into standing." He thinks the horses can feel that he likes them and therefore they calm down. "It's like the horse can feel the nervousness. When I feel that tension, I let this horse relax, feel that I'm not going to hurt him."

When he takes care of the horses at the sale, he says, he likes to do a good job because he imagines that's what they want. "I like to sleep comfortable," he says. "So they want to sleep comfortable."

As Cordell is taking his break, owners are coming and going, plopping onto the benches next to him to say hi, and then wandering away. Everybody knows him. The beginnings of many of the showings he does start with a Kentucky drawl: "How ya doin', Cordell?" He's shown some famous horses over the years, like Hansel, Summer Squall, and Curlin. "I held over fifteen horses that brought over a million dollars," he says. Mrs. Whitney, though, sent him three hundred dollars and a picture of him with her Storm Cat filly, which he held for her. The most valuable horse he ever showed to advantage in the Keeneland ring was an Awesome Again colt that sold for eight million dollars. "I was thinking maybe somebody would give me a hundred dollars, but nobody did."

Across the street, the race meet has started and those who were able to get away have left. Frank and his wife, Kim, who's working the welcome desk this year, are having a barbecue tonight. (Her added challenge today was figuring out how to shuck enough corn for fifty people.) Sam

Pollock, neighbor, client, and the person whom Frank describes as his best friend, stands up slowly from where he's been sitting all afternoon. He's worried he doesn't have enough fresh tomatoes for the barbecue and is off to pick up more from the farm stand. He's got two horses selling here this week, one of his own and one he owns in partnership.

The sun is on its way down, and the light has softened. It filters through the trees and into the stabling area, dappling the walkways, the horses, and the staff as they finish up for the day. Because it's slow, Kim has come under the tent, as well. Sheri Pitzer, the farm photographer, has pulled out her camera, taking advantage of the quiet time to squeeze out a few portraits. Eleven-year-old Chris Taylor and the friend he brought with him for the week are chasing each other with the horses' water bottles. "Quit that," his mother yells at him. The boys pretend to put the bottles down, but as soon as she's not looking, they pick them up again.

"Frank needs the day of travel to get caught up on phone calls," says Kim, who's chatting with a client who has also spent the day under the tent, explaining why her family makes the trip from Lexington to Saratoga by car—a seventeen-hour drive. "I drive. We put *Scooby Doo* on for the kids and Frank solves every problem in the world."

"Well, good," the woman says. "I'll give him a list."

Kim yells at the boys again, and this time, the grooms appear, sliding the water bottles out of the boys' hands and replacing them with rakes.

Everything is slowing down. Clients murmur to one another, concerned, and to Kim. In the yard, Chris has given up the rake and taken up the hose. He sprays down the walkway and then, seeing his father standing at the end of it, is overcome by temptation and starts flicking the water closer and closer to him. It dots the bottom of Frank's pants, but Frank doesn't notice, and then a buyer arrives and Chris has to put away the hose.

Frank joins his wife under the tent and reads through his phone messages. Sheri needs a photo of the Katherine Seymour filly who's been causing some trouble today, and Mario brings her out into the yard. Seeing that Mario's having trouble getting her to stand square, Cordell gets up to help. Frank glances up and then yells at Chris to go hold that horse. The Katherine Seymour filly belongs to a client of his eldest daughter, Katie Taylor Marshall, who is getting her own start in the business. Mario and Cordell shoot him a look as if to say, Do you see who this is? Chris isn't interested.

"Get over there and hold that horse," Kim tells her son.

Four feet tall and wearing the little-boy version of the khakis, light blue shirt, and burgundy Taylor Made tie, Chris takes hold of the lead shank. Her curiosity aroused by the novelty of being anchored to something she could pick up with her teeth, the filly lowers her head toward Chris, blowing out a hot breath.

"Hold that shank up," Kim reminds him.

Chris is so short that he has to hold the long end of the shank above his head to make sure it's level with the filly's nose—where it's supposed to be. The filly follows it up. In the photos, she'll appear to be gazing off at some far-distant vista.

Millimeters outside the shot's frame, Mario and Cordell are leaning forward, their hands out, bodies poised to leap out and grab both the filly and Chris should the filly explode. Chris grins, Frank is on the phone, and Kim watches serenely from the benches as her youngest child poses for a photograph that may, depending on the filly's fate, end up becoming iconic.

Sheri gets her shot, and as soon as she lowers the camera, Cordell's and Mario's hands slide forward, taking the shank and nudging the boy away from the horse. Along the perimeter of the yard, Iris is tossing straw bales into the stalls that need to be freshly bedded for the evening. In thirty minutes, the Jim Dandy Stakes will be run, and the grooms are trying to get through their chores so they can get across the street in time to place their bets. Mark Taylor is standing in front of the TV monitor. He'll watch the race from here.

Chris and his friend have found the water bottles again. Kim stares at them, giving up, until she notices that the boys are trying to spray each other so that it looks like they've peed in their pants. Exasperated, sighing, she tells them to quit, just quit.

It's Sunday, August 1, the day before the sale, and by 7:30 A.M., the stalls are cleaned, and the horses fed and bathed. Teresa Little is hanging around the welcome desk and telling Kim and Sheri that Frank sent her to her room last night. She was on her way out with Paige, one of the younger women working the sale, and Frank told them to get back up to their room and no climbing out the window. "Thank God!" Teresa says. She'd never be able to make it through the day if she'd been out drinking last night, she jokes.

"See?" Frank arrives with Finn Green in time to hear the end of the story. "I'm starting to mature." Frank's eldest daughter, Katie, is having a baby in November. Frank will soon be a grandfather.

Chris has also arrived bright and early, complaining that there's nothing left for breakfast after his father goes through the kitchen in the morning. Grinning, Frank tells everyone that yesterday Chris called him at 6:30 in the morning to accuse him of eating all of the toaster strudels.

"He leaves the empty box!" Chris says indignantly.

"They were little, itty-bitty toaster strudels, weren't they, Finn?" Frank says.

"Little bitty," Finn concurs.

🐎

By 7:50, the yard is busy. It's overcast, and the cool weather has excited the horses, making them jumpy. In the crowded showing area, Cordell and Julie run into each other while trying to turn their horses around. Julie's horse kicks, almost clipping Cordell. He yells at her to walk on and she yells at him that it's his own fault for coming too close behind. They both stomp off in opposite directions. Their horses, chastised, follow them closely and obediently.

Kim Taylor is back at the welcome desk. She doesn't usually work the sale, she says, but her kids are older now, the farm's trying to save money, and, it's "better to be working than shopping," she says. From her command behind the welcome desk, she manages not only the showing of the yearlings but the requisite social activities. Seeing a friend arrive, Chris's older sister, twelve-year-old Gracie, tells her that her outfit is really cute.

Chris appears, pink lemonade in hand, and lets his mother know that he's already been working very hard.

Around Taylor Made, the other stable yards are quiet, their stall fronts washed clean, and the grass glistens in the early-morning dew. The pots of hanging flowers, their leaves wet from their morning watering, pop bright pink and red against the dark green of the barns. The stinging, sharp smell of the pine-oil cleaner that everyone uses lingers in the air. Denali Stud, immediately adjacent to Taylor Made, is empty, its salespeople sitting around and chatting in their bright blue shirts. Eaton Sales, the only consignor as large as Taylor Made, has just one horse out and one on deck. Across the road, in between the stabling areas, Woodford Thoroughbreds is empty. "We always show more than everyone else," Frank says. "I don't know if it's because we got more horses or because we get them out faster."

Saratoga's racetrack sits on the edge of its historic and picturesque downtown. The sale takes place right next door on a sales ground that holds a single pavilion, just nine barns, and has room for only two hundred horses. The sales company is older than Keeneland, and was once the company that handled the September sale until Keeneland took it over. Boutique, exclusive, a little fusty, and distinguished by hard partying, the sale got a big face-lift last year when Sheikh Mohammed bought a controlling share in the company. That purchase was followed by over $100,000 worth of repairs and upgrades to the barns, and this year, they've opened the new Humphrey S. Finney Sales Pavilion. But the scale of the operation is so small and so discreet that even from a couple of blocks away, a visitor in the neighborhood would have no idea what is going on. Tidy blocks of Victorian cottages are decked out in their summer best—wind chimes and wicker, tumbling, sexy little flower gardens extravagantly overrun with wildflowers: black-eyed Susans, purple coneflowers, bee balm. Neat lawns square off against freshly painted fences. A woman in last night's party dress, barefoot, her hair frizzed out behind, strappy high-heeled sandals dangling from her fingertips, pads down the street barefoot, talking on her phone. "I appreciate anything you can do," she says. It is supremely peaceful. The only sign that something unusual might be going on are the out-of-state license plates on the parked cars: Florida, Ohio, Wisconsin, Texas, Tennessee, New Jersey, and, of course, Kentucky.

Monday morning, August 2, is the first day of the two-day sale. Barrett is prowling the yard, making sure that the staff has enjoyed breakfast. It's overcast and warm and everyone is already worn-out, and the sale hasn't even started. Every chance they get, staff members retreat to the breezeway between Taylor Made and Denali Stud and flop on a hay bale or into a plastic chair. They smoke, give one another back rubs, or sit back-to-back, propping one another up, their eyes closed. Noelle is excited—she had her first cheesesteak last night.

The horses are tired at this point, too. They stretch out fully, their gentle snores whiffling the straw in front of their noses. The Malibu Moon filly lies down the minute she's unclipped from her lead shank. Iris needs to show that Malibu Moon filly and rattles the lead shank to wake her up. "C'mon, sister," she says.

At this point, the buyers are coming back for a second or third look. Or in some cases, says Mark, a principal has just arrived and an agent or trainer is taking him or her around to see the short list. Grouchy and annoyed, the Malibu Moon filly bites Iris's arm just as she's about to march her up and back, up and back. While the buyer checks her out, Iris examines her arm, looking for a mark. "You bit me *hard*," she complains to the filly.

The Malibu Moon filly back in her stall, Iris stands in front of Resplendency, waiting for Nacho so they can get the horse out for a showing. She pats his broad face. "You're too big to play with us," she tells him.

Tom Hamm has posted the evening's assignments on the walls of the breezeway. With every hip number, a leader is listed, as well as a follower, a second groom who carries a water bottle, a rag, and an extra lead shank. The grooms, footsore and tired, have a one-hour lunch break today, so they can race home and get fresh clothes, and maybe a quick nap before the sale starts at 7:00 P.M. Noelle returns in a rush, freshened up after a nap, her makeup fixed and her hair combed. Freddy and Chilo offer to help her with her tie. It's not a problem, they insist. Noelle glares at them. "I can tie it myself," she says.

An ice-cream truck pulls up, jingling and spooking the horses. The grooms abandon their posts for a sweet.

At 4:15, Bob Baffert shows up, alone. "There's the man. There's the man," Teresa Little calls out, and Baffert smiles. He's the last person left who's still looking at horses, and he wants to see hip number 126—the Awesome Again filly that's been dragging everyone around the stable yard for five days. Noelle retrieves her, then walks up and down the path, her blond ponytail bobbing behind her, and sets the filly up for Baffert to look at. Mark Taylor is at his side; Wally, Teresa, and Jacob have faded away. Baffert reaches up to touch the filly's back, and she spooks, kicking at him and scrambling away. Noelle hauls on the lead shank, keeping the horse's head close to her and getting her back under control. Ever charming, Baffert smiles warmly and congratulates her. Noelle blushes to the tips of her ears, and Mark leans in to let her know she almost killed a Hall of Famer. Baffert smiles and finishes. By 4:30, the yard is empty and Mark sits down with his notes, but no sooner does he open the notebook than the gate clangs and two more people walk in. "I know it's a long day," they say, apologizing. "But we'd like to look at one."

"And we'd love to show you one," Mark says energetically.

The horses don't want to walk for buyers anymore. They're tired. The game has gotten boring and aggravating. They stretch their necks out, plant their feet. It takes two people, one clucking and walking, the other marching up from behind, to get most of them moving out.

The grooms are whipped, too. They're half sprawled on bales, ties loosened, eyes closed. Ellen has pulled off her shoes and is rubbing her feet. Only the Taylors have the same level of energy that they did this morning.

The buyer satisfied, Mark returns to his notebook, in which he's written comments on the horses: "18—not good; 27—looking good; 36—hit or miss, three scopes; 37—hit or miss, Live Oak and Sheikh Mo.; 43—2 scopes."

Mark's information comes from the data mining that the farm does. When buyers give the welcome desk person—in this case, Frank's wife, Kim—their names and the list of horses they want to look at, she types it into the computer and a convenient ticket is printed out that the farm can hand off to their front men; all that information also goes into a database. Behind the welcome desk, in the barn's office, are the office staff—the proverbial men behind the curtain—who are making sense of that information. Along with the IT guys who keep the database going are Patrick Mahan, who's doing regular updates on the horses and preparing the advertisements for the next day's dailies, and Tom Hamm, who's managing the crew.

When Mark runs a report on a horse, he gets lists of the people who asked for a showing and who those people's associates are, and that can be linked to their buying history.

The database that keeps track of people's connections is especially useful when the person looking is a bloodstock agent and could be looking on behalf of any number of people. It's also especially useful when they know who the vets are. The horses' X-rays are in the repository, and it's unusual for a potential buyer to rescan a horse. But everyone scopes them. Brief and relatively inexpensive, the vet examines the horses' breathing apparatus using an endoscope. The number of scopes a horse' has reflects the amount of serious interest it's attracted. Knowing the name of the vet, and the people that vet works for, tells the Taylors who is likely to compete for their horse in the auction ring.

As far as Mark knows, Taylor Made is the only farm that maintains such an expansive database.

By 6:45, everyone has returned to the sales grounds. The grooms have washed, eaten, and, in some cases, changed. Tammy Frasier will be doubling as controller tonight, as well as topping off the horses before they go to the sale. Salesmen and account reps have donned their navy blue blazers and have washed their faces. Frank is on the phone. "She could bring two or three hundred," he's saying. "She could bring four hundred. You know how it is up here. You don't know what the fuck is going on. About half of them you feel good about; the rest are questionable."

Frank, Jeff Hayslett, Mark, and Finn Green all look a little grim. Mark says he's not optimistic, and, as Finn points out, the Europeans and the Japanese, who propped up this sale last year, are not all that visible this year. Sheikh Mohammed is here, but it takes more than one bidder to make a sale.

The first horse in the consignment is a bay filly out of a mare named Brooklynsangel and by Corinthian. Iris is helping Tammy Frasier top her off while Julie holds on to the jumpy filly. Tammy rubs baby oil around her nose and eyes, and mineral oil is smoothed on her tail. Iris has a spray can of vitamin E hair oil. She demonstrates it on herself by shining up the ringlets she wears clipped on top of her head. Before she sprays it on the filly's tail, she says, "Shhhhhhhhhh," longer and louder than normal. Her voice, which the filly trusts, will mask the sound of the aerosol, which the filly doesn't like.

Since the oil makes the horses sticky as well as shiny, they can't go back in their stalls after they're sprayed. Julie will take up this filly, and Mario Ramirez, who's been pulled away from the farm because, like Freddy and Chilo, he's part of the A team that works all the sales, waits nearby because the next yearling is his. He admits that he's a little nervous. Everyone is a little nervous. The air is charged.

Iris is underneath the filly, daubing at stray white hairs and nearly invisible scabs with a black marker, coloring them in. The filly gets a little Vicks in her nose to keep her from scenting any horse of the opposite sex. Tom Hamm swings by and tells Tammy to remind all the followers to carry an extra lead shank.

Jamie McKechnie is sending the horses to the ring tonight. He's one of Taylor Made's front men, hired just to work the sales. Small, wiry, soft-spoken, and with an Irish accent, he used to ride horses for Niall Brennan at his training stable for two-year-olds, and once did a little pinhooking on his own. "Low level," he explains. Five, ten, fifteen thousand. But not now. He shakes his head. "Not in this market."

The loudspeakers pop on with a buzz and a crackle and the announcer summons the horses to the ring.

Wisdom would suggest that if you're about to bid tens or hundreds of thousands of dollars on a horse, you might want to pass on the cocktails. But this is Saratoga, where the bar is next to the walking ring. It's a beautiful night—soft, cool, and green. Cocktails in hand, buyers crowd around the walking rings and edge onto the balcony outside the owners' club. Women teeter in their high heels and sleeveless dresses, beaded clutches tucked under arms that are tanned and gym-toned. The men stand with their hips square, their slacks puddled into a single fold over their loafers. Leaning back, they look coolly at the horses. Those who are actually buying make their way through the crowd, heading toward the arena. In and among the crowd are the uniformed grooms, leading their horses, trying to keep them calm. Fasig-Tipton maintenance staff prowl, keeping garbage cans empty. Clocked-out barn staff members linger around the edges, as do Sara-togans who've figured out that this is the most interesting spectacle of the race season. Outside the second and smaller of the two walking rings, a young woman in jeans, a faded blue polo shirt, and tatty sneak-ers, her hair scraped back into a ponytail, composes a text: "Honey, I'm gonna buy a racehorse, okay?" and then smiles as she hits send.

Julie appears with hip number eighteen, the bay filly. Behind her, walking quickly, despite a limp, comes Louis Germany. He's also part of Taylor Made's sales team. A decade ago, he was an exercise rider working for Tom Hamm when Hamm was a trainer. The Brooklyns-angel filly by Corinthian walks with purpose, her body close to Julie, as if she's comforted by being close to the only person she knows here.

🐎

A frisson of excitement agitates the crowed when the second horse in the ring sells for $775,000. No one is expecting this sale to be good, but you never know. Hip number eighteen sells to a racing syndicate for $130,000. The highest-priced horse of the evening comes about halfway through the sale, when Taylor Made's hip number forty-seven, the Street Cry colt out of Don't Tacha Me who marched and posed like a rock star all week, sells to Sheikh Mohammed, via his agent John Ferguson, for $800,000. In 2006, five horses at this sale sold for over a million dollars each.

🐎

Outside the pavilion, it's dark and warm, the night peaceful. The loudest noises in the stable yard are the crickets and the laughter of the grooms. The grooms have arranged the plastic chairs in a semi-circle around the TV monitor mounted over the doorway that leads to the back of the barn. Their backs are to the road and the pavilion across the way, their heads tilted back, and when there's an extra empty chair, someone will grab it and prop his feet on it. On the other side of the yard, sitting on the green benches under the tent, one of the Taylors' clients sends e-mails on her phone. A self-described "behind the scenes kind of girl," she's here to watch the sale of her mother's horses, the first of which already went through the ring and did not meet its reserve.

Though the auctioneer's voice drifts over from the pavilion, it's not loud enough to drown out the crickets. In their stalls, the horses who are cataloged for Tuesday night are lying down, their lights off, asleep. The warm brown of the stall walls, along with the yellow straw and incandescent light, contrasts with the deep, cool green of the grass, now damp with dew.

Chris Taylor takes a chair and joins the line of blue shirts and burgundy caps. His shoulders are narrower and he's two heads shorter than the others, his feet barely touching the ground. Gracie, who's very pretty tonight in a white eyelet dress with a pink sash and low platform sandals, has also returned to the quad. She sits in one of the tall chairs by the welcome desk, watching the sale on the monitor there.

Tammy is still on her feet, topping off the horses. Hip number seventy-six, a filly out of Katherine Seymour and by the stallion Gone West, enters the auction ring. Gracie has a special interest in this horse because it was prepped by her sister Katie, who's started her own Thoroughbred selling business and has consigned the filly through her family's farm. The filly brings just $165,000. "Tammy, what's going on here?" Barrett asks. "This is supposed to be a good filly."

The filly goes unsold. "What the hell?" Barrett says. "This is another RNA." He means a horse whose reserve has not been attained.

Spectators from the sale, dressed up, cocktails in hand, wander into the yard and peer into the stalls. One of the van drivers buzzes through, letting everyone know that the computers he's selling will be arriving tomorrow—laptops, two hundred bucks, in case anyone is interested.

"Where are they?" Tammy yells out for the next groom and follower pair, who are due in the ring soon. "They better hurry up," she adds, marching down the shed row to get them.

"That filly done whipped 'em," one of the grooms jokes.

The filly by Malibu Moon heads out, and Tammy sends off the last of the colts. Once she's done, she wants the grooms to start raking the yard. The grooms don't want to. They want to wait until the horses are back, in case one of them poops, or they have to take it out for the vet. That's what they usually do, but Tammy is determined to get them started.

They ignore her.

She stands with her hands on her hips, the exhaustion showing on her face.

In her sandals and white dress, Gracie gets up, picks up the rake, and starts scraping the tines over the crushed stone.

Noelle stands in front of the grooms with the rake in her hand. "I have to go to the ring," she says, and then lays it over Freddy's legs.

"Agh." Iris gets up with a sigh. "Where's the big rake?" A groom named Hollywood grabs another one, and then Ellen. Under the rolling chant of the auctioneer comes the *scratch, scratch, scratch* of half a dozen rakes.

They finish raking and plop back down, their eyes on the screen, their feet up if they can find a chair, telling jokes in Spanish, waiting for the day to end.

There's only one gate big enough for the horses, so the Lane's End grooms have to cut through the Taylor Made yard on their way to and from the pavilion. The Lane's End groom, her ponytail bobbing behind her, leads a big colt down the shed row. He has his head down and is walking cautiously through the unfamiliar yard, past a dozen grooms he's never seen. Head lowered, he blows out a long breath, slowing to a halt, spooked. Without getting up, the Taylor Made grooms whistle at him, chasing him along, while the guy following squirts the back of the colt's legs with a water bottle. The whistle that was directed at the horse, once he starts moving, threatens to morph into a wolf whistle as the girl walks on.

"Quit whistling at the girl, y'all," the Lane's End follower says, chastising them. The Taylor Made grooms burst out laughing.

Hip number ninety-eight, a bay colt by Street Sense, heads up to the ring. He's the last of the Taylor Made horses for the night.

Barrett, who in addition to driving the supplies up from Kentucky for this trip and being the on-call driver has also been put in charge of providing food for everyone, slouches down into a chair, his long, rickety frame threatening to collapse in on itself like a marionette dropped on the floor. He arrived in Saratoga three nights before the house rental was available and spent those three nights sleeping on a couple of chairs pushed together. In the morning, he'll get breakfast on for everyone. He's exhausted and he's been having some health problems lately, though now that he's quit smoking, Frank says, they don't have to worry about him crashing the truck because he can't see through the windshield.

Hip number ninety-one sells, and hip number ninety-two, the penultimate horse in the consignment, appears in the ring.

"It's almost beer thirty," Iris observes noting that it's almost quitting time. She lets Tammy and Jamie know that they've done a good job getting all the horses to the ring.

"I know you're mad at us and want to cry," she says to Tammy, who's just settling down now from having been ignored about the raking.

"Nobody's gonna cry," Tammy says.

One by one, with groans and heavy sighs, the yearlings go down in their stalls, stretching out to sleep on the fresh, sweet straw.

Tom Hamm summons the team around him while they wait for the last horse to come back. He sold to John Ferguson, the agent for Sheikh Mohammed, for just $230,000. Tom reminds the grooms that hip numbers thirty-six, thirty-seven, forty-three, and ninety-one are all RNAs. No one will be arriving to take them away tomorrow, and they need to be prepped in case someone comes by who is interested in a private sale. They'll start at 6:00 A.M., he lets them know, and then dismisses them.

The sale isn't a disaster, but the market's not roaring back to its old form, either. Not a single horse sold for over a million tonight.

"There wasn't anybody under the Arabs," Finn Green says, shrugging.

🐎

Tuesday morning, the last day of the sale, starts out quiet. It's a dark day at the track, and by now buyers have had their fill of looking at the horses they're interested in. It's a good day to shop, sightsee, or conduct some business on the golf course. The day's hazy and warm, and rain seems imminent. Eating his breakfast from a plastic plate, Frank watches the horses walk. They look sleepy, too. Their heads hang low, and they don't quite seem awake. Once again, Barrett is checking in with everyone to see if they like their breakfast.

"I'm a jack-of-all-trades," he explains. "Whenever they yell, I just go see what I have to do."

By 9:30, the grooms are standing around without much to do. The ice-cream truck jingles its bell, summoning Julie and Iris. Cordell is at the welcome desk, changing channels on the TV. Kim Taylor is taking the kids to nearby Manchester, Vermont, to shop at the outlets. The grooms are sprawled around the breezeway, chatting, twirling the ends of the lead shanks. One of them wants to know if Ellen has a boyfriend.

"I don't neeeeeed a boyfriend," Ellen tells him.

Jamie McKechnie likes the Resplendency colt, even though he walks all over everyone who goes into his stall. He's not mean, Jamie says, just big. Like most everyone else, Jamie thinks the horse could be a good racehorse, but the money in racing is in the two- and three-year-old races. A horse who might end up needing an extra year to mature into a big body would be at a great disadvantage.

By 4:00 P.M., Sam Pollock has spent the better part of the day sitting under the tent, watching the horses and visiting. Hip numbers thirty-six and thirty-seven, both his, did not meet their reserves last night and are back in their stalls and *not* on their way to new owners. He's not sure what he's going to do with them. If someone doesn't step up here today, the colt will probably go to the Timonium sale in Maryland—a step down from the elite sales. He has partners on the Street Cry filly, so he doesn't know what they're going to do with her.

"I thought the sale would be better," he says. "I thought we'd reached the bottom."

It's a hard time in the industry, he says. "I think we're going to lose a significant number of tracks."

In 1990, according to the Jockey Club *Fact Book*, the total amount of money bet on racing in the United States—the pari-mutuel handle—was $9.3 billion. Twenty years later, at the end of 2010, that handle was up by just $2.1 billion. But during that same time, off-track betting became more accessible, so the burden of covering that handle has fallen to the tracks. In 1996, on-track money was $2.94 billion, and off-track was $8.7 billion. By 2009, $1.3 billion was from on-track betting, but almost $11 billion came from off-track betting. When gambling revenue is shifted away from the track that is responsible for covering the expenses of racing, those expenses take a bigger bite out of the track's profits. Legalizing slot machines has drawn gamblers back to the tracks, but not necessarily because they're interested in racing. Their perspective is well-represented by a racetrack attendee interviewed by the *Pittsburgh Post-Gazette* at Mountaineer Casino, Racetrack & Resort in Chester, West Virginia. "I've got no faith in the horse racing system. . . . I wouldn't have the patience to figure it out. I don't have the knowledge."

During its heyday, in the 1940s, Thoroughbred racing was one of the country's most popular sports. But it was also the country's only legal form of gambling. People were more urban, and tracks were accessible by train—as they still are in places like New York, Boston, and Chicago. A day at the track was a day out of the city.

Because the foal crop is bigger, and the handle is smaller, the average racehorse wins about $19,000, and the cost of the average racehorse is $40,000. By his calculation, says Sam Pollock, it costs about $15,000 to keep a mare. From birth to sale, the foals costs around $35,000. Stud fees, even now that they have dropped, average around $55,000 for a top stallion, and there's no way to make money in the business unless you're at the top end. "There's no way to make money on cheap mares," he says. The goal of this sale is to get these horses sold because racehorses lose money.

Mark is going over the day's data and getting ready to set the reserves—the minimum acceptable bid—for tonight's horses. Fasig-Tipton, Jeff Hayslett explains, takes 5 percent of every horse that walks into the ring, whether or not it meets its reserve. Keeneland takes 2.25 percent of the reserve and 4.5 percent of the final price if the horse sells. The commission price is based on the final bid.

From the consignor's perspective, Mark explains, you want to set the reserve high enough to get what the horse is worth, but not so high that you drive away bidders. There are two ways to set reserves, explains

Geoffrey Russell, the director of sales at the Keeneland auction house. With a "live money reserve" the auctioneer responds only to real bids coming in from buyers in the pavilion. An "all the way" reserve occurs when a consignor has authorized the auction house to bid on the horse. On a horse with a $99,000 reserve, for example, the auctioneer might run that bidding up to $97,000 or $98,000 by calling out those bids as if they are coming from the buyers. This is why, Mark Taylor explains, "Everyone could go out for a coffee break at the same time, and the bid spotters would still be going, Yo!"

The benefit of this kind of reserve is that the auction house can push the bids beyond the horse's real market value—all they need is one person willing to keep increasing their bid. In live bidding, you need at least two. Whether the horse sells or not, the auction houses still base their commission on the last bid the horse received. So the downside of an all the way is that the owner of the horse could end up paying a higher commission on a horse they didn't sell. Russell doesn't know the exact percentage of live versus all-the-way bidding, but he estimates that there's more all-the-way bidding than live bidding.

From the selling standpoint, Mark explains, if you set the reserve at $299,000, those bids are going to go through 100, 200, 250 pretty quickly—one of the ways that the bidders could guess that they're not bidding against a live bid. But the actual seller of the horse might be bidding on it as well. It's perfectly legal to bid on your own horse, though no one likes to admit to it.

The goal is to get as much "live" bidding as possible. Say you have a bidder who's set his limit at $300,000, Mark explains. If you've set the reserve at $299,000, the auctioneer drives bidding up to that point too fast for that guy with the $300,000 limit to get into the game.

But set the reserve at a $199,000, Mark says, and the auctioneer slows down. That guy with the $300,000 goes on the board at $100,000. By the time bidding gets to $250,000, he's two or three bids into it. Bidding hits $275,000 and he's in again at $300,000—his limit. But the bidding rolls on and now that horse is his horse, goddamnit! "Maybe it's the one," Mark says, grinning. So here comes $350,000 and he's still in the game because he can't bear the idea of someone else getting his

horse. This could be the next Zenyatta, the next Curlin, the next Unbridled's Song. And the guy, who has demonstrated financial prudence
in just about every other area of his life, throws in a bid that's a *hundred
thousand dollars more* than his limit. Ryan Mahan, Keeneland's head
auctioneer, (and father of Taylor Made's Patrick Mahan) says that when
he's running the bids, his main job "is to make sure the guy knows
that his arch enemy is bidding against him."

Jeff Lewis is quite firm that colts are not part of the business plan
for the Bob and Beverly Lewis Trust, and he sets the reserves accord-
ingly. His Unbridled's Song colt that pounded up the ramp of the
truck a week ago with an estimated value of $450,000, will go into the
ring with a reserve of $199,000. "He's done it to himself," Hayslett says.
"He came up here and became a big goofball."

Maybe something happened on the truck. Maybe he's sore. Maybe
it's a growth spurt, but the massages and the extra baths have not succeeded in getting the big bay colt to settle into his pantherlike walk.
"He left the farm looking like Michael Jordan," Hayslett explains, "and
he gets up here and he's looking like Elmer Fudd."

By 7:00 P.M., the air is heavy and humid, and rain still seems imminent.

"It always rains on us up here," Tammy says as she moves horses
through her grooming station.

The team has gathered around the monitor. The first yearling, a
bay colt by A.P. Indy, sells for $1.2 million. He's followed by a Medaglia
d'Oro filly, who sells for $450,000. Suddenly, it feels like old times
again. An Awesome Again colt goes for $350,000, but within a couple
more sales, they're down to $150,000.

Beverly Lewis and her son, Jeff, are seated in the pavilion. Beverly is conservatively and elegantly dressed in taupe and Jeff wears a
navy blue jacket. They have catalogs in their laps and are watching
the horses go through the ring. Jeff is a great admirer of his late
father, who was famously passionate and competitive at the sales,
blasting past his limits so regularly that Ryan Mahan says that Lewis
was his favorite bidder. "I own all the Budweiser in Southern California,"

says Mahan, laughing, as he describes the look on Lewis's face when he got outbid. But Jeff is disciplined and has a plan that he's sticking to.

"Okay, Mom, here we go," Jeff says when the Resplendency colt walks into the ring.

"Here's an Unbridled's Song colt out of the good-running mare Resplendency," the announcer begins. He runs through the pedigree, pointing out that the sire's progeny have won $63 million.

Characteristically, Resplendency '09 has entered the ring with his tongue hanging out of the side of his mouth.

Walt Robertson, at the time Fasig-Tipton's chairman and auctioneer, opens the bidding at $200,000 and then drops quickly to $25,000 before he gets a bid on the board. The bids move up incrementally: $50,000, $100,000, $125,000, $135,000, $150,000, $175,000. The bidding hangs at $175,000—well short of the colt's reserve. Then the bidding picks up again: $185,000, $190,000. "Bruce is winning!" the auctioneer warns, his little hammer tapping like a woodpecker. "You're out of there."

"Yep, one ninety-five," he says at the next bid. "Bruce, you're out of there."

"Yep, two," he continues. He's made the reserve. The auctioneer pushes up to $210,000, then drops back. "Two oh five. I'll take two oh five, right quick." His chant pauses and he rolls back. "And outside. Tommy, two hundred thousand right here."

The gavel falls, the sale is done, and Jeff Lewis is disappointed, although relieved to send the colt on his way. "He may be changing," he says about the colt's less-than-stellar showing at Saratoga. "He may be growing or off his game. He's kind of dopey," he adds, though Lewis says that "he doesn't have any particular flaws."

Because the colt was a foal share—the Unbridled's Song syndicate contributed the stallion's stud fee—the Lewises will clear about $90,000 after the commission. They'll come out with a little bit of profit, though the syndicate took a hit—Unbridled's Song's stud fee was $150,000 when the mare was bred. "I hate taking horses home," Lewis says, adding that the buyer just got a very good deal on a very nice horse.

Outside the pavilion, it's raining buckets. The glitterati are hovering under the eaves, cocktails in hand, women teetering on their high heels. Bleary-eyed, her hair out of place, one looks like she's about to throw up, the boyfriend next to her watchful but embarrassed. Out in the stabling area, they're using the breezeway to prep the horses, but just as quickly as it descended, the storm departs, leaving behind glistening green grass, humid air, and the smell of saturated earth.

In his stall, Resplendency '09 finally gets to rest. A vet comes by to draw blood. The horse was so uncharacteristically lethargic that Frank was worried he might have EPM (equine protozoal mycloencephalitis)—a bacterial infection that causes neurological damage. He warned the horse's buyer, Ahmed Zayat, who is picking up some bargains at Saratoga even though his farm, Zayat Stables LLC, is in a bankruptcy action with Fifth Third Bank. Zayat, who, like Bob Lewis, made his fortune with a beverage distributorship, has sent a vet by to test for EPM before they ship the horse home. The test will come back negative.

The grooms are sprawled out again. They'll finish late tonight and come back tomorrow to pack up. They're taking more horses back with them than they want to, but, Mark explains, their expectations were low. And, as everyone says, you don't assess the market with the "boutique" sale. The real measure is coming up next month, at Keeneland.

9

August 2010

 JOHN HALL IS DISAPPOINTED THAT RESPLENDENCY'S colt didn't sell for a higher price.

It's the middle of August, and he's in Yearling Complex C with Cesar and the grooms. They've got showings scheduled for one of their clients this morning, who's bringing his farm's new manager, Scott Kintz, along with him.

The navy blue of Scott's Bass Pro Shops T-shirt and jeans suits him. And he looks handsome and energetic when he gets out of his new Ford F-250 and teases Cesar that his old truck, which Cesar inherited, needs to be cleaned. The grooms raced through the chores this morning so that they would be ready for Scott, though Danny admits that it was more for the owner of the horses than for Scott. "Maybe in a couple years," he adds, smiling.

The horses are pulled out of the barn and walked in the heat. River Drive '09, everyone agrees, is gorgeous. But he's still walking like he's dealing cards. Indian Charlie's fillies are doing great. The Elusive Quality filly they find a little blah—nothing terrible, but nothing great, either. Ever optimistic, John Hall points out that Europeans like a laid-back shoulder and deep pasterns.

Scott and his new employer go inside to check out the barn. Their new barn is being rehabbed and modernized, and Scott has a question about how to hang the outside doors.

Looking down at Queen in the next stall, who's been sound asleep and snoring, not bothered by the fly that has landed on her lip, Scott's new employer notices that she's slept through the interruptions, the strangers, and the noise of them talking and banging doors.

"She jogs from the barn to the grass only," John Hall jokes.

On Tuesday morning, Sam and Jo Pollock are coming around to see their horses. At Yearling Complex C, Danny isn't working today, and his brother Marshall is covering his shift. Like his cousin Joe, Marshall just graduated from the University of Arizona's racetrack-management program and has returned to the barn. He's got the same energy as his brother Danny, but he has an added enthusiasm for the horses. "I love this business!" he tells visitors. "Love it!" When they work on the farm, the Taylor children need to navigate the barriers between staff and management. When they're grooms, they need to act like, and get along with, the other grooms: work hard, show well, care about the animals, and offer an opinion only when it's requested. But they are also Taylors, which means they then must swap hats. When he's introduced as a Taylor, Marshall strides out to greet visitors cheerfully, hand extended. When he's a groom, he's silent.

He's out back with the grooms this morning, bathing the horses before the Pollocks come by. He moves quickly, chatting in Spanish with the other grooms. He's taken on the messier job, scrubbing and cleaning the horses, while Mario, who's been with the farm for twelve years, holds the horses' lead shanks. Another pair of grooms works in the neighboring wash stall. Danny moves quickly, scrubs vigorously. Before he finishes with the horses, he offers them water from the hose, which they often like to lap up with their long tongues because it's cold and fresh. Finishing up with one colt, he drops the hose to the ground, where it lands on its handle, sending up a shower, which lands on the grooms and sends the Distant Roar colt to the other side of the wash stall, his ears downward and straight out to the sides and his eyes closed to keep out the water that's spraying him in the face.

"Sorry about that!" Marshall jumps to pick up the hose. The grooms are laughing even as they get wet.

This morning, everyone's talking about Zenyatta. She's just won her eighteenth race, the Clement L. Hirsch Stakes out at Del Mar, and has tied Eclipse's record for consecutive wins. The record for consecutive wins is held by a mare named Pepper's Pride, who, Marshall is pleased to point out, lives at Taylor Made.

🐎

The Pollocks start their tour at Bona Terra A. They've got mares, weanlings, and yearlings in most of the barns on the farm. They climb down from their Escalade, along with Frank, Jeff Hayslett, and Charlie Boden, Darley's head of sales. The first weanling of the day is a Lady Echo colt.

"This is the first time we've seen him," Sam Pollock says.

While they're admiring a walk on an Elusive Quality colt, Frank points out the unpainted boards that dash throughout the farm's blackboard fencing. The repair was completed by the Taylor Made staff. In the past, Frank says, before the recession, that job would have been contracted out, but they saved that money by having the farm staff repair them. "It's a new day at Taylor Made," he says, beaming.

Sam Pollock wants to know if that's why, when he returned yesterday evening from playing golf with John Hall and Steve Avery, they saw Frank out in the fields with the tractor, dumping topsoil, long after everyone else had gone home.

They head off to Bona Terra B, where Frank admires a Tiznow foal out of a mare named Dirty Rush. "I love this mare," Frank says. "This is the best foal yet."

Back in the cars, Frank following behind, they head down the lane to Bona Terra C. "Saratoga didn't go very good," he says, "and I didn't expect it to do very good. I don't know what the new plan is—just keep working and try not to worry."

Taylor Made's RNA rate was just slightly higher than that for the overall sale, meaning that strategically they did a good job of setting rates. If the RNA rate is too low, then they're selling the horses too cheap. If it's too high, then their reserves are not realistic. But just getting the horses sold doesn't mean that some of their owners, who breed at the top of the market, didn't lose money,

"I can tell you on about two fingers the number of horses that went past their reserves," Frank adds.

Frank and the Pollocks have been together a long time. Originally from Alabama, Sam, like many racehorse owners, made his money with car dealerships. Though you'd think that you'd need to make Wall Street money to be in the Thoroughbred game, a lot of owners in the industry make their money in car dealerships, beverage distributorships, or cell-tower leases. Maybe it's because finance people are already gambling, or because they can't hang around the barn because they have to watch markets all day, but there are not a lot of stockbrokers in the business. Ben Taylor thinks that "a lot of guys are in the business because they run mundane businesses that make a lot of money." And the whole scene is fun for them. The wealthy, he says, "are in these structured lifestyles where they never talk to a regular guy. Plus," Ben adds, smiling, "they know they can't take it with them."

Sam and Jo first started with exotic cattle in the sixties. Jo came from a family who'd had racehorses in Ohio, and they had a neighbor in Alabama who had racehorses. They bought their first one in the 1970s and started going to the yearling sales regularly, hauling a cattle trailer up from Alabama, staying in a local hotel, and, paying no more than the stud fee, buying as many yearlings as they could fit in the trailer.

Then Frank "found us," says Sam, and talked them into getting out of the low end of the market. Their original goal, says Sam, was to "have fun and make money." Frank got them started on a little pinhooking—buying at the yearling sale, starting the horses in training, and then selling them a few months later as two-year-olds. "That was profitable," Sam recalls.

From there, the business grew. They bought an apartment in Lexington and then, about eleven or twelve years ago, Frank found their farm for them—adjacent to the Taylor Made property. Frank built a house, and they built one next door, leasing the land back to the Taylors in a deal that Ben Taylor, who manages the farm's real estate as well as the stallions, describes as a "complete screwup," but, he says, "that's what happens when you're a nice guy."

The patter between Frank and Sam as they move from barn to barn is about the deals they've made and the deals they're going to make. When they dispute each other, they turn to Jo for arbitration.

The colt in front of them at Bona Terra C is by Unbridled's Song and out of Return to Paradise, though he's on a nurse mare now: a black-and-white Paint of appealingly round proportions.

"I'd like to ride her," Jo says. The mare looks agreeable: wide-eyed, ears up, her back broad and flat, relaxed and cheerful with the giant colt at her side. And, most important, she's close to the ground.

"May colt," Frank says. "That's a strong booger."

Frank got a share in this colt by putting up the stud fee. Sam teases that it's not an equal partnership: Sam's costs are bigger because he's maintaining the mare.

"A hundred and twenty-five into half of anything is a lot these days," Frank says, reminding Sam about the stallion's fee.

They need to get him sold, Sam says. "Can't keep him at thirty-five dollars a day. Frank says he can't make any money at that rate." He'll be stuck out there, "riding the tractor late at night, while his managers play golf."

Looking at the colt, who comes halfway up the nurse mare's flank, Frank says to Sam, "Good thing is, this horse prays every day. He's got to get down on his knees to nurse, and he does it while he's down there."

The foal has huge ears. They point this out to Charlie Boden, who has already shared with them that his boss, Sheikh Mohammed, likes horses with big ears, believing that they're a sign of intelligence.

They bring out yet another Songandaprayer colt.

The Pollocks have another partner on this one, but he's in financial trouble. Frank and Sam argue about the details until Jo confirms the correct ones. "Better get a lien on him now," Sam Pollock says, so they'll be first in line to get paid when the colt gets sold.

In the current recession, Ben Taylor explains, the banks have departed from their normal practice of paying servicers first. With so many farms going bankrupt, the banks are taking their money first; what's left goes to partners and servicers like Taylor Made. There are so many horse owners in trouble, he says, that the yearlings coming into Keeneland are plastered with liens from the multiple debts of the horses' multiple owners. It will take months for people to get their money, if they get it at all. Ben runs the stallion seasons, and has had to shift people into pure collections, and they can't be the same people who are selling those shares. It's a nightmare.

The next horse out of the barn is out of Marina de Chavon and by Malibu Moon. She's got a 2009 yearling going to the September sale. Watching the weanling, Frank tells Sam that initially he was excited about this mare, thinking, he says, "Right here, this is going to be your next mare that's going to make it, and then this foal started walking funny."

It's too late to modify the walk by putting in screws, but Frank thinks it might get better on its own. Watching him turn and walk back toward him, Frank adds, "It could get worse, too."

Distant Roar comes out with her filly, which is so aggressive, Frank initially thinks it's a colt. "Don't let him paw you," he says to the groom, who's dancing to keep his feet and shins out of the filly's way. "Don't be afraid to knock the crap out of him," he says.

Frank realizes his mistake when the weanling walks away. "Oh, it's a filly," he says.

"That foal wants to be in everybody's business." Jeff Hayslett points out that she's covered with bite marks from the other horses.

This mare is the only one left out of the five-mare purchase that the Pollocks made with the proceeds from Contrive. The rest, like Queen, were sold last year.

"If you hadn't done that Contrive deal," Sam says to Frank, wishing aloud that he could take it back and have Contrive again.

That Frank advised them to first sell Contrive, and then minimize the tax penalty by reinvesting the profits in five different mares—none of whom have done well—is a little nut of contention that Frank and Sam like to pass back and forth.

Frank points out that if Sam hadn't been greedy, if he'd just been willing to pay a little tax instead of reinvesting, then he wouldn't have gotten stuck with those five mares. If he'd just paid the tax, he wouldn't have ended up with the foals who lost money and then had to sell the mares, who also lost money. And maybe (clincher), if he hadn't been so greedy and just paid that tax, Obama wouldn't have been elected.

"How much money did you make on that transaction?" Sam asks Frank.

"I made my five percent," Frank says forthrightly. "That was a good deal, and I paid my taxes."

Frank's ankle has been bothering him, and he's asked one of the vets to meet him at Bona Terra C with the portable X-ray. In the barn, Frank strips off his shoe and sock to have his ankle scanned. There's nothing unusual on the screen. "Hell, I'm all right," says Frank. While they're looking at Frank's ankle, Charlie Boden rolls up his sleeve to shoot a picture of an old break in his arm. Frank admires it, and then rolls up his own sleeve.

"Check this out," he says.

The men amuse themselves by looking at the pictures of their broken bones until the vet tells them it's time to quit.

Done with the weanlings, the Pollocks head over to Mackey Pike to see Royale Michele, who's been retired this year and bred to Unbridled's Song. She's on her way to the November bloodstock sale. Her dam, Michele Royale, says Sam Pollock, is his favorite horse. They bought her for $140,000 eleven years ago. She was in foal to Unbridled's Song at the time and they thought the colt would bring $100,000. He sold for $1.4 million. Her next foal, the best on the farm that year, was struck by lightning. In between years, she slipped a foal, and one year she didn't get pregnant. Then, in 2004, in foal to Elusive Quality, the mare colicked in her paddock overnight. She hit her head, and the vets thought she needed to be taken to Rood and Riddle and put down.

Jo wouldn't allow it. "That mare," she said to Sam, "owes me nothing, and I owe her everything." She refused to ship her off the farm and have her put down, asking that the farm keep her comfortable and peaceful. The next day, Sam says, he called up to get the time of death for the insurance claim, only to be told that the mare hadn't died. "She's up and trying to eat hay," he was told.

And she didn't lose the foal. They thought they'd get a $200,000 to

$300,000 filly, but they ended up buying her back for $35,000. They sent her to Todd Pletcher to be trained, but he didn't think she'd amount to much.

So Scott Kintz stepped in. He liked the filly and the mare, and asked the Pollocks if they would let his brother Matt take over her training. She went off to Mountaineer Park, won a couple of claiming races, then an allowance race, and finally a Grade 2 stakes race, accumulating $230,000 in winnings. Of the horses they own outright—no partnerships or shares—Sam says she's been their biggest winner. On their way to see her this morning, they're going to pass her mother in her paddock.

Speeding ahead in a separate car, Frank pulls over at the mare's paddock. Despite his sore ankle, he climbs over the fence and jogs up the hill to where the mares are standing. Curious, ears pricked, they watch him approach. Since it's not customary for middle-aged men to climb into their paddocks and chase them, they regard him with suspicion, and when he reaches for Michele Royale, she walks out of his reach, turning back to watch him from a distance of about ten feet.

Frank stops, rethinking his approach. With the midmorning heat and humidity bearing down, cicadas whirring in the grass, a thick grayish haze coating the sky, he and the mare regard each other. There's no point in chasing a racehorse—no point at all. They can't be caught, but they can be tricked. Frank backs away from her, doubling over and crouching low. Ears pricked, curious and unable to resist, she lowers her head to see what he's doing and then reaches her nose into his hand. She sniffs, and slowly his fingers curl over her halter.

By now, the Escalade has pulled up behind Frank's car and he leads the mare down to the edge of the paddock. She stands compliantly, looking around, accepting admiration, and when Frank lets her go, she turns and lumbers back up the hill.

At Mackey Pike, they gather to see her daughter, Royale Michele, as she walks out of the shade of the cool barn into the heat and light of the day. She's lean, fit, and a little footsore. Lindsey points out that the farrier was just here and the mare always gets a little sore when she's being trimmed. Royale Michele will be going to the November sale, in foal to Unbridled's Song.

"I tell you," Frank says. "That mare right there is the best-looking mare on the farm."

They watch her walk out and back and stand again. "I wouldn't change anything about her right now." After a pause, he adds, grinning at Sam and Jo, "Except maybe her ownership."

Now it's all the way over to the other side of the farm to check in on the Critical Cat colt by Malibu Moon who did not meet his reserve at Saratoga.

"I don't know why he didn't sell," Frank says as they watch him walk out at Eagle Creek A, where they are housing the Saratoga horses who returned from there. "This horse is worth a hundred thousand."

Jeff Hayslett points out that someone did bid $100,000 but that the reserve on the horse was $125,000.

John Hall has caught up with them at Eagle Creek. He came out the winner in the golf game earlier this week, and when he sees Sam Pollock, he grins and pats his pocket. "Want to ride with me, Sammy, and visit your money?" he asks.

Sammy believes that he will.

At Eagle Creek B, the Dirty Rush filly by Medaglia d'Oro is already out for everyone to see. "She's just gonna be little," Frank says, offering his only criticism. She's well-bred but small; they think she'll do okay selling in the second week, where her pedigree will make her a big fish in a small pond. Jo thinks she'll bring around $20,000. Jeff thinks she won't go over $50,000. Looking at the small but well-built filly, Sam says, "Let's just race it, Frank."

But Frank is sticking to the plan, and the filly heads back into the barn.

It's a hundred degrees by the time they pull up in front of Yearling Complex C. A late-summer drought has made the grass crispy, and it crackles like a dry cough in the hot wind blowing through it.

Frank retrieves a couple of white plastic chairs from the office and places them under the tree, whose rattling leaves offer what little shade there is. Sam folds up his long body and sits down, Jo behind him, as the grooms bring out the first filly, out of Distant Roar and by Unbridled's Song. "Oh my goodness," Sam says when he sees the substantial filly. "Here's a different story."

After her comes Marina de Chavon's Indian Charlie filly and then Queen's 2009 filly by Street Cry. Waiting for the grooms to bring her out, Frank dials a trainer he knows who already has a colt by Marina de Chavon to let him know that they've got an Indian Charlie by the same mare. He slides the phone back onto his hip and stares at the gray filly set up in front of him.

"God, I can't believe how good her front end came out."

When Mario turns the filly to walk her, she lets her neck stretch all the way out before she gets enough energy to lift up her feet and walk.

"I think everything out of this mare is lazy as hell," Frank adds.

Jeff Hayslett opens with his appraisal. "Buck and a quarter."

Golden Temper, Maddie's Charm, Chartreuse—the rest of the Pollock's yearlings march out one by one. Despite the heat, they give them a thorough appraisal, and thank Mario for his skillful handling.

Whatever the dry, hot weather has done to the grass has made it very appealing to butterflies; the bluegrass is overrun with them this summer—Swallowtails with their long black stockings trailing behind them, pale yellow Cabbage Whites, Viceroys and Monarchs, velvety and vibrant Red Admirals. In the high, sunny window of Eagle Creek A, two giant yellow Swallowtails sit in the corner of the pane as Frank begins yet another round of evaluations. The woman whose husband just loaded up their property with sixty racehorses is with him again.

There are two new colts in Eagle Creek A, shipped in from a breeder who wants to consign them with Taylor Made. They're a mess—small and sun-bleached, coats full of burrs, feet cracked and uneven. Shaking his head, Frank says, "These people have absolutely no clue. Didn't feed 'em. Didn't take care of 'em." He tells Cesar to go ahead and worm all of them.

Watching the walk of a colt by Master Command, Frank says, "We can't make them any worse. That's for sure."

"Get a gallon of mineral oil," he tells Cesar. "And just soak them in it."

He points out that the colt is a half brother to two stakes winners.

A Da Lovely colt by Any Given Saturday comes out. He's been on the farm since birth, and Frank's guest points out that he looks much better. "Honestly," Frank says to her. "This horse isn't near as good as that horse." He points to the small and half-wild colt with the dried-out, cracked hoofs, who's got a date with a gallon of mineral oil.

In Eagle Creek B, the grooms pull out a filly by Unbridled's Song and Frank begins her evaluation exactly the same way he's begun it since last year. "The stud fee still isn't paid on this one," he tells everyone. That unpaid fee has been the lens through which he's seen this horse for its entire life.

The filly is walking with her body curved away from the groom, and Frank wants to know if she's been shanked—her ribs smacked with the end of the lead to get her to move forward. "That's an absolute no-no," he tells his visitor. "You see it all the time. It works once or twice," he says, but then you end up with a horse that won't get close to its handlers.

Ryan Mahan, head auctioneer and part of the inspection team for Keeneland, says he can always tell if a groom has worked for Taylor Made, because they all walk the horses in the same way. Three pats on the shoulder to alert the horse that they're going to walk, and then a walk. Noelle, who has already been training show jumpers in Ireland, was also impressed with the discipline and consistency of how they handle horses at Taylor Made. Once they signal a yearling to stop, they get only three steps—one for the signal, the second to slow down, and the third to end up squarely over their hooves. Taylor Made was one of the first farms to embrace the natural horsemanship techniques popularized by horsemen like Monty Roberts, and the way the yearlings are handled there has evolved from those techniques.

Frank, John Hall, and Cesar love the walk on the Grand Slam colt. He gets a B++. When Folklore's chestnut colt comes out of his stall, the men agree that he's one of the best on the farm. He's not very big, but Frank believes he's balanced. A touch soft in his pasterns, perhaps, but according to Frank, "this colt looks like a runner." Frank moves in to examine some wavy hairs over the colt's pasterns. Little irregularities in hair growth could be an indication that there is scar tissue forming. But there's nothing there, just some wavy hair. Frank, who gives him an A–, thinks he'll bring $500,000, maybe even $1 million.

"It's not how many you get," he tells his visitor. "It's how many good ones. Horses are assets that eat."

Flying Glitter, Miss Speed, Halo Tyra, Sleepytime—Frank runs through them, pausing at Alidiva's Giant's Causeway filly.

"I'm starting to like her a lot," Frank says. She's put on weight since her last evaluation, and has settled down in her stall, is less fretful. She's grown into her head and gotten strong through her hip and loin. The screw in her knee has straightened out the leg.

"That's the most improved horse on the farm," Frank says.

Officiate gets an A–. Joy Valley is one of Cesar's favorites. Neither Angela's Love nor Glenarcy look particularly promising. Glenarcy's filly by Master Command is just too big. She's got a plain head, Frank says, though a decent neck. He likes her heart girth, though she's back at the knee—one of the more serious conformation flaws. She's a little weak through the hocks and the best he can hope for her is that someone will buy her, break her, then let her spend another year in the paddock growing into her body. She gets a B–.

At C barn, Collect Call '09 comes out of his stall. "This horse will be in the Kentucky Derby," Frank says. "You wait and see. He's a racehorse."

🐎

The sales meeting is next, and everyone spins off, getting last-minute phone calls made before they gather in the conference room. The agenda has seventeen items, with an additional fifteen subitems, somewhat inconsistently divvied up among bullet points, numbered points, and boldface lists, indicating either that someone cut and pasted bits and pieces of other people's lists or was indecisive about how to format the outline.

Today, they need to figure out where all the signs are, who's hanging them, and where the ring stakes are that will divide the long rows between the sheds into four separate "rings." They need to staff the welcome center and concierge positions. Horses they've picked up for the consignment are being shipped in and need a place to stay, and they'll need room for the RNAs after the sale. They have to coordinate release forms, repository X-rays, and get the vet to assign grades.

The team pauses and looks around.

"I believe in full disclosure," Duncan reminds the team. Duplicates of the reports on the horses X-rays will be available in a bulky ring binder for interested buyers to see, but the problem is either that people don't know what they're looking at or they know just enough to get themselves into trouble. Tom Hamm points out that in his experience, buyers look at the vet reports and then ask him what *he* thinks they mean. All agree that not *everyone* on the nearly two-hundred-person sales staff needs to be pawing over the vet book. Perhaps the book is better off in the hands of people who know less. Staff members, who know enough to interpret the reports, are going to get pushed into doing so by an aggressive buyer. They agree that they will share the information, but the binder will stay in the office, shared when requested, and only by certain staff, those who know to show the reports, but leave the interpreting to the buyers and their vets.

Paperwork will be handled in the office, as will the schedule. Jimmy will be sure to deliver enough tables and chairs for the front-man meetings.

They've assigned two days, a week apart, for on-farm appraisals prior to the sale. Off-farm appraisals will be handled by account managers. The research department will handle what's on the front-man cards. They'll have a client room, hang pots of flowers, make sure everyone on the crew gets a Taylor Made tie.

The room is packed. The members of the research department, who show up late, have to squeeze into the chairs by the door.

The horses are batched according to their catalog, or "book." Keeneland is trying out a new format this year: Book 1 will be a "true" select sale. The offerings will be slim, with just over four hundred horses, and they will be the best of the sale and the sales company will auction them off at night—an attempt to create a sense of glamour and drama akin to that at Saratoga.

The batched horses are then assigned to one of nine separate barns. Barns 3 and 4 are northeast, and downhill from the pavilion, and the other seven barns are clustered more closely together, uphill and northwest of the pavilion. There are a total of forty-nine barns on the grounds, and for the September sale, Keeneland has cataloged more than 4,800 yearlings. Once the horses are sold, they will ship out to their farms or training centers, and new horses will be shipped in. Tom has organized the crews taking care of the Taylor Made horses into "layouts." There are eleven in total, and each one has two to three controllers, between three and eight quad leaders; the balance of the staff, between 125 and 135 people, are grooms and showmen, roughly divided into a 2:1 ratio. Moving chronologically, any given barn will be busiest in the day or two before its horses go to sale. The day of the sale, once everyone has made their decisions, buyers will move on to the next barn and Tom will be able to shift people around—half-staffing the less busy barns so that the busier ones are fully staffed. His budget for this sale doesn't include the full-time employees who will be coming out from the farm. So far, he's under budget.

In 2006, at the height of the market, when everyone was less worried about money, the farm spent thirteen hundred dollars per head to bring a little over six hundred horses through the sale. Last year, Tom got the price per head down, and this year he hopes to be lower. He can't cut pay and hold on to his best staff, and if he doesn't give them the hours they want, he runs the risk of losing them to another barn, so instead, he's hiring fewer people, which means that everyone will have to double up on work: Sales staff will be mucking out stalls, quad leaders can show horses, and for the two days when the auction runs at night, staff members who work until the end of the day will get only an additional twenty dollars added to their day's pay.

Every layout has a full cohort of office equipment—computers, printers, swipe cards, card stock for printing out daily updates, plasma TVs, handheld DVD players (for showing off the horses' relatives)—as well as office staff to manage the database, advertising, and payroll. Saratoga was a bivouac and Keeneland is an occupation, and the sale is approaching like a distant storm, getting louder and more ominous and more exciting as it draws closer.

In an early-morning fog, Cesar is driving the grooms from barn to barn to bring in the horses. The fog is thick over the paddocks, and the grooms disappear in it as they hunt down the horses. They whistle to the horses, who snort in response, their hooves pounding over the damp grass as they run away from the grooms. Noelle appears first as a shadow in the mist, a filly leaping and bounding at the end of the shank as Noelle throws her weight against it, stepping along in big leaps as she tries to anchor the filly.

"Two hundred." Cesar is looking out over the paddock where his grooms have just disappeared, trying to catch the horses who don't want to come in. "There're only two, but it feels like two hundred," he says.

The horses who've just been shipped in don't know the routine and don't want to be caught.

"Ho, papa. Ho, papa!" Danny calls to them from the fence line.

Two colts are cantering toward the gate. Cesar throws it wide open and stands back, inviting the colts to canter out of the paddock and follow their buddies into the barn, where their food is waiting for them.

The colts decline, disappearing again into the fog.

The five grooms who've been chasing them swish back through the wet grass. They chase the horses through the gate again, pushing them toward the barn, where Cesar and three other grooms have made a blockade of their bodies. The horses veer into the barn, where another line of grooms keep them from running out the other side. Their only out is into their stalls, where breakfast is waiting for them.

Across the lane at Eagle Creek B, the fillies have helpfully crowded up to the gate and are waiting their turn to come in. The colts, who get aggressive when they're left alone, come in first. Dominic pauses for Cesar to inspect the one he's holding, and young Joe gets dragged around the corner by another one. Cesar throws up his arms. "Hey!" he yells, stopping the horse in his tracks long enough for Joe to get his head down.

In a more ladylike fashion, the fillies step through the fog and wait patiently while Cesar checks their legs. In minutes, the barn's twenty-six horses are closed in their stalls, eating their grain. Once the horses are in, the grooms linger by the entrance while Cesar delivers the day's instructions in Spanish. The grooms who need to return to the other barns climb into the back of the truck. Noelle and Chilo stay behind to do chores.

"Hi, Tom Tom." Noelle leans over to pat the orange-and-white barn cat. "Want breakfast?"

10

Keeneland, September 2010

THE FINAL SHOWING DAY BEFORE THE START OF Keeneland's 2010 yearling sale is Saturday, September 11. Ryan Mahan, Keeneland's head auctioneer, remembers nine years ago, when the sale opened on the same day as the September 11 attacks. Keeneland officials gathered around the televisions and wondered how to respond. Cancel the sale? Delay it? In the end they decided to go ahead with it, although the opening session was delayed for a day. "We're selling an agricultural product," Mahan explains. It has been grown and prepared for sale on this day and during this week. If they'd been selling wheat or produce or cattle, they wouldn't have been able to delay the sale, and they couldn't delay the auction of racehorses, either. Making it even harder was that there are strong ties between New York's financial community and Lexington's horse industry. People were selling horses as they were hoping to hear about friends and family in New York.

On this Saturday in 2010, everybody is here. The bivouacked staff of sales workers number about 170 by Tom Hamm's calculation. There's a two-person kitchen staff. Tom's wife is managing the supply room. There are two vet assistants—skilled horsemen who handle the yearlings for veterinary procedures. The farm's permanent employees are in for the duration—John Hall and Tom Hamm, as well as grooms Mario, Freddy, and Chilo. Sheri Pitzer is shooting photos. Patrick Mahan is prepping marketing materials. The IT people are keeping the database going. Iris, Cordell, Julie, Tammy, Jamie McKechnie, Lou Germany, Hollywood, and, of course, the Taylor brothers—Duncan, Ben, Frank, and Mark—are also here. For Dominic and Noelle, the first week of the sale will be their last as Taylor Made interns. Dominic will be heading back to school, and Noelle, once she finishes out the semester, will go back to what she was doing before Taylor Made, training and riding show jumpers and finishing school. She's had enough of being a groom.

Everyone is wearing their light blue shirts, khaki pants, and burgundy ties.

Barns 3 and 4 house the "select" horses for Book 1. It's a long walk from the pavilion, and a little dip down from the next-door consignment, Lane's End. On this final Saturday before the sale begins, buyers are rolling down the hill like ants. It's a perfect fall day, warm, the skies bright blue. The buyers come, catalogs in hand, sometimes alone and sometimes trailing a posse. They walk brightly, or trudge, depending on how they feel about all this shopping.

Taylor Made is ready. The burgundy-and-gray valances are up, as are the new posters. Plants have been hung and watered, and the table with cold iced tea and tasty cookies has been set out.

Wise to the ways of the Taylors and not wanting to show their hands, not all the buyers are willing to give their names at the welcome desk. "They give aliases now," Ben Taylor says, smiling. Others willingly sign up for the frequent customer card and enter the giveaway for a free steak dinner at Malone's, the favored watering hole for industry types.

It's the end of a long day, and the grooms have already been showing the horses for three days. Footsore, they lean against the walls or rest in the few chairs that are available. Alidiva '09 comes out of her stall for a bit of grazing. In the first book, she is hip number nine. She's just been pawing her straw and is agitated, a bit of sweat on her flanks—an early sign of colic—and she's being walked around a bit until Bart Barber arrives. The air and the grass seem to help her, and she relaxes, returning to her stall after a stroll. Quad leader Jamie McKechnie thinks that maybe all she needed was a little something to do. "The idle mind can be the devil's runabout," he says.

The grooms wander over to the welcome desk for the end-of-the-day meeting. They've loosened their ties and are smoking. Tom Hamm tells them they'll start at 5:30 A.M. tomorrow. The auction starts at 7:00 P.M. tomorrow and most of them will work until 11:00 P.M., he warns them. He suggests a change of clothes for the grooms and showmen going to the ring.

"Check your schedule, the layout," says Tom. "We'll have food in the afternoon. Hopefully, you like pizza." The Book 2 horses will be arriving at barns 33 and 34 tomorrow and half the team will be sent up there at midday to get set up. "If I don't see you when they're done shipping in," he warns them, "it'll be a half day's pay."

The grooms depart and the brothers arrive and check in with Tom about Alidiva '09 as everyone gathers outside her stall. Bart Barber arrives with his wife, who's working as his vet tech today. Dean Proefrock, one of the two vet meds, stands by, twitch in hand, while Bart checks the filly's gums, listens to her heart rate, and gives her a once-over exam. He thinks she's okay and gives her a shot of Banamine. The horses also get a small dose of the sedative with their food, along with electrolytes to protect them from stress and dehydration. "I take Advil and they take Banamine," Frank jokes. Laughing, he adds, "And a fifth of vodka at night."

The Taylors are all heading home for the night. They used to party more than they do now; as Frank jokes, "I'm maturing."

🐎

Sunday, September 12, the first day of the Keeneland yearling sale is bright and warm. In a walk that they have practiced all their lives, the horses at barns 3 and 4 are led up and down, up and down, for the buyers.

The buyers are full of purpose as they march up to the desk. There are thousands of horses to look at, and the sale is just starting. In the middle of the grassy median, Kiaran McLaughlin, who trains horses for Shadwell Farms, which is owned by Sheikh Hamdan bin Rashid Al

Maktoum, brother of Sheikh Mohammed, the ruler of Dubai, watches a colt walk. The Shadwell retinue faces him from the other side of the crushed-stone walkway. They are young men, neatly barbered and wearing well-fitted polo shirts, pressed jeans, and mirrored shades. They, in turn, are trailed by the burly white guys who are the sheikh's bodyguards.

A buyer flags down one of the showmen and wants to know if an Unbridled's Song filly has been scoped. The showman freezes: He doesn't know; doesn't know if he's supposed to know; or if he did know, whether he should say. He tracks down Tammy Frasier, quad leader and thirteen-year veteran, and she, in turn, summons Dean Proefrock. There's a book with that information in it, and just as they're wondering aloud where that book is (and the buyer is wondering why the consternation over what seemed like a simple question), Frank Taylor strides onto the scene with a thick binder in his hand.

John Tinsky, one of what Ben Taylor estimates to be about 125 Taylor cousins, is assigned to Collect Call's racy-looking and high-spirited colt. He's out on the row now with nine other horses. Most of the Book 1 horses have designated handlers, especially ones like Collect Call '09. He marches and poses, marches and poses, and then, annoyed with all this going in circles, stops, rears, and scrambles backward. Hanging on to the lead shank, Tingsley politely apologizes to a group of buyers as the horse drags him by. With a growl and a snap, he gets Collect Call back in hand. The colt drops his head, peeks out from under his forelock, and flicks his ears left to right, chastened. On the walk back, he plugs along mulishly, embarrassed and resentful.

Cot Campbell is here, as is Debbie Easter. Todd Pletcher and Nick Zito will drop by, as will John Ferguson on behalf of Sheikh Mohammed, who will end up skipping the sale this year. Demi O'Byrne and the Coolmore crowd have already been by. Charlie Gordon-Watson, a British bloodstock agent, has stopped by more than once. And later, the white-haired and charming Bob Baffert will motor in with his bowlegged walk.

A few dozen buyers are strung out all up and down the shed row, and a dozen horses are out of their stalls, walking, posing, or waiting their turns. The grooms are cajoling, clucking, snapping lead shanks, growling. At the edge of her ring, Queen '09, who's been standing quietly, drops her head and bucks, her hind hooves snapping out like whips and skimming the air a foot away from Finn Green, who's looking down at his sales book. Everyone laughs, but the grooms converge on her, growling. "Watch her," one of them says. "If she's done it once, she'll do it again."

Unharmed, Finn grins.

In handling colts, you watch the front end—a male horse's natural defense is rearing and striking. With fillies, you watch the hind end, because they resort to bucking.

Alidiva '09 and Collect Call '09 are in and out, in and out. Folkore's chestnut colt is turning into one of the "hot" horses. Her and hip number 144, a filly by Smart Strike, are the two most looked-at horses in these barns.

Beverly Lewis and her son, Jeff, check in with Frank. They've got eight horses in this sale, four with the Taylors and four with Denali. Like his father, Jeff Lewis believes in spreading out the business, sharing both the risk and the rewards. Unlike the grooms, they like the evening format. They went to the welcome party last night, and are more than pleased to hear that their colt has had the most vet work so far.

"He looks as good as he can," Jeff says. He's got the balanced and compact body that promises speed—what Keeneland buyers are looking for. Fit, shiny, his walk loose and powerful, his head low, there is no evidence left of the abscess that could have ruined him. He's a little on the small side but is calm amid the chaos, exerting a certain authority, his ears flicking from side to side, as if it is his job to appraise these buyers.

Up the hill from the pavilion, in the distinctly less modern barns numbered 22 and 23, Mark and John's team is showing the first half of the horses in Book 2. Because Keeneland restricted Book 1 to the truly select horses this year, Book 2 now lists thirteen hundred horses. It has the heft of a small dictionary.

John has requisitioned the full-time help for his team. Mario is here, as are Chilo and Freddy, Noelle and Dominic, Danny and Marshall. They've pulled other Taylor Made employees away from their regular responsibilities, like administrative assistant Audra Tackett. Just west of these barns are barns 32, 33, and 34, which hold the second half of the horses from Book 2, and the first chunk of horses from Book 3. Within each layout, the horses are divided by gender: fillies in one section, colts in the other.

The place is packed, festive, and abuzz with a sense of urgency, best compared to a crowded restaurant in a busy and stylish city. The buyers waiting their turns are in the long line forming outside the velvet ropes. Some of the people in it are very, very rich, some also very, very important. Some would be considered rich in other company but are not considered rich here. Some have scrambled for years to come up with the cost of this dinner. And somewhere in the minds of all of them is the thought that this particular expenditure could culminate in the most amazing experience of a lifetime, one that is so rare that only one person in the whole world per year gets to experience it, but the experience is *guaranteed* to go to someone. Every year, someone wins the Kentucky Derby.

Inside, the barn seems like a normal high-quality restaurant. Everyone is uniformed, with subtle modifications that reflect differences in rank. But in this case, the "meal," or product, that everyone is ready to buy is a Thoroughbred racehorse.

Like a restaurant, the barn is divided into back of the house (stalls, grooms, quad leader, top-off station, vets, food, offices, break room) and front of the house (controller, show ring, salesmen, showmen, and customers). Once the order is placed, the product is triaged from the back of the house: The controller calls the hip number, the groom retrieves the horse, the quad leader and grooms dress, or plate, it, then hand it off to the showman to bring to the front of the house.

The most attractive staff are those who "serve" the horse to the customer—the showmen. They are skilled, neatly dressed, fit, and spiffier—their haircuts are stylish; they wink with a touch of glitter from earrings, a bracelet, a nice watch, or a fancy belt buckle. Some of them, usually the women, have modified their uniforms to show off long legs, a narrow waist, or slender arms. Like the best entourage, they are not so stylish that they detract from the star, but enough so that they confirm that beautiful people are that star's most appropriate company.

The front of the house (or quad) is sectioned off, and the staff assigned to each section is made clear only to the employees, though an observant customer could figure it out, and some often do, crowding around the manager, helpfully pointing out an empty space in an attempt to jump a line that is not quite orderly, or even visible. If they are sufficiently important, they will be allowed to do so.

At its busiest and most crowded (on the first day of the sale, that's barns 33 and 34—the decisions have already been made about the horses in barns 3 and 4), the barn is like a family-owned diner. Instead of clattering plates and the crash of silverware, there is the sound of whinnying, skittering hooves, the constant jingle of the Chifneys in the horses' mouths. Frantic to keep up with the crowds, staff members cross over the lines of their job descriptions. Salesmen call in orders that they've overheard—sometimes helpfully, sometimes not. Hip-number requests sometimes zip though the headsets, but often they just get shouted across the quad. A product goes missing—mistakenly served to a different customer who ordered the same thing—or arrives in the wrong order. On the receiving end, grooms respond to the next item they hear ordered, not necessarily the one intended for them.

Lead shanks snap; hooves skitter in the crushed stone. Voices shout "Watch it!" and "Whoa!" Horses whinny, kick, rear, and erupt, scattering the customers and clearing the way for members of the staff, who close in, pressing the horse into the groom holding the lead shank—the fail-safe, the last person between a minor scuffle and a major catastrophe: a panicked adolescent member of the world's fastest, strongest, most excitable, and, pound for pound, most valuable species on the planet, running loose and wild.

For the customer, the experience is not nearly so hectic—the chaos under the surface, a steady hum behind the amiable greeting and chit-chat. Handshakes are exchanged all around, which the English and Irish grooms hate. Why do they do that? All those viruses! Are Americans just not worried about disease? There are friends with whom to catch up, rivals to reassess: Who's gotten fat, or thin, or divorced? Who's lost a farm, trading a lifetime of sole proprietorship for the steady paycheck of the corporate employee? Who's been visited by tragedy? Who's grieving? They are gathered together for the yearly cash throwdown, the biggest gamble for, essentially, professional gamblers, and they're horsemen to boot, busting at the seams with stories:

half-truths involving cars, planes, horses, children, brothers, sometimes sisters, more horses, spouses and others, golf matches, booze, sex, and "Oh my God! Did you hear she left the photos on the bar?" Horses, horses, and always, a little bet, just pocket change, an over-under on the side.

There is much for Frank to be worried about at this sale. Those stud fees are hanging over his head as he meets to set the reserves on the horses going on opening nights. Distorted Humor, the sire of Folklore's colt, has dropped from the $300,000 the Lewises paid in 2008 to $100,000 in 2010. The sire of Collect Call's racy bay colt commanded $100,000 when he was bred in 2008 and now the asking price is just $50,000. Giant's Causeway, the sire of Alidiva's chestnut filly, has slipped to just $25,000, and the sire of Queen's pudgy gray filly has actually had his fee increased, from $100,000 to $150,000.

But those horses are the best of Taylor Made's consignment; that's why they're going in Book 1. But even those stallions who were the best of the bunch in 2008 have dropped in value: A.P. Indy, who was once second only to Storm Cat, has dropped from $300,000 to $150,000. Ghostzapper has gone down to $30,000 from $125,000. Mr. Greeley has dropped from $125,000 to $50,000. And, probably the most discouraging, Taylor Made's own stallion, Forestry, has dropped from $100,000 in 2008 to a mere $17,500 for 2010.

It's a long and painful correction, because there are two long years between when the horses are bred and when they are sold, and another one to two years before they start racing and really establish their value. Rod and Lorraine Rodriguez, who own Collect Call, are happy to race their horses if they don't get the price they're looking for. Last year, they kept their Ghostzapper colt. The Pollocks also race, but they are not interested in adding to their racing stable now. And Jeff Lewis is very clear: They race fillies and keep the best for breeding; the colts have to go.

Alidiva and the other horses owned by Charles Wacker were left in shares to his employees, and these shares represent their retirement funds.

The Taylors are operating as leanly as possible right now. They haven't had to lay off, but they haven't replaced staff members who've left; instead, they've off-loaded their work onto others, and they've cut hours. Because the Taylors pay in cash for their real estate, they carry no debt, which puts them in a much stronger position than that of most of their peers. But they still feel the burden of those employees who support their families on their Taylor Made paychecks and who would have a hard time, in this economy, finding other work. Some of the staff members grumbled about the decision to cut hours rather than lay off, but the Taylors are trying to do the most for the greatest number of people. "They have very Christian values," says Jeff Lewis. "And they live by those." He adds, "I mean that in a good way."

But even those still in the game are not necessarily paying their bills. "Some are; some aren't," Mark Taylor says, shrugging. When board bills aren't paid, you can't stop feeding the horses. When the year's income is going to come from the sale of a couple of yearlings, you can't stop prepping them for sale because the owners aren't paying their bills. If a stud fee isn't paid, the only way to get it back is to sell the foal. The liens on the horses coming through Keeneland right now, says Ben Taylor, mean that settling up on overdue accounts "is a nightmare."

When the yearling prices drop, he says, everyone yells at the stallion syndicates, but the current market was created by everyone in it. "Everybody's greedy. Everybody's breeding horses they shouldn't be breeding," says Ben. "Now there're way too many horses."

By his reckoning, the current situation is a result of not only the hormone and ultrasound technology that reduced the number of times a mare had to be covered before she got pregnant but also of the business practices of the wealthiest farms. When Coolmore started booking two hundred mares per season, it put pressure on everyone else to keep up. Stallion owners like Sheikh Mohammed would offer discounts on their top-priced stallions to mare owners who were willing to send three or four of their nice mares to their lesser stallions— keeping the books full and hopefully producing some nice yearlings, who would boost the value of those stallions. As long as the prices were going up, owners could make enough money on one or two horses— perhaps by selling them to Coolmore or Sheikh Mohammed—to justify the losses on the others. The owner, says Ben, "only needed to get lucky with one of them. Five million to make forty million," he says, for a colt who became a successful breeding stallion. Shrugging and smiling, he adds, "That's the colt's game."

There are fourteen Taylor children just among the four brothers who run the business, and five more from the sisters who aren't in the business. "We got more generations. If there is anyone who wants to be in the business, should they be in it? The dynamics aren't too good."

In the sales pavilion, the staff is busy with finishing touches before the 7:00 P.M. sale. The lunch room is busy, but the arena is dark, a single employee checking tags for the reserved seats, though not many people spend much time in their reserved seats. Under the bulletin board where the results are posted in hard copy as the sale takes place, a woman in a Keeneland polo shirt sits on the floor with brass polish, buffing up the foot rail.

Before the horses left the farm, the team compared the final assessments. Collect Call's, says Mark, "was all over the place." He claims that he put in the lowest assessment, at around $400,000 to $500,000. Frank's, he says, was something like $1.3 million. Adopting the deeper voice and frown of his older brother, Mark imitates him. "'This is the best son of a bitch on the farm! He's going to win the Derby!'"

Alidiva's, he says, was around $700,000 and Queen's just at a $150,000. All three of these horses will go tonight.

By 2:00 P.M., barns 3 and 4 have slowed down to a steady but manageable clip—just the buyers who want one more look before tonight. For better or worse, the decisions about the Book 1 horses have been made.

Tammy Frasier, who's worked the sales for Taylor Made for the past thirteen years, is the controller for these barns. A big woman, she wears her curly blond hair clipped back, is rarely separated from her dark glasses, and has a laugh that comes up from so deep in her belly that she has to stop what she's doing, put her hands on her hips, and throw her head back to keep from being knocked over by it. When she's not working the sales, she's a barn foreman for Steve Asmussen when he races at Keeneland. Like most of the people here, she's not the first generation of her family to make her living in the business.

Right now, she's yelling at one of the salesmen through her headset. On the other side of the quad, he's leaning against the wall, chatting.

Tammy marches across the quad, yelling at him to turn up his damn radio. He yells back that it is up—he just can't hear her. Her hand flies to her hip and she lets out a raspy guffaw. "That's because my radio is off!"

Apologizing, she heads back to her side of the quad.

In the dead spots between rushes, there's not much for the grooms to do. They hose the walkways to keep the dust down. They rake the stone in the aisles and in the quad. They smoke and flip through the sales book, shifting their weight from foot to foot because there are not enough chairs for them to sit down all at once, and they're not allowed to sit on the walls. They squat down, rolling their shoulders forward to stretch out their sore backs.

Two women, Missy Robertson and Suzanne Johnson, have been sitting on Taylor Made's benches all day, shifting their positions as the sun moves across the sky so that it's not in their faces. They are the proprietors of Copper Cap Farm and have just eight horses. Missy Robertson works as a salesperson for a book distributor and they have a third partner who does all the farm chores. "It's a miracle," they joke, that a farm as small as theirs has a horse in Book 1.

Not small, Suzanne corrects, "boutique." Both women roll into giggles again. They've been doing it all day.

Initially, says Missy, she was a little worried about consigning with Taylor Made because they're so huge. But she needed someone to help her sell the horse, and she likes the Taylors. There's nowhere else in the world she'd rather be, says Missy, than watching these horses walk up and down all day long.

The staff has taken notice of them and pop over from time to time to see if the women would like a cookie or some freshened-up iced tea. But they mostly leave them to sit. Like everything else in the business, the sales are a family affair. A visitor whom Duncan knows arrives with his young children, and Duncan takes their hands and escorts them to the cookie tray. How's school? he asks. How's their uncle, the priest? He sends them on their way with a cheerful reminder to go to confession. Everything will be right if you go to confession.

Most of the people working in barns 3 and 4 are what Mark calls the "A Team" and have worked together for over a decade. One of the surprises of Saratoga, says Noelle, was seeing what really good friends they all are. They come together and work side by side, exhausted, in bad weather and good. They've seen one another and worked with one another when they were exhausted and crabby, or energetic, or lazy. They've had bad attitudes and can-do ones. These are the people, guaranteed, that Tom Hamm will provide work for from the first to the last day of the sale because he's too afraid to lose them to someone else. "Some might complain about Lou Germany"—he singles out a groom with a wicked tongue—"but he's there when you need him, and he works." Their faces are sunburned and worn—some bear the wear of too much smoking, or too much drinking, or too much bad luck. Some, like Iris, have only ever worked the sales. Others, like Lou Germany and Jamie McKechnie, have landed here after careers as exercise riders. Some, like Cordell, are celebrities in their own right. They travel from sale to sale, country to country, setting up a base in Lexington and calling the bluegrass home.

For now, early in the sale, they're not yet frazzled and are cautious and courteous with one another. They ask for one another's help, call one another "baby" and "love." They squish together, hip-to-hip, on top of a cooler, and it is the privilege of the older men to provide the shoulder on which the young girls, exhausted by the work and newness of the experience, can lay their pretty heads and close their eyes, just for a moment, for a little rest.

Finn Green thinks his final number for Collect Call was $874,000. The horse, he says, is a little straight in the pasterns and a little over at the knee, but neither of those flaws bother him. It was at this auction in 2005 that Finn first spotted Zenyatta and, he says, "fell in love." She was hip number 703, a Street Cry filly out of Vertigineaux, and was well out of the Book 1 select sale. When she walked for him in front of barn 28, she was big and gangly, but—he cups his hand to demonstrate— she had huge bone and substance.

Finn is an emotional man, and he stands square-shouldered, a half smile on his face, as he delivers this piece of information and waits for it to sink in with his listener. Every time he hears about the mare, which in the business is at least a dozen times a day, every morning when he wakes up, there it is. He was one of just two people to see the value in the filly—she only had two bidders. But he had only fifty thousand dollars to spend. He went over that by seven thousand dollars, worried about what his wife was going to say, but then dropped out, letting Jerry Moss get the filly for sixty thousand. The sting of that is alleviated somewhat because he heard that Moss was willing to go to $200,000—way more than Finn could pay. But he still sees it as a lost opportunity to have been the owner of one of the greatest race fillies of all time. Instead, his eyes damp, he accepts his lot with cheerful resolve, grateful that even after his setbacks, he was able to move into the shelter of a commercial farm, one that leaves Derby dreaming to its clients.

Finn thinks that Queen might be the surprise of the sale. This morning, he says, Shadwell wanted to see her, and just as they were pulling her out, the Coolmore vets arrived. Finn made the call to show the filly to Shadwell, forcing the vets to cool their heels. "The Irish haven't been spending much money around here lately," Finn jokes. The Arabs, on the other hand, have.

Sam Pollock has arrived, taking a seat on the bench next to the welcome center desk. During the sales, he spends his afternoons watching the action on his horses. Jo has stayed home for the showing, but will come to watch the sale tonight. In between showing and sale, he may try to squeeze in a few holes of golf. Sam loves his filly's walk. She overreaches by eighteen inches and he thinks she's got the best walk of any horse here. What the buyers aren't going to like about her, he suspects, is that she's European-bred—meaning more stamina, less speed.

"We loved the mother," he says. They thought they'd be able to do a European/American-bred—best of both worlds—but given what her first foal looked like, they decided to go all out for a European model on the second.

As Sam's watching the buyers watch his horse, Frank appears and murmurs to him that he has an "outside chance," because he's got the ingredients for a perfecta—both Coolmore and the Arabs are interested in the horse.

As Frank recalls, his assessment on Collect Call was $1 million and it was Mark's that was $1.3 million. Finn also remembers $1.3 million as the top number, but he can't recall if it was Frank or Mark who made the claim. "It's not going to happen," says Frank. In fact, it won't even be close. A lot of people have looked at the colt, but he's not getting vetted, at least not by the right people. Those conformation flaws that don't bother Finn bother the buyers enough that they're not following up with scopes.

Queen walks for a buyer and Frank sidles up to Sam, who has stood up to watch. "I can't believe we fixed them knees," he says, barely able to keep it under his breath. Shrugging, he adds, "She might be the surprise of the sale."

Rod and Lorraine Rodriguez have shown up to talk to Frank about the reserve for Collect Call. Frank opens his notebook and smoothes out the printout, which reveals that even though the colt has been one of the most looked at in the barn, he's only been scoped once. That means that the buyers have seen something on the X-rays in the repository that they don't like, and Frank suspects it's the minor sesamoiditis in the horse's ankles. The farm's vet didn't think it was a problem, and in the past, horses with the condition have sold well, but in this market, it means he's a smidge less perfect. The Rodriguezes glance at each other over the book. Trim and attractive, they visited their mare at the farm this morning and saw her with her 2010 Curlin foal. Rod, a New Yorker who relocated to California, has his head bent over Frank's notebook. Graying, well-groomed, his slacks pressed, he doesn't allow his look to give anything away. Lorraine, her dark hair bobbed, is wearing jeans and a crisp white shirt. She says that she leaves the setting of the RNA to Rod. Frank is shaking his head. Only one scope means only one bidder. He looks at his watch—the day's not over yet; a vet could still arrive to look at the colt, but he's not hopeful.

Overhearing Frank as he walks up behind him, Duncan says, "There's a vet with him now."

"What?" Frank spins around.

"He's being scoped now."

Riding that wave from gloom to glory, Frank's face breaks into an ear-to-ear grin. He looks at Rod and Lorraine as if they've already made a million dollars. "Well, there's hope," he says, bursting into a deep and extended cackle. His excitement is almost more than he can stand, and he walks back and forth in front of the wall, still laughing, notebook in hand. Duncan smiles serenely; he and Mark cling to the middle road, leaving the lows to Ben and the up-and-down ride between the lows and the highs to Frank.

"That changes everything," Frank says to them. He points to the data in the far right column on his chart. It's labeled "Associates" and under it is a list of all the known associates of the vet who has just asked to see the horse. It's a long list, and it's the A list. The Rodriguezes look a little bemused, as if they're not sure how to respond to the news that their million-dollar colt went from a million to nothing and back up to a million in the course of ten minutes. They stand at the same height, and their heads line up next to each other as they look over Frank's list. Lorraine steps away to let Rod, who, like Sam Pollock, started his fortune in car dealerships, set the reserve. "He's the salesman," she says.

This year, Sherry, the groom who handles the top-off, is wearing a T-shirt that reads, I'M NOT OPINIONATED. I'M RIGHT. By the time Alidiva's 2009 filly by Giant's Causeway comes under Sherry's hands, her reserve has been set at $349,000. Finishing up, Sherry lays down the filly's mane with the brush, flattens the hairs in a whorl on her crest one at a time. Her white stockings have already been powdered, and Sherry is using some VO5 at the edge of the marking, both to keep the powder from creeping up her calf and to increase the contrast between her chestnut coat and her white stockings.

A showman named Dennis is walking her to the ring; his follower is Juan. The filly is apprehensive on the long walk up to the pavilion, venturing out into a part of the world she's never seen before, her herd mates left behind. She is startled by imaginary dangers, her shoes skitter, stopping on the pavement, her body arced away, while her nose, still curious, curves toward whatever scared her. She snorts and spooks at a rubber mat laid over some electrical cords. Juan shakes his head. "They all spook at that," he says.

Duncan has already started shaking hands all around. Well-wishers crowd around him. Audra Tackett, who's clocked out for the day and is drinking a beer at ringside with Noelle, watches him move through the crowd. "He's a quick little booger," she says.

Alidiva's filly is in the outer walking rings. The horses enter at the middle of a figure eight and turn right, walking clockwise around the top loop. As their turn gets closer, they move to the bottom loop and walk up and down on one side, pausing from time to time for people to look, the buyers perhaps making a last-minute decision about how high they're willing to bid. There the horses are moved up a short ramp to a small walking ring inside the barn, where they move counter-clockwise.

It's hot in the walking rings, and even though part of the rationale for moving the sale to the evening was to bring back some of its glamour—the kind that you see in Saratoga—most everyone is dressed no differently from the way they were during the day. There are some high-heeled women and some jacketed and dissipated sons of the ruling class, but since they're not the buyers, they don't matter. The Taylors have thrown on their navy blazers, and Finn looks sharp in a houndstooth jacket in subtle olive tones, his matching slacks pressed and creased.

The Taylors and their associates line up as Alidiva's filly enters the ring. They are just behind the T intersection, through which almost everyone on the grounds will pass at some point this evening, their eyes locked on the big screen. Her pedigree is read out as she enters the auction ring through the big sliding door, and the auctioneer starts by asking for $500,000 and cascades downward rhythmically before the first bid—$25,000—goes up on the board.

The bids increase from $50,000 to $75,000 to $100,000. Her price quickly goes up, bidding active: $125,000, $200,000, $225,000, $250,000, $275,000. She hits $300,000, then $350,000—her reserve—and hangs.

When he's rolling out his chant, Ryan Mahan says, his main job is to let a bidder know that his archrival is bidding against him, but that only works when he's got archrivals in the game. And he works in tandem with the bid spotters like Bo Black. Bo first met Mahan when the two of them were in the fourth grade. By high school, Black says, Mahan knew he wanted to be an auctioneer. He played Bo a tape of an auctioneer and told him, "This is what I'm gonna do." Mahan started with country auctions, dragging Bo along with him, where Bo would hold up the stuff for Mahan to sell. "I'd listen to him chant," Bo says, "and he got me started." Bo started out at Fasig-Tipton, but he works exclusively for Keeneland now. Nobody, he says, works for both Fasig and Keeneland.

Bo says that the bid spotters don't know what the reserves are, but he can generally tell what they're worth by who sits in his section, and he can often tell by their body language when they're going to bid. All of a sudden, he smiles and imitates the buyers. After looking around disinterestedly, they sit up, square their shoulders, and though they're trying not to look any different, he can tell they're alert. Some buyers give him advance warning by telling them whom they want to bid on—a practice recommended by Keeneland. Others settle on a signal, though that's not always useful. In one often-retold story, D. Wayne Lukas almost lost out on a horse because he told the bid spotter to keep him in as long as he had his pen in his mouth; then a kid approached him for an autograph. The buyers don't want people to know they're bidding, though the savvy watchers can usually figure it out.

As the bidding on Alidiva's filly hangs at $350,000, Mahan's assistant auctioneer reads out the accomplishments of her nearest relatives, but there are no more offers, and Mahan calls out, "Sold!" The filly has been bought by British bloodstock agent C. Gordon-Watson.

How the Taylors feel about the price is impossible to tell by looking at them. At the intersection between the walking rings and the arena, they quickly take notes in their binders, and then they break up like a flash mob—every member of the team heading in a different direction. Duncan is off to the sales office, and the others head out back to where the next horses to go are in the walking rings. They've got maybe twenty minutes before their next horse, hip number twenty-seven, Collect Call '09.

The Taylors reappear just before their next horse heads into the ring. Clustered at the intersection, the brothers lean in to talk in one another's ears. Jeff Hayslett, Jacob, and a few salesmen are here. Finn Green is off somewhere, but Mark Brooking is here.

Collect Call '09 enters the ring, goes on the board at fifty thousand, and moves up erratically. His reserve is just $84,000. His owner, says Mark, works intuitively and is going to bump the bids from his seat in the pavilion when he sees what the action is like. The bids increase: $70,000, $140,000, $160,000, $170,000. And then there's a big jump to $225,000. Then it's $250,000, $275,000, then $300,000, where the bidding hangs. Last year, this colt's half brother was an early favorite for the Derby. In the auction ring, Bo holds up three fingers—his pinkie, ring, and middle fingers—wiggling them beguilingly, as if they're worms and the bidders are fish he's trying to trick into biting. The bid spotters call into the crowd, nudging, nagging, their eyes scanning for a nod, a touch to someone's glasses, a specific kind of scratch. Silence.

Three hundred thousand. Sold.

Folkore's little powerhouse of a colt is hip number thirty-eight. He doesn't want to go in the ring. The huge door slides open, but no horse appears. It's strangely silent as the auctioneer waits. The grooms turn him around and back him in, tricking him. In the auction ring, he's handed off to Cordell, who's swapped his Taylor Made tie for his blue Keeneland blazer.

Bidding on the colt races up to $400,000 and then hangs. The bid spotters' calls are a chorus, trying to drive up one more, one more, one more. The colt whinnies and stands square, his four white socks gleaming. Watching, Jeff Lewis is worried that the colt won't make his reserve of $425,000. But the bid comes in, quickly followed by one for $450,000. Mahan doesn't wait long. Sold.

Leaning forward in his seat, Jeff Lewis explains that they spent $318,000 (including taxes) on the stud fee for Distorted Humor—a hot stallion that year. They put between $20,000 and $25,000 into the colt, including the treatment for the abscess and subsequent infection. Jeff is pleased that they're not behind, but it's disappointing that this is all they've gotten out of a champion broodmare. And he's not sure that the bids in the room were all "live," because the bidding stopped suddenly at $425,000—just above the colt's reserve.

There isn't much time to wonder, because the sale has already moved on. Jeff Lewis and his mother move out of the pavilion. The Taylor brothers are focusing on the next sale. A Taylor Made groom hands off hip number forty to Cordell and they bump fists before the groom takes his place by the exit door.

Once they're done, the horses walk back to the stabling area in near darkness, their path illuminated only by the barn lights. Just outside the sale area, at the first barn that you have to cut through to get downhill, a barn worker looms up out of the darkness. Big, bald, the flesh on his skull drawn and tight, he doesn't wear any farm insignia, but he has a shovel and a muck bucket in his hands.

"It's not good. Not good," he intones, veering into the paths of people walking down to the barn, who shoot nervous looks around, as if they're hoping to spot Keeneland security people zooming up out of the darkness in their farm carts. "People are going to lose their farms!" he warns. "Gonna lose their jobs!" Like Marley's ghost, he stands at the divide between barn and auction area, between worker and buyer, the tools of his trade in hand, pouring out his warnings for anyone who's ready to listen,

Back in the stabling area, it's dark, quiet, and almost quitting time. The Copper Cap farm entry, hip number forty-two, sold for just $100,000. Missy is disappointed. "Someone got themselves a real bargain," she says. "He's a nice horse." Because she had partners on the horse, he sold without a reserve. She walked up to the ring with him and watched him sell. "I like to take my punishment head-on," she jokes. She's saying good night to the grooms, thanking them. She'll go back to work tomorrow. "I'm a salesman." She shrugs. At first light, she'll be back on the road.

The grooms sprawl over the plastic lawn chairs and in their stalls the horses nibble their hay. The Alidiva filly has tucked herself so far back in her stall that in the darkness, it looks like it's empty. She's tired, cranky, done. Her buyer will send someone to pick her up tomorrow.

The grooms have gathered around the welcome desk, waiting for the nightly meeting before they leave.

Lou Germany and Tom Hamm go back decades.

"Nineteen ninety-four, I finally pried him off," Tom jokes. "And I get here, and here he is."

"We worked for four dollars an hour today," Lou shoots back.

There are about fifteen grooms gathered around Tom. They've been working since 5:00 A.M., and they're being told they're expected back tomorrow at the same time. Worse, in addition to showing the horses in barns 3 and 4, half the team will be sent up to barns 32 and 33 to show horses in Book 2. "If you're in thirty-two, thirty-three," Tom explains, "you're going home at the start of the sale. Some of you—John, Leandro, Arturo—are coming back."

The grooms who work until ten o'clock will get an extra twenty dollars.

Tom apologizes to them for the computer problems encountered during the day, explaining that the new guy doing the computers was having trouble with the new system, though—and here he seems to be thinking out loud—if the guy is new and the system is new, then there shouldn't be any confusion about the difference between the old and the new system, but, anyway, it should be better tomorrow.

The grooms wander off. It's not quite time to go, because the last horse has not returned. The night watchman has started his shift and is topping off the water buckets. One of the grooms lets her body topple over on the bench. "We might as well stay here," she says. "We'll save an hour's drive."

The row of three barns, each with thirty-six stalls and a gap between, stretches out about a tenth of a mile against the edge of a now half-empty parking lot. Visible from a hill on the other side of the lot, the barn's lights bounce up into the trees, illuminating their still-green leaves from below. Faint stars prick the night sky and an orange crescent moon hangs low behind one pale brushstroke of clouds. The auction area is silent. The only sounds are those of the doors on the grooms' cars creaking open and their old engines and bad mufflers coughing and spitting into life as everyone heads home.

🐎

September 13, 2010, 9:30 A.M.

Monday is beautiful—clear blue skies. Morning temperatures are cool enough for everyone to stay comfortable while they do their chores and freshen up the horses. Everyone has their Taylor Made vests or jackets on over their blue shirts. Barns 3 and 4 are half-staffed today: The action has moved uphill to barns 32 and 33.

Striding speedily down the hill from the Lane's End consignment, streams of Japanese buyers, in two different groups, arrive at the sales area in funky sneakers and techno vests. Behind them comes Sheikh Hamdan with his fifteen-person entourage, all wearing pressed jeans and mirrored shades. With them is their American trainer, Kiaran McLaughlin. He has multiple sclerosis and stands with his weight unevenly distributed, one hip propped out, while he watches the horses walk. He watches them alone while the entourage lingers near the half wall that runs down the outside of the shed.

Up the hill in barns 22 and 23, the horses look sleepy. Getting out of their stalls is so much work. They stretch out their necks, the weight shifting from front to back with the speed of a giant pendulum. They slept so heavily last night that the straw has left crease marks in their coats. As the day warms up, so do the horses. They march up and down, up and down. Audra Tackett is here again, pitching in until she's needed back at the office. All this marching reveals as much about the grooms' conformation as it does about that of the yearlings. Audra's walk looks a little rubbery this morning, her hips loose and jangly.

One of the grooms breaks away and sinks into a plastic chair. He has an open water bottle in his hand, and before sipping, he says, "Ahhhhh, break." After drinking, he presses his hands to his face, rubbing his eyes, his forehead. Coming around the turn, Audra calls out to him, *"¡Ayuda me!"*

"I'm tired," he replies.

"Yo tambien," she calls over her shoulder as she heads back up the path.

Watching her walk away, he sighs. Then, quickly and brightly, he heaves himself up and out of the chair and makes kissing noises to the horse Audra is leading, sparking it into a bright and energetic walk.

The music of accented English chirps to the surface in the chaos of the stabling area. Kentucky accents, British, Irish, Spanish, Jamaican—and those are just the grooms'. Hip numbers are called and the horses are moving. Tired, they line up on deck, their glossy butts hip-to-hip with those of their stablemates, their heads leaning against the shoulders of their grooms. And the customers keep coming and coming. The wooden gate to the stabling area creaks open and bangs shut again and again and again.

When it's her turn, hip number 549, a filly by Hard Spun, led by Julie, is suddenly airborne, a hoof flying straight out behind her, skimming just past the shoulder blades of a groom named Louis, who's been following behind.

The crowd settles into a worried "Oooooooh."

When a horse blows up, the people with their backs to it dart away, offering a perfect reflection of the horse's flight response. Once safely away, they turn and look. The people facing the horse move toward it, closing a circle down around it, kissing, clucking, growling, slapping their hands on their notebooks, waving their rags, pressing the horse forward, into its handler, into obedience.

Around 1:00 P.M., Frank enters the stabling area, laughing. Mark sneaks off to the far end of the barn to get a plate of food from the caterer. They're not completely happy with last night's sale, but they performed about where they expected and their RNA was consistent with that of the overall sale.

When the horses don't sell, they come back to the stabling area for a day, in case anyone missed their chance last night. And then they either go back to their owners or stay on at Taylor Made, where about a week after the opening night, the barn hosts its RNA party—beer, barbecue, and horses. It's where, private sales administrator Pat Bellairs says, you get to see Frank in his glory as he goes to whatever lengths he needs to to get the horses sold.

Downhill, at barns 3 and 4, the action has slowed to a halt. Half of the stalls have been left empty by the horses who were sold last night. Lou Germany has his shoes off, his feet resting on them. He's staring down at them when they're joined by another groom, who slides down the wall to a squat and leans forward to stretch out his back. "Since you're sitting down, do you have time to rub my feet?" Lou asks him. The groom shoots Lou a disgusted look.

Out in the parking lot, by the loading ramp, the van has pulled up for Collect Call '09. The colt, sick of walking up and down and getting nowhere, runs away from the Taylor Made grooms when they come to his stall, but he's curious about the van driver, whom he's never met. The driver snaps on the lead shank and marches the colt away. Turning left at the intersection instead of right puts Collect Call '09 on alert. He's never walked out *this* way before. His head goes up and his nostrils flare. He steps more lightly, up on his toes, as if he's prepared to flee at a moment's notice. The driver leads him up the chute and the colt plants his feet, refusing to go forward. The driver circles him around, heading back up, and the helpers start closing in behind the colt who's having none of it. He scrambles backward, scattering the men.

Hearing that the colt won't load, Lou Germany and another groom head out toward the van. Quad leader Sherry hollers out to them, reminding them not to touch the horse. He belongs to someone else now. If anything goes wrong, the Taylors aren't covered.

Lou and the other groom stand in the driveway. Collect Call '09 is circled again, and this time he heads quietly up the ramp. Seeing that the driver has the situation under control, the grooms head back to the barn. But the Collect Call colt doesn't walk right onto the trailer. He stops one more time, lifting his head over the side of the chute and looking back toward the people he knows, and who know him, and who, so far, have treated him like the champion he might become. He gives one last look before he drops his head and follows the driver onto the van, bound for his new owner and his new life, where he may or may not be a very big deal.

By evening, the horses are ready for the ring. Taylor Made has several horses going early, and the team has taken over the intersection: Duncan, Teresa Little, Frank and his very pregnant daughter Katie, Finn Green, and two other younger salesmen. They have left their jackets off tonight, and though the pavilion is less crowded, it's almost more festive than the first night. Heading into day two of the sale, most people are still in business.

Once a horse sells, the Taylor team disappears into the crowd. Most of them aren't very tall, so they disappear quickly. Then, just a horse or two ahead of one of their own, they reappear to command the intersection: Duncan, Finn, Frank, Teresa Little, Shawn Collins. Ben Taylor arrives, though he's the sole member of the team who doesn't wear the blue shirt and tie. After hip number 142 sells, Jeff Hayslett and Tammy Frasier arrive, though Frank leaves. Finn is getting kissed and hugged by a steady stream of people. Hip number 144 goes in—a Smart Strike filly who's had a whopping twenty-two scopes. She goes on the board at $150,000, then moves up to $175,000, $200,000, $250,000, $275,000. At $325,000, bidding hangs. Then it goes to $335,000, $350,000. Mark Taylor joins his brothers. Now it's $360,000 $370,000. "Three seventy," the auctioneer says again and again. At $370,000, the horse is sold.

No one smiles. This was the hot horse of the night.

Hip 145, a filly by A.P. Indy whose fee when she was bred was $300,000, enters the ring and sells for $350,000.

There's a break of five horses and everyone disappears again. Then Nacho arrives, leading hip number 151, an Unbridled's Song colt who's the same gray as his sire. Just Ben is in the ring when the colt appears. Then Duncan arrives, followed by Shawn Collins and then Teresa. The horse goes into the ring. Finn appears as bidding hits $160,000. Jeff Hayslett arrives when the bidding reaches $220,000. The horse is sold at $250,000, and everyone jots that down in their books. They confab through the sale of the next horse, who doesn't belong to them. It's 8:45 and they're almost halfway through the night's consignment.

By the time Denali Stud's hip number 154, another Street Cry colt, enters the ring, the Taylor Made team is gone. Duncan returns to watch hip number 155. And the rest of the team reassembles in time for hip numbers 157 and 158, and they take over the intersection entirely for a Pulpit colt that they've consigned for Fares Farm. The brothers' lips are pressed together in identical frowns as they watch the bidding end at $200,000.

They leave and return for hip number 162, an Unbridled's Song filly. She enters the auction right at 8:59, waits patiently for her bio to be read by the announcer, who lets the audience know that the filly has a mild opacity on her left cornea. Ryan Mahan has to drop the bidding all the way down to $10,000 to get the filly on the board, but three minutes later, at 9:02, she sells for $300,000.

Out in the walking ring, Jo Pollock is watching her Queen filly walk. Dennis is leading the filly and she looks relaxed. What looks like laziness on the farm looks like unflappability here. The others yearlings are leaping at the ends of their shanks, blowing up and snorting, but Queen '09 is strolling along.

Seeing the Pollocks, Dennis sets the filly up and Jo blows her a kiss. She won't stop by the barn later on to say good-bye, she says, because it's too sad. Scott Kintz, representing his new employer, appears behind the Pollocks to say hello and wish them luck.

If Jo knows whether or not Frank and Sam have agreed to bump the bids on the filly, she's not saying. They've done so in the past, she says, then adds, "You never know what Sam is going to do."

Queen '09 passes through the giant doors and into the auction ring at 9:50 P.M. and is handed off to Cordell, who's working for Keeneland tonight. When the filly left the farm, they thought she'd bring about $125,000. Because Coolmore and the Arabs expressed so much interest in her, that reserve went up to $249,000. Her bio is read and the opening bid for the pudgy and lazy filly is $100,000. The bids increase: $150,000, $200,000, $225,000, $250,000. Ryan Mahan's chant rolls on uninterrupted: $275,000, $300,000, $325,000, $350,000, $375,000, $400,000. Bidding lingers and Ryan Mahan calls $400,000 one more time and the hammer falls. The filly is sold to Shadwell.

Sam Pollock arrives, cheering. Jo beams, but Sam throws his fist into the air, whooping. Frank is grinning, and Jo gives him a hug. They didn't sell either of the two horses they took to Saratoga, and they were worried they were going to have to keep this one, too. The Pollocks disappear and Frank heads back into the intersection. Taylor Made is not done yet.

Hip number 191, the River Drive colt, whom Frank described as walking like he was dealing cards, goes for $250,000—the problem never completely resolved. Then comes hip number 196, a filly by Sleepytime and one of those willed by Charles Wacker to his employees. Bidding opens at $50,000 and jumps to $175,000. From there, it goes to $200,000, $225,000, $250,000, $275,000, $300,000, $325,000, $350,000; then there's an impatient leap to $450,000. The bidding moves up to $500,000, $525,000, $550,000, $575,000, $600,000, $625,000, then pauses. A second call. At $625,000, the filly is sold. For the first time, the team members allow themselves to smile. Like Alidiva's 2009 filly, Sleepytime will be handed off to British bloodstock agent C. Gordon-Watson.

In the ring, the filly pitches a fit, running backward and rearing. The Taylors watch the monitor helplessly. It goes on long enough that their best sale might actually end in disaster, but the filly calms down and heads back to the barn.

There's one last horse, a Staraway colt by Hard Spun, who goes for $120,000. One more confab and the team is done for the night.

Sam and Jo arrive with more hugs and kisses for Frank. Sam's got two vodka and orange juices and he hands one to Frank. Frank smiles and gets pulled away by well-wishers eager to congratulate the farm on the sale of the Sleepytime filly. Seeing that Frank is busy, Sam hands the other cocktail to Finn and asks that Finn hand it on to Frank. Finn looks momentarily confused, because Frank already has a drink in his hand, but he smiles agreeably, promising to hand it off as soon as Frank's free.

By Tuesday, the "select" sale over, Keeneland is back to business. The pace has picked up; they're now showing and selling at the same time. After lunch, Sam Pollock arrives to take up his post on the bench outside barn 33. Though these barns are smaller, the aisles narrower and the ceilings lower, they hold the same number of horses as barns 3 and 4. The grooms don't like them because they're crowded and hectic.

Sam is enormously relieved to have sold the Queen filly. He's not having a very good year. "I hadn't sold anything in New York," he says. And he explains that there are two or three horses out at the farm "that I'm gonna have to take to a different level," meaning that he might end up racing horses that he was expecting to sell. "I don't know what anything's worth in this economy," he says.

He's vague about the possibility that the bidding on Queen '09 was bumped. "A lot of time, I'd rather not know," he says, then goes on to say how much he likes Taylor Made. "I think that Taylor Made has something that no one else does."

Sam can't immediately say how many horses he owns. There are those he owns outright, but he's also got shares and partnerships in others. He owns parts of from fifteen to twenty stallions—the most profitable of his Thoroughbred holdings. He's got the same number of mares in partnerships, plus three racehorses and some two-year-olds in training. He's got about a dozen yearlings to sell this year. The first two were in New York, one of which sold to a pinhooker privately after the sale, the other of which is in the RNA barn at Taylor Made.

As he's looking off, counting in his head, the colts around him are wheeling and spinning. Across the row, one rears up high and just hangs in the air, a look of panic spreading across his face as he starts to lose his balance and realizes that he could tip over. For the fraction of the second that he hangs there, everyone in the yard goes still. The groom plays out as much lead as he has, giving the horse his head. There's nothing anyone can do for him now. His fate is entirely up to him. He can't quite get back down to the ground and he starts to scramble backward with his hind feet, ready to tumble, when his butt backs into a tree and he gets bounced forward onto his front feet. He's safe on all fours, but now he's in trouble. His groom glares at him, insults his intelligence, and walks him back into the barn. Chagrined, the colt glances around under his forelock.

The barns get progressively crazier as the sale goes on. There are more horses, and less valuable ones, whose owners have not had the means to provide them with the level of care and training that they get at Taylor Made, though it's not as bad as it used to be. "Remember when it was like they'd never seen a human before?" says one groom, cackling.

Sam is sitting at the top of the walk, exactly where the grooms turn the colts around. Every time a colt turns around, its hocks, just a couple feet away, are directly in line with Sam's face. The grooms seems to be well aware that he's in direct range of a snapped hoof, and they're trying both to show the colts to advantage and to keep them from killing Sam.

"I've sat here for years and years," Sam says, watching the shiny hindquarters in front of him "Someday they'll get me."

The market has changed, but Sam's plan has not. "I do not want to own any mares that will not produce something that's eligible for Saratoga or Book One or Book Two." Like Jeff Lewis, Sam's aiming for the top of the market, understanding that aspiring to that level still means that you're going to get horses that fall below it. Queen '09's sale last night, he says, was a good sale. "It wasn't a home run," he adds, qualifying this remark, but it was a good sale and he's relieved that he doesn't have to take the horse back home.

Around him, the colts are spinning on their heels, rearing and bucking. When it's pointed out to him that he could get killed where he's sitting, he replies, "It's a good way to die."

Sam says that once his horses are sold, "I don't look back. If they were nice enough to buy my horses, I want them to do well and make money with them."

Over the years, he's had his favorites: Staraway, whose current owner sold a filly through Taylor Made just last night; Octave; Belle Nuit; and, of course, Royale Michele.

Duncan meanders over to Sam and Sam tells him he's been sitting on the bench, waiting for someone to look at his Marina de Chavon filly. He wants to see her, but he doesn't want to create work by asking for her. Duncan points out that he hasn't seen her because he's sitting in the colt's quad. "You have to go over to the fillies," he tells Sam.

Sam straightens out his long body, settling himself securely over his comfortable shoes, and heads into the middle of the fray. His pastel polo shirt, tan pants, and white hair are in stark contrast to the dark bodies of the colts leaping and spinning around them. Like Mr. Magoo, he aims himself toward the other side of the chaos and sails through untouched.

On the filly side, the first thing Sam notices is the ambulance. A Taylor Made groom named Dana was just taken out by one of the fillies. Tammy, who summoned the ambulance, did so because Dana was dazed and jabbering in the bathroom, where they went to see if the skin was broken under her clothes. The filly jigged backward, kicked, and took Dana's legs out from underneath her, slamming her back and head-down onto the pavement.

Duncan walks into the quad, sees the ambulance, and makes his way over to the groom, who's seated on a plastic lawn chair. The paramedics are on their knees, looking up at Dana in her chair. They're checking her pupils, asking her questions. Bart Barber wanders in, sees the paramedics, and moseys over to offer his help. Dale Brown, who's been prowling around looking for customers, says it won't be the first time a vet has treated one of the humans.

Bart Barber wanders in and goes over to say hi to Dale Brown. The ambulance packs up and moves on. Dana's shaken but okay. With Iris to keep her company, she rests in the chair and has a smoke.

Frank arrives just as everyone is settling down, and he wanders over to keep Sam company. "Sammy's in charge of everything that goes right," says Frank, characterizing their partnership. "I'm in charge of everything that goes wrong."

Finn finds the men. He stares across the lane toward barn 28. Right there, he says, is where he saw the filly who would become known as Zenyatta. He gazes toward the barn as if that day is a nice memory for him, the moment long past, another life, perhaps.

A filly by A.P. Indy walks by on her way to being shown. Both Frank and Sam turn to watch her. "I'm gonna buy that filly for Sam," Frank says. "But he don't know it yet."

"He says they're mine." Sam and Frank like to talk to each other through intermediaries. "But they're really half his."

"How much money did I make you last night?" Frank laughs.

Sam stands up, getting ready to leave. Finn Green stands next to him. "Twenty-two dollars," he says.

"I'm not paying it." Sam frowns.

"Ohhhhhh, now Sammy," Finn chides him.

"I already paid it."

"You didn't pay all of it.

It's the lingering balance on a bet from Saratoga. The story starts on the golf course at twilight, with poor Shannon Potter, who didn't want to play eighteen holes, and Frank, who'd paid for the game, insisting that they play all eighteen, and there was Finn's drive, which landed in the rough, and the bet was between Sam's difficult putt and Finn's seemingly impossible one, in the dark, in which the ghostly white ball disappeared up a rise in the gathering dark, becoming visible again only as it rolled back down the green and plopped into the cup.

"Twenty-two dollars," Finn says again, grinning.

"No."

Sam asks if Frank wants steak and vodka, and Frank passes on the vodka. "I'm maturing. I'm maturing," he jokes. He looks down at his ankle. He's pissed off at it because it hurts and he can't figure out why.

Sam turns from Finn to Frank. "Golf?" Frank is reluctant. He's working early. He's in the middle of the sale. It's already late, and though he doesn't say this to Sam, his ankle hurts.

"Not enough time," Frank says, though he thinks steak is a good idea.

"Nine holes?" Sam counters.

"Okay, nine holes."

Sam heads off to the parking lot, moving through the middle of the shed row and out into the lane with the same charmed aplomb that got him through the chaos of spinning colts, unscathed.

Down in the sale pavilion, which is nearly empty, there are just a few horses left to sell for the day, which you wouldn't know if it weren't for the broadcasting of Ryan Mahan's voice. Mark is trying to get a bite to eat over by the Taylor Made counter. The farm is doing okay, Mark says, but the market isn't going back to what it was.

Responding to the suggestion that one million is the new two million, he smiles. "Everything new is half of what the old used to be."

The only horses that they're really struggling with, he says, are the ones who should have been placed later in the sale but whose owners insisted that they go in Book 2. His comment reinforces Sam Pollock's observation that the way people get in trouble in this business is by not listening to the professionals whom they hire.

Scott Kintz is sitting in the little courtyard outside the walking ring. One of the last horses of the day, consigned by Taylor Made, belongs to his new employer. He gets up to watch her in the walking ring before she heads off to the sale.

The bars are already crowded. Nick Zito is leaning against the wall and chatting. Bob Baffert's at the bar, Coke in hand. The Taylors are finishing up their day and haven't yet left. Up in barn 22, as the grooms get the horses tucked in for the night, Patrick Mahan is settling down to update the numbers and send out notices for tomorrow's ads. He'll be working long after everyone else is gone. So will Tom Hamm. In the offices at barns 33 and 34, he is going over the payroll, figuring out which employees he'll keep and whose hours will be cut. He works back from the end of the sale, giving his senior employees full hours and full wages for the duration; then he tries to juggle everyone else in, splitting hours where he can so everyone gets at least some work. He doesn't have to do this. The spectators are gone and it's down to business. The last horse goes through the ring with no fanfare and Ryan Mahan brings down the hammer on the last bid of the day. "We conclude another session. We thank you very much. Your purchase must be removed from the sales grounds by noon tomorrow. Good evening, everyone," he says.

No one responds to the end of the sale, even though everyone is still here.

Out on the farm, it's quiet, the chatter and chaos of the sale far, far away. It's eight o'clock. Popcorn clouds drift across the sky, followed closely by flat, more threatening clouds from the west, their edges lit up by the last of the day's sun.

Terry Pellin stops to chat with Dan Kingsland during her nightly rounds. The farm hasn't laid anyone off, but they've cut her hours, and she's not sure she can survive on a hundred bucks less a week than she already makes. She's been enrolled in a fifteen-month certification program to become a massage therapist, and she's almost done. The farm has offered her day work, but it will delay the completion of her program. And she likes her solitary work, the quiet nights, the dark, her time alone with the horses and her thoughts.

This is what she always wanted to do and it's why she moved to Kentucky, but the days of these big commercial farms might already be past. The days when an eager girl form Massachusetts could head to the bluegrass and easily get a decent, if not lucrative, job, with benefits, might be over. Ben Taylor thinks that by the time the market is "corrected," the annual foal crop is going to be half of what it once was—down to about 25,000. The business is heading in the direction that everyone thinks it should, something akin to the old family dynasties: owners who breed to race and then take their best runners home to breed, racing the best of those and selling the others to cover expenses. Since the generous credit available to everyone in the industry appears to be gone for good, in the future, the endeavor will be funded entirely by the discretionary income of those families wealthy enough to support it.

The yearling side of the farm is lonely—the yearlings out at the sale and the weanlings from the broodmare side have not yet arrived. The horses to be sold next week occupy the half-empty barns. Glenarcy and a stablemate graze contentedly in their paddock. Her medium-quality pedigree and conformation problems have put her almost at the end of the sale. She's hip number 3363 out of a total of 4,857 horses. For now, as far as she knows, she lives on this nice farm.

But the colt up at Eagle Creek A is upset. Surrounded by empty paddocks, he runs the perimeter of his, whinnying frantically to the other horses, who whinny back at him from their stations on the farm: Eagle Creek C, up the hill, or across the lane, where the chestnut filly out of the mare Extend whinnies back, as if to say, We're here. Don't worry. You're not alone.

🐎

At Whitehouse upper, where the foals of Alidiva, Cherry Bomb, Collect Call, Folkore, and Resplendency drew their first breath in the winter of 2009, the broodmares are out in their paddocks, their bellies showing their pregnancies, even as some of them still have their 2010 foals at their sides. While their mothers graze, the foals who will be weaned as soon as the September sale is over race one another across the paddock.

As always, the farm is still, serene, and surreally beautiful as night descends. Somewhere on the farm, Dan, Charlie, and Barb are prowling, checking on horses, filling water buckets, listening.

Out in the paddocks, which are desperately in need of rain, the mares graze the legendary Kentucky bluegrass, which really isn't that special at all. In another week, the last of the 2009 foals will have been dispersed to their destinies and just one among them will be the next Derby winner. The 2010 foals, some of whom are still playing at their mothers' sides, will move over to the yearling side and into John Hall's capable, work-worn hands. Right now, they graze peacefully. Their mothers are pregnant—again. They don't know yet that they will be taken away, or that they are racehorses and in the hands of these gamblers, anything could happen to them—sale, the racetrack, death by misadventure, or the Kentucky Derby. Anything is possible.

You never know.

Glossary

Abscess: Localized bacterial infection in the sensitive layers of the horse's hoof that creates a painful pus-filled pocket.

Account managers: Like stockbrokers or financial advisers for Thorougbred bloodstock, account managers assist owners in the management of their Throughbred holdings.

Ace: Shorthand term for antianxiety and sedative acepromazine.

Auctioneer's stand: High podium behind which an auctioneer sits.

Back at the knee: Conformation flaw in which the horse's knee sits slightly behind the cannon bone (the bottom shaft of the horse's leg). Opposite of over at the knee.

Banamine: trade name for the nonsteroidal anti-inflammatory flunixin. Produces a mild analgesic effect.

Barren: A mare who has been bred but has either not conceived or has lost the foal.

Belmont Stakes: The oldest and longest of the three Triple Crown races. Inaugurated in 1867, the race is one and a half miles long and is run on the first or second Saturday in June at Belmont Racetrack in Elmont, New York.

Bid spotters: Individuals who spot the bids in the crowd and announce them for the auctioneer.

Blackboard fencing: The characteristic black-painted boards that most Kentucky horsemen use to fence their pastures.

Bloodstock agent: Individuals who specialize in advising buyers about horses and who purchase horses on their behalf.

Bloody long johns: Colloquial name for a placenta that has been turned inside out for inspection, exposing its red interior. Extending the two horns of the placenta from the bottom of the central sac creates the appearance of bloody long johns.

Bone: In conformation evaluations, horsemen use the word *bone* to describe the size and substance of a horse's leg bones.

Books: The individually numbered catalog books of a sale. The Saratoga yearling sale, which lasts only two days, has one book. The Keeneland September sale, which lasts about two weeks and catalogs more than 4,500 horses, has six books.

Bowed tendon: Tendon that has a bowed-out appearance due to an injury.

Breeders' Cup: Officially the Breeders' Cup World Thoroughbred Championships, these two days of racing are the brainchild of the late John R. Gaines, of Gainesway Farm. Held every November, the races are timed to come just before Keeneland's annual bloodstock sale and are held at a different track every year. Horses need to qualify for the events, and distances for the fifteen races range from a five-furlong sprint to a one-and-three-quarter mile marathon. Its featured races are the Mile and the Classic, and the results of the races heavily affect not only the year-end Eclipse Awards but also the values of the horses running the races, as well as the stud fees of their sires. Purses for these races range from $500,000 to $2 million. Before the races were spread over two days, the event was known as the richest day in sports.

Broodmare: Mare who is used for breeding stock.

Bute: Shorthand for phenybutazone, a common anti-inflammatory and analgesic.

Caslick's: Routine surgical procedure in which edges of a mare's vulvar lips are stitched and sewn together. The edges adhere when they heal, blocking air and debris from entering the mare's reproductive tract.

Catalog: The listing of horses for sale, includes their vital information and their pedigrees.

Chant: What the auctioneer does to drive up bidding.

Chifney: Round bit made of brass that circles through a yearling's mouth and under its chin. It provides gentle but effective control and helps prevent rearing. The bit is attached by snaps, thus creating a cheerful jingling noise.

Claiming race: Race in which a horse can be bought, or "claimed" by anyone who pays the established fee before the race is run.

Clarithromycin: Antibiotic used to treat *Rhodococcus*.

Clubfoot: A foot that grows straight up and down.

Colic: Colic describes any kind of gastrointestinal distress. This can be something mild—such as gas that's easily relieved by movement—or in severe cases, may indicate intestinal blockages that can be remedied only by surgery. Complications from colic can be fatal.

Colostrum: Mare's first milk, rich in antibodies.

Conformation: The overall appearance of the horse.

Consignor: Thoroughbreds are auctioned through a consignor. Most consignors, like Taylor Made, also offer other services like boarding, and many of the larger farms, whose proprietors breed and own their own horses, such as Lane's End or Three Chimneys, also consign their horses themselves. A small breeder will usually consign his or her horses with someone else, and owners who don't have their own farms will also use the services of a consignor. The standard commission is 5 percent on every sale.

Coronary band: A band of soft tissue between the horse's hoof and the bottom of the horse's leg out of which the hoof grows.

Cross-ties: Ties that clip to the either end of the aisle outside the horses' stalls. They are used to restrain horses for grooming or care. Rarely used with Thoroughbreds.

Currycomb: Rubber or plastic circular comb used to draw up dirt and dust from a horse's coat. Also provides a good scratching.

Dam: A horse's mother.

Differentials: Shorthand for differential diagnoses, a systematic process of elimination used to identify the source of a medical condition.

Drift: The process by which mares, due to postnatal recovery periods, get pregnant a month or two later every year. Because of the January 1 birthday for all Thoroughbred foals, mitigating drift increases lifetime productivity for broodmares.

Dummy foal: Common term for a foal with neonatal maladjustment syndrome. The foal will display abnormal behaviors after birth, such as irritability, disorientation, and a failure to suckle. The condition is associated with insufficient oxygen before birth. Severe cases may cause seizures.

Dystocia: Difficult or abnormal delivery caused by any number of reasons— breech, a large foal and a small mare, abnormal alignment of the foal in the birth canal.

Eclipse Awards: Annual industry awards given to Thoroughbred horses and horsemen.

EPM: Equine protozoal myeloencephalitis, a disease in which protozoa from opossum feces cross the blood-brain barrier and infect the central nervous system. Noncontagious but debilitating. Treatment effectiveness increases dramatically if caught early.

Extender: Commercial preservative used to extend the life of a stallion's semen.

Farrier: A blacksmith who is also a specialist in equine hoof care. At highly managed farms, the farriers are like veterinarians for the horses' feet; they are also able to shape shoes for them. After attending farrier school (some farriers go straight to apprenticeships), farriers apprentice to a journeyman farrier. Apprenticeships can run anywhere from a few months to five years or more.

Fetlock: The joint above a horse's hoof that attaches the hoof to the leg. Comparable to the ankle joint in humans.

Foal: A baby horse. Males are colts; females are fillies.

Foaling kit: A large plastic toolbox with everything needed to deliver a foal.

Foaling log: Log of the foals' births.

Foaling season: The time of year between January and May when the foals are born.

Foal share: Financial arrangement in which multiple owners share the costs and sale or race proceeds of a foal.

Forelock: Clutch of mane that grows forward and lies over a horse's forehead.

Frog: Triangular-shaped soft tissue in the center of a horse's sole.

Gaskin: Meaty part of a horse's thigh between the hock and the stifle.

Gastrogard: Trade name for omeprazole, a drug used to treat ulcers in horses.

Handle: Total amount of money wagered on a race, or a day's schedule of races (a program), a particular race meet, or as a measure of the amount wagered during a particular period or in a particular place.

Hayrack: Rack that holds hay off the ground for horses to eat. May be attached to the wall of a stall or be freestanding in the middle of a paddock.

Hip number: Number assigned to horses in a sale. These numbers are attached to the hip of the horse.

Hock: The joint that connects the lower bone (the cannon) of a horse's hind leg to the length of leg that connects to a horse's hip (gaskin).

Hoof pick: Curved metal pick used to clean out a horse's hooves.

Hoof testers: Large round pinchers that farriers and veterinarians use to squeeze parts of a horse's hoof to isolate the source of lameness.

Jockey Club: Breed registry for Thoroughbred horses in the United States, Canada, and Mexico. Various racing jurisdictions (Britain, Japan, Hong Kong, etc.) have their own Jockey Clubs.

Jaundice-positive: Mare who has been found to be producing anitbodies to the foal's red blood cells. Highly dangerous to foals, who will absorb those antibodies, which will then attack their own red blood cells, from the colostrum when they nurse after birth. Although antibodies will clear out within the first twelve hours, foals with jaundice-positive dams need to be fed a milk replacer immediately after birth.

Kentucky Derby: The first of the three races of the Triple Crown. Takes place on the first Saturday in May at Churchill Downs, in Louisville, Kentucky, and the distance runs one and a quarter miles. Inaugurated in 1875.

Kentucky Oaks: Race restricted to fillies. Run the day before the Kentucky Derby, it's often referred to as the "fillies' Derby."

Laminitis: Condition that occurs when the blood supply to the hoof is constricted, causing separation between the laminae of a horse's hoof. In severe cases, pressure on the hoof can cause the hoof to separate from its underlying tissue, exposing the bone and creating opportunity for infection. After a year of fighting to recover from his broken leg, Barbaro was eventually euthanized because of severe laminitis.

Live bidding: Bidding that is connected to an actual bidder who intends to buy the horse he or she is bidding on.

Live cover: The physical mating between a mare and a stallion.

Lead shank: Leather lead with a chain attached to the end that attaches to the horse's halter and is used to walk it around.

Live foal guarantee: Also called stand and nurse, live foal guarantees come with the stud fee. If the foal does not stand and nurse, the fee is forfeited. Foals are often insured for the stud fees.

Maiden: Mare who has never been bred.

Milk replacer: Feeding formula for foals.

MRLS: Mare reproductive loss syndrome was first identified in 2001, when mares were losing their pregnancies (early fetal loss, or EFL) or aborting near-term foals (late-term abortion). Though a definitive cause for MRLS has never been determined, it is believed to have been caused by an unusual weather cycle and eastern tent caterpillars, conditions that combine to create a toxic fungus in the pastures. The loss of these foals to the industry was estimated to be about $500 million.

Muck bucket: Any kind of large tub into which soiled bedding or other barn debris is dumped.

Mud: Clay pack smeared on horses' lower legs to tighten tendons, reduce inflammation, and protect from flies.

Naval dip: antiseptic dip made of diluted Nolvasan used to disinfect a foal's umbilical stump after birth.

Neck straps: Leather straps with engraved brass nameplates that buckle around horses' necks for identification.

Night watch: Staff that works overnight and specializes in the delivery of foals.

Nurse mare: Lactating mare that nurses a foal that is not her own.

OCD: *Osteochondritis dissecans* is a joint disorder in which blood deprivation causes cracks in the cartilage and subchrondal bones below it. Fragmentation of the dead bone causes bits to lodge in the joints, causing pain and inflammation. A special concern for Throughbreds because the condition may be related to feeding and breeding for early growth.

Offset knees: Knees that are offset in one direction or the other, suggesting that they will wear down unevenly once the horse starts running.

Out: A horse who has been withdrawn from a sale after it has already been entered in the catalog. Usually done because the seller has good reason to believe that the horse will not bring the anticipated price.

Overreach: Distance that a horse's hind foot reaches over into the footfall of his front hoof—an indication that the horse has a long stride.

Over at the knee: Conformation flaw in which a horse's knee sits slightly over the cannon bone (the bottom shaft of a horse's leg).

Oxyclorosine: An antibacterial used for cleaning wounds.

Paddle: Excessive horizontal movement of a horse's forelimbs. Resembles the swimming motion of the dog paddle.

Paddock: In racing, the paddock is where the horses are saddled up. On the farm, a paddock is the area in which the horses are turned out. Although technically the breeding farms turn their horses out in pastures, horsemen often use the words *paddock* and *pasture* interchangeably.

Palpate: To examine an organ or part of the body by touch or pressure. Mares' reproductive organs are palpated through the rectal wall.

Parrot mouth: Oral deformity in which a horse's upper jaw is longer than the lower jaw.

Pasterns: The short length of leg between the hoof and the fetlock. It encompasses the pastern bones and the paired ligaments. Conformation evaluations always include an examination of the angle of the pastern to see if it's too low (or soft), or too straight.

Physitis: Swelling in the growth plates of a horse's long bones. Occurs in foals during the first year of life.

Pinhooker: Industry term for an individual who buys a horse with the intention of selling it later for a higher price. Most typically refers to those who buy yearlings, start their training, and then sell them as two-year-olds. Has been used as a derogatory term in the past. May also be used as a verb—e.g., "I started out in the business by pinhooking two-year-olds."

Potomac horse fever: Contagious bacterial infection.

Poultice: See Mud.

Preakness: The second of the Triple Crown races. Run at Pimlico Racecourse in Laurel, Maryland, on the third Saturday in May. The shortest of the three races, it's one and three-sixteenth miles long.

Pulling straps: Straps that tighten around a foal's legs so that the grooms can help pull the foal out of the mare during a difficult delivery.

Purse: Prize money given to the winners of a race.

Race meet: A gathering of horses for a series of races.

Rasp: Farrier's tool used for filing down a horse's hooves.

Red bag: The appearance of the interior red tissue of the placenta rather than the exterior white tissue, indicating that the placenta has prematurely separated. Premature separation disrupts the foal's oxygen supply, and the mare's amniotic sac must be ruptured manually.

Regu-Mate: Synthetic hormone use to regulate a mare's ovulation cycle.

Repository: Central location on the sales grounds in which consignors file radiographs of a horse's joints for inspection by potential buyers.

*Rhodococcus***:** Bacteria that causes pneumonia in foals. Can be endemic on some breeding farms.

Rompun: See Xylazine.

RNA: Reserve not attained. Also called "buy-back." The sellers of the horses establish a reserve, or minimum price, before they enter the ring. The RNA rate, or buy-back rate, is the percentage of horses who did not meet their reserve. An RNA sale is a sale comprised of horses who did not meet their reserve at the auction. The RNA barn is the barn in which those horses are housed in preparation for the RNA sale.

Scope: Short for endoscope, the surgical tool used to examine a horse's breathing apparatus for irregularities. Procedure is requested by buyers before they bid on a horse for sale.

Screws and wires: Colloquial term for the popular surgery in which screws and sometimes wires are inserted into a foal's ankle to stabilize one side so the other side can catch up as the foal grows.

Select sale: A specific sale (e.g., the Saratoga yearling sale), or part of a larger sale (e.g., the first two days of Keeneland), in which the best, or most select, horses of the auction are offered for sale.

Sesamoid fractures/Sesamoiditis: The sesamoid bones are located at the back of a horse's fetlock, or ankle joint. The bones can be broken, or the joint can have bony spurs adhering to it.

Short-cycled: The practice of using synthetic hormones to bring a mare into heat early, usually when she skips a heat after giving birth.

Showman: Groom who specializes in showing horses to their best advantage at the sale.

Silks: The jockey's uniform, whose colors and patterns represent the horse's owners. Also the name of Scott Kintz's dog.

Sire: A horse's father.

Slab fracture: Vertical fracture of the surface area of the bone.

Slant-load trailer: Horse trailer in which the horses are angled sideways inside, allowing for more horses to be hauled in one trailer. Slant-load trailers are often more comfortable as well, allowing the horses to rock from side to side, rather than from front to back, to keep their balance.

Stallion syndicate: Group of individuals who own a single stallion in syndication.

Stifles: Joint that attaches a horse's hind leg to his hip and is responsible for the spring that propels the horse forward. Comparable to a human knee.

Stripping knees: Surgical intervention in which the tendons on one side of a horse's knees are stripped away from the bone, allowing the bone on that side of the horse's knee to grow freely.

Stud fee: The fee a mare owner pays to the owner of a stallion. For racing-quality Thoroughbreds, these fees range from around ten thousand up to a couple of hundred thousand. At the height of the sales market, Kentucky's top sire, Storm Cat, commanded a $500,000 fee. The stud fees are published annually, and their fluctuations reflect not only the overall market but the rising and falling fortunes of a particular stallion. Stud fees are frequently negotiable in the complicated syndicating, packaging, and marketing of certain horses.

Sweating gel: Gel rubbed over any area of a horse's body that needs to be sweated. Used often on colts with thick crests—the line at the top of their necks.

Tattoo: Thoroughbreds registered with the Jockey Club have an identification number tattooed on the inside of their upper lips.

Teaser stallion: Teaser stallions are used to evaluate the mares' readiness for breeding. They are also used to accustom maiden mares to the process of being "jumped" by a stallion. On the farm, managers regularly introduce teaser stallions to their mares to see if the mares demonstrate that they are ready to be bred.

Toeing in: Common conformation flaw in which the toes of a horse's hooves turn in.

Toeing out: Common conformation flaw in which the toes of a horse's hooves turn out.

Top-off: The process whereby a horse is given the final grooming touches before going to the ring.

Triple Crown: Three-race series comprised of the Kentucky Derby, the Preakness, and the Belmont Stakes—for three-year-olds, run in the spring. Although there are comparable races for fillies around the same time, fillies may also run in the Triple Crown races.

Turnout: Putting the horses out in their pastures. Turn out is used as a verb—e.g., "Who will turn out the horses in the morning?" and also as a noun—e.g., "How much turnout are the mares in that barn getting?"

Twitch: As a noun, this is the pole or shaft, a couple of feet long, with a short rope loop that is used to restrain a horse by twisting the rope around the lip and applying pressure. It is considered a humane form of restraint because it activates an acupressure point, usually causing the horse to relax and focus on the pressure. With more difficult horses, the twitch is sometimes used on their ears, though this is not considered a good practice, because it hurts the horse and makes it head-shy. Twitch is also used as a verb, as in "Can someone twitch this mare?"

Walker, or exerciser: Large pole spindle topped with spokes to which horses are attached for exercise. More elaborate versions leave the horses' heads free but separate them by hanging gates so they don't bump into one another as the spokes turn, pushing the horses into motion.

Walking rings: Series of rings with padded flooring in which the horses are walked by grooms and showmen for inspection by potential buyers.

Wash stall: Stall designated for washing horses. Indoor wash stalls have a drain.

Wastage: Term used to describe the elimination of horses from racing due to death or career-ending injury while they're racing.

Waxing: Waxy secretions that gather on a mare's teats usually within twenty-four hours of foaling.

Weanling: Foals who have been weaned but are not yet yearlings.

Wing fractures: Fractures in the small bones of a horse's hooves.

Xylazine: Equine sedative. Sold by Bayer under the trade name Rompun.

Yearling: A foal becomes a yearling on January 1, regardless of when it was born. They will be called yearlings until the following year, when they turn two.

Where Are They Now?

At the time this book went to press, the 2009 foals had begun training, though many of them were still unraced. The fillies of Alidiva and Queen were shipped to England and though they have different owners, they're both trained by Sir Michael Stoute. Collect Call '09 is trained by D. Wayne Lukas, Folklore '09 is trained by Eric Guillot, and Resplendency '09 is trained by Todd Pletcher. The details of their careers are listed below.

Alidiva '09: Alidiva's 2009 filly by Giant's Causeway was bought by British bloodstock agent C. Gordon Watson for $350,000 on behalf of Kazakhistani businessman Nurlan Bizakov, who bought England's storied Hesmonds Stud in 2011. The filly, now named Albanka, is trained by Sir Michael Stoute. Hesmonds Stud's farm manager, Tony Fry, reports that she is a "lovely looking filly," and is on the farm until she can grow and mature. At the same sale, the farm also bought Sleepytime's '09 filly by Mr. Greeley for $650,000. She was named Lashyn, and Fry reports that she's a "smashing filly." The two horses, he says, "are peas in a pod," and the farm is looking forward to racing them as three-year-olds.

Angela's Love '09: Angela's Love's filly by Forestry was bought by Jack Dickerson for $16,000 at the Keeneland September sale on behalf of Louisiana trainer Richard Jackson. Named No Not Angela, she began breezing at Louisiana Downs in July of 2011. She was unraced as of November 2011.

Collect Call '09: After selling for $300,000 at Keeneland's September sale, Collect Call's Empire Maker colt was named Honor Call by his new owners Robert C. Baker and William Mack. He is trained by Hall of Famer D. Wayne Lukas. His first attempt to break his maiden came on June 9, in a Churchill Downs maiden special weight race, where he came in seventh. On July 30, he improved his position, but still failed to break his maiden at Saratoga, coming in fourth in a maiden special weight race. On a third attempt a month later, he came in fifth in an August 20 maiden special weight race. Chart comments described the race: "bump st, 3w, run to lead." As of October 2011, his last recorded workout was in August at Saratoga, and his year-to-date earnings were $5,368. He's taking a break, says his assistant trainer at Lukas's stable, but they're aiming him for Oaklawn Park. "He's a very nice horse," says his trainer. "A lovely horse."

Folklore '09. Bought by Southern Equine Stables for $450,000 at Keeneland's September sale, Folklore's bright little chestnut colt by Distorted Humor was named Immaculate. He is trained by Eric Guillot of Southern Equine and as of October of 2011, had worked out at his second 5/8ths of a mile. Guillot says, "He's compact. His conformation is very straight. He's efficient." Guillot thought the colt would have gone for more at the September 2010 sale: "I probably got him for half price. I thought he was going to go for seven or eight hundred thousand." He's still calm and steady. "He's lazy," Guillot says. "Like a pony horse." Guillot expects that he'll be going for his maiden win in late fall of 2011.

Glenarcy '09: The big bay filly by Master Commander was sold at Keeneland in September to Gregory Peck for $16,000, and was named Once in a Jillian. As of November 2011, she was unraced and had no registered workouts.

Queen '09: Queen's 2009 filly by Street Cry was bought by Shadwell for $400,000 at Keeneland's September sale. She was named Yanabeeaa and, like Alidiva's 2009 filly, is training in England with Sir Michael Stoute. In her first race in October at Kempton Park Racecourse outside of London, she came in second. Stephanie Snell, spokesperson for Sir Michael, reports that she will not run again as a two-year-old, but "should be capable of winning a race next year."

Resplendency '09: Resplendency's big 2009 colt by Unbridled's Song was bought at Saratoga for $200,000 by Zayat Stables, LLC, and named Z Vilna. He started early training at McKathan Brothers Thoroughbreds in Citra, Florida. Says a very busy Ron Williams of Shadwell, who describes himself as "bookkeeper slash everything else," the colt was doing very well. As of October of 2011, he was just getting ready to ship to Palm Meadows at Gulfstream Park to begin training with Todd Pletcher. "He's ready," says Williams. Z Vilna recorded his first official workout on November 3, 2011, when he breezed three furlongs at Palm Meadows.

Other notable foals encountered during the course of the book include:

City Fire '09: City Fire's feisty colt by Rock Hard Ten, who wrestled mightily with Dan Kingsland, Dale Brown, and Arielle Cheshire, was sold at Keeneland for $80,000. He was gelded and named Mr. Threewit. His first attempt to break his maiden under trainer Chuck Peery and owner Michael Jawl came at Keeneland on April 14, 2011, where, ridden by jockey Victor Lebron, he placed eighth out of eight horses. According to the chart for that race, the gelding "saved grnd to no avail." On June 25, he made a second attempt at Churchill Downs and came in ninth out of eleven horses under jockey Miguel Mena. He trains at Keeneland's Thoroughbred Center.

Deputy of Wood '09: Forestry's filly, who shared the barn with the 2009 foals of Alidiva and Folklore, was named Claresmiezie. After failing to break her maiden at Keeneland, she moved to Hastings Race Course in Vancouver, where she broke her maiden in May of 2009, and came in first in the Lassie Stakes there in July. At Hastings Park in Alberta, she won the Princess Margaret Stakes, also in July, and returned to the United States where she came in fifth in Monmouth Park's Sorority Stakes in September of 2011. She is owned by Riversedge Racing Stable and is trained by Greg Tracy. Her career earnings as of November of 2011 are $76,773.

Clay's Rocket '09: Clay's Rocket's colt by Bluegrass Cat who was born at Bona Terra A, sold for $300,000 at Keeneland's yearling sale to Willis

D. Horton. Named Laurie's Rocket, he is trained by Dallas Stewart. The colt came in second in a maiden special weight race at Churchill Downs on May 30, 2011, racing for a purse of $49,000. He broke his maiden at Saratoga on July 23, coming in first for a $52,000 maiden special weight race under Kent Desormeaux. On September 5, he came in fourth in the Grade I Three Chimneys' Hopeful Stakes at Saratoga, and eighth in the Grade 1 Champagne Stakes at Belmont on October 8, 2011. On October 30, he won an allowance race at Churchill Downs. As of November 2011, he had earned $83,100.

Dream of Summer's 2009 colt by Giant's Causeway, who sold for $135,000 at Keeneland's September sale, broke his maiden in the Grade I Norfolk Stakes at Santa Anita. Named Creative Cause, he is owned by Heinz Steinmann and trained by Mike Harrington. He ran in the Grade I Grey Goose Breeder's Cup Juvenile where he came in third, trailing the leader by just one length. As of November 2011, he had earned $521,000 and was ranked 73rd among North American 2011 starters.

The names of the 2009 foals can be looked up on the Jockey's Club's registry database equineline.com by entering the name of the foal's dam and the year of birth.

To find out about the horses' race records, use the Jockey Club's racing database, equibase.com, where you can access records for the horses' official workouts and race results.

Directory

American Association of Equine Practitioners
http://www.aaep.org/
4057 Ironworks Parkway
Lexington, KY 40511
859-233-0147
aaepoffice@aaep.org

American Horse Council
http://www.horsecouncil.org/
Newsroom:
1616 H Street NW
7th Floor
Washington, D.C. 20006
212-296-4031

American Veterinary Medical Association
http://www.canterusa.org/
Headquarters:
1931 North Meacham Road, Suite 100
Schaumburg, IL 60173-4360

Phone: 800-248-2862
Fax: 847-925-1329

Governmental Relations Division:
1910 Sunderland Place, NW
Washington, D.C. 20036-1642
Phone: 800-321-1473
Fax: 202-842-4360

Bill Pressey
Thoroedge Equine Performance
http://thoroedge.com

Blackburn Correctional Complex
Kentucky Department of Corrections
3111 Spurr Road
Lexington, KY 40511
859-246-2366

Blandford Bloodstock Agency
http://www.blandfordbloodstock.com
6a Rous Road

Newmarket, Suffolk, CB8 8DL England
info@blandfordbloodstock.com

Bob Baffert Racing Stables
http://www.bobbaffert.com

Calumet Farm
http://www.calumetfarm.com
Calumet Farm
3301 Versailles Road
Lexington, KY 40510
Phone: 859-231-8272
Fax: 859-254-4258

Canter
http://www.canterusa.org/

Churchill Downs
http://www.churchilldowns.com
700 Central Avenue
Louisville, KY 40208
502-636-4400

Claiborne Farm
http://www.claibornefarm.com
PO Box 150
Paris, KY 40362-0150
859-987-2330
bernie@claibornefarm.com

Coolmore America
Ashford Stud
http://www.coolmore.com/farm.php
?country=America
5095 Frankfort Road,
Versailles, KY 40383
Phone: 859-873-7088
Fax: 859-879-5756
info@coolmore.com

Darley Stud
Jonabell Farm
3333 Bowman Mill Road
Lexington, KY 40513
859-255-8537
info@darleyamerica.com

Eaton Sales
http://www.eatonsales.com

1510 Newtown Pike, Suite 108
Lexington, KY 40511
859-233-4021

Fair Hill Training Center
http://www.fairhilltrainingcenter.com
Manager: Sally Goswell
sally@fairhilltrainingcenter.com
719 Training Center Dr.
Elkton, MD 21921
410-398-2992

Fasig-Tipton Sales
http://www.fasigtipton.com
Kentucky Office:
Fasig-Tipton Company, Inc.
2400 Newtown Pike
Lexington, KY 40511
859-255-1555
info@fasigtipton.com

Gainesway
http://www.gainesway.com
3750 Paris Pike
Lexington, KY 40511
859-293-2676

Jockey Club
http://www.jockeyclub.com/about_tjc.asp
40 East 52nd Street
New York, NY 10022
Phone: 212-371-5970
Fax: 212-371-6123
Online Fact Book: http://www.jockeyclub
.com/factbook.asp

Jonathan Sheppard
Steeplechase Trainer
National Steeplechase Hall of Fame
363 Lamborntown Road
West Grove, PA
610-869-2799

Keeneland Racetrack, Sales and Library
http://www.keeneland.com/default.aspx
Keeneland Association, Inc.
4201 Versailles Road
PO Box 1690
Lexington, KY 40588-1690

Phone: 859-254-3412; (toll-free)
800-456-3412
Keeneland Library: http://www.keeneland
.com/visit/lists/copy/research.aspx

Ken McPeek Racing
http://mcpeekracing.com
2650 Russell Cave Road
Lexington, KY 40511
office@mcpeekracing.com

Kentucky Equine Education Project
http://www.horseswork.com
4037 Iron Works Parkway
Suite 130
Lexington, KY 40511
866-771-KEEP

Kentucky Horse Park
(also houses the National Museum
of the Horse)
http://kyhorsepark.com
4089 Iron Works Parkway
Lexington, KY 40511
800-233-4303

Kiaran McLaughlin Racing Stables
http://www.kiaranmclaughlinracing.
com/trainers/mcl/public/index.cfm
?menuid=47
Belmont Park
2150 Hempstead Turnpike
Elmont, NY 11003
mclaughlinracing@hotmail.com

Lane's End Farm
http://www.lanesend.com/
1500 Midway Road
Versailles, KY 40383
859-873-7300
lanesend@lanesend.com

Len Ragozin
The Sheets Handicapping tool
http://www.thesheets.com
212-674-3123

Maker's Mark Secretariat Center
http://www.trfinc.org/Makers-Mark
-Secretariat-Center-c18.html

**Maxwell H. Gluck Equine Research
Center**
http://www.ca.uky.edu/gluck
Department of Veterinary Science,
University of Kentucky
Lexington, KY 40546-0099
859-257-4757

Mountaineer Racetrack and Casino
http://www.mtrracetrack.com
Mountaineer Circle,
Chester, WV 26034
800-804-0468

**National Thoroughbred Racing
Association**
http://www.ntra.com/home

New York Racing Association (NYRA)
http://www.nyra.com/index_saratoga.
html (Web site for Saratoga, Belmont,
and Aqueduct racecourses)

Niall Brennan Stables
http://niallbrennan.com/images
/niallbrennan.com/default.aspx
?contentName=Home%20Page&news=1
/9119 NW Hwy 225A
Ocala, FL 34482
352-732-7459
nbstables@aol.com

Old Friends
http://www.oldfriendsequine.org
1841 Paynes Depot Road
Georgetown, KY 40324
502-863-1775

**Philadelphia Park (and Pennsylvania
Horseman's Association)**
http://www.parxracing.com
2999 Street Road

Bensalem, PA 19020
215-639-9000
Pennsylvania Horseman's Association:
PO Box 300
Bensalem, PA 19020
http://www.patha.org
215-638-2012
Turning for Home:
Barbara Luna, Program Administrator
turningforhome@patha.org

ReRun
http://www.rerun.org/
ReRun, Inc.
PO Box 113, Helmetta, NJ 08828
732-521-1370
info@rerun.org

Rood and Riddle Equine Hospital
http://www.roodandriddle.com
2150 Georgetown Road
Lexington, KY 40511
859-233-0371

Saratoga Racetrack
http://www.nyra.com/index_saratoga
.html
267 Union Avenue
Saratoga Springs, NY 12866

Shadwell Farm
4600 Ft. Springs Road
Lexington, KY 40513
859-255-9757
info@chadwellfarm.com

Stone Farm
Arthur B. Hancock III
http://www.stonefarm.com
200 Stoney Point Road
Paris, KY 40361
859-987-3737
info@stonefarm.com

Taylor Made Sales Agency
2765 Union Mill Road
Nicholasville, KY 40356
www.taylormadefarm.com
859-885-3345

**Thoroughbred Owners and Breeders's
Association (TOBA)**
http://www.toba.org
Mailing Address:
PO Box 910668
Lexington, KY 40591
Street Address:
3101 Beaumont Centre Circle
Suite 110
Lexington, KY 40513
Phone: 859-276-2291; (toll-free)
888-606-TOBA
Fax: 859-276-2462
toba@toba.org

**Thoroughbred Retirement
Foundation**
Headquarters:
PO Box 13218
Lexington, KY 40582
859-246-3080
info@trfinc.org
Development:
PO Box 3387
Saratoga Spring, NY
518-226-0028
info@trfinc.org

Three Chimneys
http://www.threechimneys
.com
PO Box 114
Midway, KY 40347
859-873-7053

Todd Pletcher Racing
http://www.toddpletcherracing
.com
PO Box 66
Elmont, NY 11003
stable@toddpletcherracing
.com

Vinery, Ltd.
http://www.vinery.com
4241 Spur Road
Lexington, KY 40511
859-455-9388
info@vinery.com